Citizen Participation: Effecting Community Change

PRAEGER SPECIAL STUDIES IN
U.S. ECONOMIC AND SOCIAL DEVELOPMENT

Citizen Participation: Effecting Community Change

Edited by
Edgar S. Cahn
Barry A. Passett

Published in cooperation with the
New Jersey Community Action Training Institute

PRAEGER PUBLISHERS
New York • Washington • London

The purpose of Praeger Special Studies is to make specialized research in U.S. and international economics and politics available to the academic, business, and government communities. For further information, write to the Special Projects Division, Praeger Publishers, Inc., 111 Fourth Avenue, New York, N.Y. 10003.

PRAEGER PUBLISHERS
111 Fourth Avenue, New York, N.Y. 10003, U.S.A.
5, Cromwell Place, London S.W.7, England

Published in the United States of America in 1971
by Praeger Publishers, Inc.

Library of Congress Catalog Card Number: 76-143242

Printed in the United States of America

CONTENTS

v

PART II: GENERAL CONCERNS REGARDING CITIZEN PARTICIPATION

FEDERAL STANDARDS AND REGULATIONS
Daniel M. Fox

Part III: SPECIFIC ISSUES IN RESIDENT PARTICIPATION

ECONOMIC DEVELOPMENT: THE SWAFCA COOPERATIVE ..145
Stanley Zimmerman

Acknowledgments

The idea for a casebook for trainers on the experience of citizen participation in the 60's -- the motive force behind this volume -- came from Dr. Thomas Broden, Chief, Division of Training and Technical Assistance, Community Action Program, Office of Economic Opportunity. He approved the allocation of funds to the project from a CAP Grant, #8307, which was administered by the New Jersey Community Action Training Institute.

Barry A. Passett, then Director of the Institute (CATI) and now President of Systems for Change, Inc., and Edgar Cahn, Director of the Citizens Advocate Center in Washington, assumed the responsibility for organizing the work.

Glenn Parker and Albert Fleming, now Director and Deputy Director of CATI, respectively, were involved at the early stages.

Cahn made most of the monograph assignments and with his wife, also a noted Washington attorney, wrote the central essay. Passett handled much of the editing, the production, and logistics.

Major editorial assistance was provided by Ronald Bailey, Patricia Wood and Joan Nicholson. Mrs. Amie Boyd led the competent typing staff.

This publication was originally produced under a grant dated June 27, 1968 from the Office of Economic Opportunity. Its original purpose was to provide a resource for training and disseminating ideas and experiences in the general area of community action, but it is not required material for any Office of Economic Opportunity training program. This work may be freely reproduced and used without permission. The opinions expressed herein are those of the authors and should not be construed as representing the opinions or policy of the Office of Economic Opportunity or any other agency of the United States Government.

There has been no attempt to editorial uniformity (except in regard to length) nor have attempts been made to censor views with which

Government officials (or the editors, for that matter) disagree.

Because of the breadth of the topic and its intimate relation to the mainstream of American history, no comprehensive bibliography has been attempted. Each author has indicated key sources in the text or in footnotes.

Citizen Participation: Effecting Community Change

INTRODUCTION

CITIZEN PARTICIPATION

by: Joseph Wilkins and
Barry A. Passett

*"I know histhry isn't thrue, Hinnessy, because it ain't like what
i see ivry day in Halsted Sthreet. If any wan comes along with
a histhry iv Greece or Rome that'll show me th' people fightin',
getting drunk, makin' love, gettin' married, owin' th' grocery
man an' bein' without hard-coal, I'll believe they was a Greece
or Rome, but not befure. Historyans is like doctors. They are
always lookin' f'r symptons. Those iv them that writes about
their own times examines th' tongue an' feels th' pulse an'
makes a wrong dygnosisk. The' other kind iv histhry is a post-
mortem examination. It tells ye what a counthry died if.
"But I'd like to know what it lived iv."*

Mr. Dooley

We are hard upon the two hundreth anniversary of our Independence. The historians "that write about their own times" often look
to headlines and newscasts only to see fearsome symptoms of a deadly
decay. In protests and demonstrations, picket lines and pamphlets, the
institutions of American life have been damned and derided.

Students laying siege to campus buildings, farm laborers on the
march, black garbage collectors seeking better conditions, PTA's challenging school administrators--all hold up the banner of "participatory
democracy."

To many observers such challenges are a menace to the Republic.
But to others, angry demands for community control are far superior

1

to a listless inattention to the affairs of government. Demonstrations protesting unilateral and insensitive policies are infinitely more preferable than what Erik Erikson has termed "the twilight smoothness of a dying civilization."

Does America thrive on riots and violence, militancy and confrontation? We are clear about their existence and pervasiveness of late. Do the shrill screams of a cursing mob always constitute the voice of the people? Even the most sympathetic supporters of "community involvement" shy away from violent confrontations.

Yet throughout the land, and in many other lands whose people often act out their own version of the great American drama, there is a growing, freshening rejection of centralized authority. In France, Japan, Czechoslovakia as well as in Brooklyn, there is a concommitant demand for a role in decision-making by those whose lives are affected by the decisions.

The movement takes no readily definable form, nor is it confined to particular areas or concerns. The blacks in major cities are visibly campaigning, with growing coherence and articulation, for power over their own affairs. So too are the youth, the voters, the consumers, the clergy, the Mexican-Americans in Texas and California, and the embattled patch farmers fighting strip mining in Appalachia. Perhaps the only common denominator is the shared feeling that the major danger is not the immediate evil, but the exclusion from power of those who must suffer that evil.

"What is Past is Prologue," reads the inscription on our National Archives building in Washington. "Study the Past." But if the inscription is true, we must still ask what in our past is prologue to identifiable present events and trends. Is a demand for community control over public facilities rooted in Jeffersonian concepts, or is it the modern version of Samuel Adams' inflamed mob attacks against any and all authority? Is resistance to opening new channels of communication and control founded on Hamiltonian ideals of dispassionate efficiency and even-handed administration, or on nervous insecurity and protection of ineptness from public scrutiny and correction?

The answer, in popular phrasing, is that "it depends." In some instances the conflict is real and ideological. In others, what appears to be a conflict is merely a shouting match between demagogue and bureaucrat.

What, then, is the touchstone?

The question is hardly academic. We are a free people and even the officials we ourselves elect trespass against our rights at their

2

peril. Yet we are a busy, thriving people; and we demand of our government services and programs to accommodate our needs. For our commerce we demand roads; yet we challenge the right of a highway commissioner to route a course through our homes. Urgent pleas for schools and hospitals are accompanied by insistence on lower taxes. "Produce more bricks," we command, "but use less straw."

Our officials, whatever their shortcomings, must be accorded some understanding when, caught in the inherent contradictions of democracy, they react with exasperation and anger at loud demands for an intangible called "involement," or "citizen participation." A mayor is, after all, under a mandate to perform certain functions; a mandate he has won, as he prefers to see it, from the entire community. So too with the city council or governor and legislature, or other governing body or authority. To subject his conduct and decisions to persons or groups who have won no similar mandate jars with the dictates of official conscience.

It is perhaps a controversial statement to ascribe credit to City Hall for concerning itself with the validity of citizen participation in the face of charges that City Hall has done no such thing. Nonetheless, City Hall has in many respects outgrown grumbling about loss of patronage and efficiency, and confined itself to the most pertinent question: with what authority do the representatives of "citizen participation" speak?

The question is logical to many; provocative to a few, and infuriating to a great many more. "We are the people!" comes the angry retort. "We speak with the only authority there is, the authority of the people."

"Ah, yes," answers the Mayor. "But can you prove it?"

And the proof is offered -- in the form of picket lines, office seizures, protest rallies, boycotts, marches, and a dozen other devices.

And still the Mayor might ask, "Where is your proof that you represent the people? Where is your election certificate?"

Few challenge the right of the people to conduct their affairs. It is the supposed instrument of the people's will which is closely scrutinized.

But election certificates are not infalliable. We have seen false elections; we have known disenfranchisement; we share the street cynicism toward the politician. And even the most trusting voter must concede that times change; that the political representative of a century ago, or even of two decades ago, is slow to respond to our fast-changing society.

What then, is the touchstone of citizen participation? How does a conscientious official determine the validity of an assertion that this or that group speaks for "the people" of an area or a community? And what are the processes that insure accountability of such groups to their constituency?

The questions have not gone unexamined in American life. A Congressional mandate to provide "maximum feasible participation" of the people to be served by programs in their development and direction has posed the question to communities concerned with implementing the Economic Opportunity Act of 1964. The Community Action Program of the Office of Economic Opportunity has sought -- in a thousand community programs across the land -- to work out the definition of participation. Model Cities programs, Elementary and Secondary Education Act programs, and innumerable private ventures have broadened the scope of the examination, until the definition and understanding of citizen participation has achieved recognition as an issue of paramount importance.

Even without such impetus, citizens and officials in a broad spectrum of endeavor have wrestled with the conflicting calls of concern and conviction.

One can hardly hope to produce a concise and complete answer to the problem. For Hamilton and Jefferson, thousands of hours of study and work were followed by days and weeks of hot debate and public correspondence. Nearly two centuries later, we see that their contribution was not the answering, but the questioning. In our own times, the complexities of our internal differences are staggering, and who can say which of our two hundred million souls has pent up within him the best answer?

If the past truly is prologue, we are amply forwarned of the futility of seeking a final solution, in a nation where each day works changes and interactions which subtly but surely alter the dimensions and proportions of the problem.

Shall we then abandon the problem altogether? Surely out of the growing experience of the past decade we can abstract some principles, some few constants with which to prepare our plans for the future.

In the past decade, and largely within the last half of that decade, we have spent hundreds of millions of dollars in programs centered upon the concept of citizen participation. Thousands, perhaps millions of citizens in virtually every town and city of the nation have

4

devoted hours of work and effort to evolving and implementing this intangible called citizen participation. To some, the concept was a means to particular ends in employment, housing, training, or other areas. To others, the process of involvement itself transcended more transient achievements in measurable objectives.

Out of all this, some knowledge must come. Even if, like Edison, we have labored only to discover those things which are useless, some stock-taking and analysis is in order.

It is in this sense that the following chapters are presented. They set forth theories, case histories, and monographs reflecting, in their entirety, much of what has transpired in the development of citizen participation since the passage of the Economic Opportunity Act.

Part I can best be described as a contemporary extension to the Jefferson-Madison dialogue, as it projects the provisions of the democratic credo into the current conflict between government and citizen over the status of individual and community self-determinism. In philosophical terms, the realities of today's democracy are matched to the credos of the past, the needs of the present, and the options for the future. The Cahns provide an analytical framework for understanding the case studies and monographs which follow.

Part II treats a number of general concerns regarding citizen participation. Here are some academically disciplined points of view: the sociology, politics, and public administration of citizen participation.* Some of the general considerations can be thought of as commentaries on, or addenda to, the Part I essay.†

Part III is a series of monographs which treat specific issues in citizen participation. The editors attempted to select authors whose experience put them closest to the action in a number of critical areas: community organization, rural cooperatives, schools, health, highways, manpower, and others.

*For excellent theoretical work on the history, politics and economics of participation, Milton Kotler of the Institute for Policy Studies in Washington has been a seminal thinker. His new book is *Neighborhood Government: The Local Foundations of Political Life*. Howard Hallman, a Washington consultant, has also been a thoughtful commentator, and actor, on citizen participation matters.

†Obviously, the general issues in Part II and the cases in Part III are not meant to be exhaustive or even focused on the most dramatic issues. Most of the readers of this volume will be familiar with the CDGM Mississippi story, which is not included. There is no monograph on the significant participatory achievements sparked by the North Carolina Fund in many parts of that state. The editors' assumption is that books on these cases are being or will be written.

Each monograph is preceded by a *brief* trainer's guide, in the form of an editor's note, designed to tell the reader who the author is, perhaps a key point to watch, and several questions to expand the scope or applicability of the study beyond the subject matter at hand. The reader is advised to ignore these road signs if he considers them patronizing or unhelpful: the monographs are the meat.

For the traveler approaching the rocky road of citizen participation, there is no prescribed route, but the road signs and warnings are many and distinct. *Where the monographs only document the errors of yesterday but thereby prevent the repetition of those errors today and tomorrow, they will have served their purpose well.* Where they point to successful experiences, these can be taken as models and examples for future efforts. A brief discussion guide serves as the introduction to each monograph. It is designed simply as a tool to trainers attempting to make effective use of the book.*

Citizen participation does not foster halfhearted supporters. Many who have played a role in its growth have foregone the neutrality of observers for a partisan's satisfaction. Others, having lived in the crossfire of criticism and controversy, have become ardent opponents of what they see as the false reasoning and unrealistic expectations of citizen participation. Such varying viewpoints are of necessity reflected in the pages which follow.

But whether the future holds an expansion or a contraction of citizen participation, or participatory democracy, it seems certain that the greater issue will never fade: the fundamental American dialogue between the citizen and his government. This, in Mr. Dooley's terms, is what America "lives of."

---

*At least two reference works not reprinted here are most useful for an understanding of the OEO contribution to citizen participation: Ralph M. Kramer, *Participation of the Poor,* Prentice-Hall, 1969, a series of comparative case studies of community action in the San Francisco Bay area; and "Participation of the Poor. . ." *The Yale Law Journal,* Vol. 75, No. 4, (March, 1966), pp. 599-629. Most of the intellectually stimulating writing on this subject – by Peter Marris, Martin Rein, Daniel Moynihan, Edgar and Jean Cahn, Melvin Mogulof, Richard Cloward, Frank Riessman, and others – dates from the early and more optimistic years of the war on poverty, 1964 through early 1967.

Part I

MAXIMUM FEASIBLE PARTICIPATION

MAXIMUM FEASIBLE PARTICIPATION
A GENERAL OVERVIEW

by: Edgar S. Cahn
Jean Camper Cahn*

Irrespective of the political controversy in which the words "maximum feasible participation" have become embroiled, the reality of citizen participation—on an expanded and intensified scale—is here to stay. It is easy to misinterpret the words, easy to make a straw man of them, but the processes that "maximum feasible participation" have at once set in motion and highlighted must be recognized as part of a larger endeavor to reinterpret the meaning and scope of democracy for our age and our times.

The reasons for the reinterpretation are many:

. . . Life has become more complex, society more fragmented, our next door neighbors strangers.

. . . The functions of government have multiplied and expanded beyond the citizen's control and comprehension.

. . . Cleavages of race, class and region seem to threaten the very foundations of our national being.

. . . An urban, industrial society has at once rendered existence impersonal, and challenged the meaning of our federal system and of personal existence itself.

. . . The radical expansion of governmental functions, powers and programs requires redefinition of the meaning of genuine enfranchisement in a democracy.

. . . Increased expertise, specialization and professionalism all pose a peculiar threat to a democratic credo which rejects government by an elite and vests ultimate authority in the citizen *qua* citizen.

*Jean Camper Cahn is Director of the Urban Law Institute, Washington, D.C. Biographical information about Edgar S. Cahn is given in the About the Editors section at the back of the book.
We wish to acknowledge and express our appreciation for the research and editorial assistance provided by Martha Maxwell, Joan Nicholson and Joseph Wilkins.

9

"Maximum feasible participation" has given rise to a process of experimentation in an effort to cope with these factors, attempts which go beyond any single government or private program. In essence this phrase has become a catalyst for that long overdue task—the redefinition of the relationship between the citizen and his government in a democratic society founded upon individual rights and liberties.

Indeed, we stand in need of an assessment of this phenomenon. Controversial though it is, the lessons that can be extrapolated are applicable not merely to governmental programs such as model cities, freeway construction, decentralization of schools or neighborhood control of policy, but to the larger and ultimate question—the meaning of citizenship in a democratic society.

There are three general propositions which sum up the experience which has been generated by (though not confined to) citizen participation under the poverty program.

First, citizen participation is fraught with dangers and risk. Even at its best, and when most fully realized, it is precarious, fragile, vulnerable and easily destroyed or perverted. It is threatening, likely to invite retaliation, and likely to generate highly explosive and controversial situations.

Second, citizen participation in all its varied aspects and dimensions has demonstrated that it can make major and unique contributions.

Third, and finally, the values of citizen participation are such that they outweigh the liabilities, the risks and the dangers. The evidence is compelling that as a society we have no choice but to accept the risks and costs of an expanded democratic ideal, if we are to achieve the goals we have set for ourselves as a nation.

The Risks of Citizen Participation

Newspaper headlines and Congressional declamations have provided ample documentation that citizen participation has its risks.

Entrusting management control and decision-making power to the poor has led to accusations, some exaggerated, some not, of fiscal shortages, "Hate Whitey" campaigns underwritten with federal dollars, alleged "revolutionary" and "para-military" activity.

Those responsible for the programs have learned to be philosophical about these allegations. They acknowledge that some failures are inevitable, some excesses predictable, but point out that the experts have made even greater mistakes, and failed on a far grander scale in

10

accomplishing public objectives.

Money has been found missing or unaccounted. But this may only mean that the poor are less adept than professionals in juggling their accounts and providing minimal paper documentation to satisfy standard accounting procedures.

Item 1

A 1967 audit of Harlem's HARYOU-ACT, Inc., the nation's largest antipoverty program, found that more than $800,000 had been misspent, improperly accounted for or lost, in addition to many other irregularities during a two-year period. It was found that the organization's books and records were not kept in accordance with good accounting principles. Items were not properly accounted for and excessive and improper payments were made to employees.

Item 2

In the summer of 1965 the Black Arts Theater received $40,000 in anti-poverty money as a cultural component of the Haryou-Act summer program. Fifty members of the experimental theater, under the direction of Negro poet-playwright LeRoi Jones, channeled anti-white bitterness into popular street-corner drama, with whites cast as villains. It was described by OEO Director Sargent Shriver as producing "vile racist plays in language of the gutter unfit for the youngsters of the audience."

However, given the extent of racial polarity that exists in this country, our society scarcely lacks for expressions of racist sentiment with or without federal funds. When such sentiments crop up in a federally funded program, the cutoff of federal funds as a retaliation for such racial expressions may be politically necessary yet constitutionally repugnant.

In all the controversies which have surrounded the War on Poverty in general, and the phrase "maximum feasible participation" of the poor in particular, one characteristic has stood out: the unforgiveable tendency of the poor "to bite the hand that feeds them." Politicians looking for gratitude, teachers looking for appreciation, welfare workers looking for understanding, racial moderates risking community acceptance—all have been the object of attack by the poor. And few have escaped unscathed from excoriating confrontations with

11

"representatives of the poor."

Welfare workers have been subjected to blistering attacks from the combined forces of welfare rights organizations and lawyers representing welfare clients. Educators, even kindergarten teachers, have been accused of being an integral part of a system of "designed retardation," a system which consistently fails at least 30% of its poverty-stricken subjects, a system which at best performs dubiously.

Public housing administrators and private landlords have been beleaguered by tenant unions demanding lower rents, better maintenance, and improved services.

Private voluntary agencies, epitomized by the Community Chest, Red Feather and United Givers Funds, have been met with demands that a greater allocation of funds go directly to poverty programs. The integrity of their own structures has been challenged with demands that they place representatives of the poor on their board.

Hard-pressed mayors, striving to avoid middle class backlash while struggling to secure a greater measure of social justice for the poor, have been damned by poor and public alike, their sincerity and motives decried as paternalism, their effectiveness denied altogether.

Other controversies have arisen in the method of funding programs.

City governments have found themselves at war over community action programs funded without the auspices or blessings of the municipal administration. County officials have been miffed by programs which were not funded through them but funded directly to groups within the country, or funded through multi-county agencies which threatened the purity and sovereignty of the county unit.

State governments have been among the most aggrieved because, generally, state agencies have been by-passed. In emphasis, programs have been primarily urban and municipal. The states have usually been relegated to the role of spectator, with only a limited option to veto or not to veto a program, while knowing full well that vetoes, if exercised, may be overruled in Washington.

Finally, and perhaps especially, neither local nor federal poverty agencies have been immune from criticism and attack by the ungrateful poor. Almost since the program's inception, community action agencies have been the object of bitter attack by the poor. As the poor become more sophisticated, the day rarely passes, in Washington, D.C., or in the regional offices, when some delegation of the poor does not descend with or without pickets, before or after press conferences, before or following visits with members of Congress, to demand that some aspect

12

of the program be modified in accordance with their wishes.

In the Washington, D.C., community action agency, the employees held a sitdown strike in headquarters. Occasionally, a cause celebre engenders vast disaffection or revolt with OEO itself, leading to employee petitions and confrontations with superiors.

In short, the poor have struck first against those considered to be the friends and allies of the poor.

The entire pattern of controversy and ingratitude came to a symbolic head when the poor turned on the private sector, the government and Sargent Shriver, the Director of the Office of Economic Opportunity. Shriver, the foremost official proponent for implementing the mandate "maximum feasible participation," was himself booed and virtually forced out of a nationwide gathering of delegates of the poor in 1966.

In retrospect such controversies appear to be the predictable, perhaps the inevitable cost of insisting that the poor be given a voice in the management and design of programs operated for their benefit. If the poor speak, they become advocates of their own. If provided with trained advocates and technicians, they are likely to begin operating as a quasi-political or explicitly political force in their own communities. Their sense of pace and direction for change is likely to offend those who are nearest at hand, or those who view things differently. Others working for progress at a more gradual pace, or moderating between the zealous and the recalcitrant, become caught in the conflict, and those who side with the poor are bound to be caught in the middle and perhaps crushed.

The fact is not without political implications. For it undercuts, on both the local and national levels the feasibility of coalition politics, in which the so-called liberal establishment (unions, professionals, civil rights organizations, charitable groups, etc.) unite with the poor to press for social reform. Such coalitions are likely to be torn assunder by internecine warfare, some of which is generated by the poor who view the coalition as inextricably linked with "the enemy"—and who are unwilling to tolerate a "trickle-down" approach to social change.

Thus what starts off as a war on poverty swiftly may degenerate into a war between the poor and the professional poverty warriors (the experts, the volunteers, the do-gooders) who possess much of the political power necessary to launch and sustain the effort.

This "ingratitude" of the poor takes two forms. The most familiar is that of confrontation and denunciation. But this form, embarrassing

13

and politically damaging as it may be, is made far more threatening and emotional by a second form. "Ingratitude" or "rejection" means direct competition for the private and the public dollar, the power, the prestige, the roles, the employment, the image, the status, which have traditionally been attendant upon charitable undertakings.

The poor simply demand: "Give us the money and we'll do the job ourselves. We don't need you with all your high paid consultants and administrators."

In a more sophisticated way this demand manifests itself in the setting up of competing enterprises which are not extensions (or outreach efforts) of existing agencies, but which are run—in varying degrees—of, by and for the poor. This competitive approach to fighting the war on poverty underlies a major portion of the conflicts and controversies which erupt in the public press.

In Chicago or Watts it may take the form of a demand by the so-called extremists or Black Nationalist groups, or gangs, to exercise some of the functions which the police purport to perform—such as keeping law and order, preventing riots or preventing the excessive use of force. Such groups find the power to engage in such activities jealously guarded, even when a "policing" service might be performed more effectively by non-police.

Certainly the police are not the only monopolistic enterprise being challenged.

Non-professionals and aides can and do acquire sufficient savvy to question the salaries, authority and even expertise of their superiors.

Parents challenge the school system, wondering if they couldn't be more effective than the central school board.

Tenant unions demand to take over and manage the buildings in which they dwell, or engage in rent strikes to compel the management to bring the buildings up to local housing codes.

Groups challenging urban renewal and highway construction programs have, in effect, threatened the established oligopoly of highway department, real estate and urban renewal agencies, who proclaim from their official positions that their plan is the one and only way in which a city may be recast.

Competition aimed at these established monopoly groups, many of which have long operated without any effective monitoring, represents a direct threat to their power, prestige and authority. The conversation becomes less polite and degenerates into the stuff of which headlines are made: "Poverty officials blast school board!" "Mayor demands

14

investigation of Poverty Group."

Citizen participation is difficult to champion. Too often, when one begins to see signs of success and dares to boast publicly, a scandal breaks, or an attack is levied on the group in question, or the special magic that somehow bound the group together has disappeared and the whole effort disintegrates.

In other instances, precarious coalitions between different factions among the poor—factions of poor and non-poor, white and non-white, professional and non-professional, urban and suburban—come together for a moment, perhaps around a singular effort, a particular crisis or awesome challenge. But when efforts are made to institutionalize these partnerships, to give continuity to that spirited cooperation and selfless-ness, to sustain that unstinting effort and maintain those lines of com-munication, one is faced with a task of an entirely different magnitude. Yesterday's triumphs then become tomorrow's ignominious failures; yesterday's partners become irreconcilable enemies; yesterday's repre-sentatives of the poor and of the non-poor are disowned and publicly denounced by their own constituencies. And, too, organizations and individuals change in time. They drift from their original mission, lose their original sense of zeal and become bare facsimiles of their own model group of six months earlier. They become in fact a "poverty bureaucracy," and their prime goals become survival and refunding as ends in themselves.

Thus, the Citizens Alert Patrol, or the Blackstone Rangers in Chicago, were darlings of the press and even favorites of the police when they helped, in a crisis, to cool explosive situations. But a few months later they were at billy-stick length again. A CAP program in Southeast Georgia, Action, Inc., which had once been the pride of blacks and whites, officials and the private sector, began organizing welfare rights groups. Then it became the "tool" of a "trouble-mongering" cadre of three or four "outsiders" who had to be gotten rid of or the program shelved.

Such are the risks of genuine citizen participation on the occasions when it has actually functioned. It is small wonder that politicians of all persuasions and parties find themselves asking whether they can afford the price of democracy—particularly in their own backyards.

Their reservations and their objections are usually couched in other terms:

(1) The government cannot subsidize "revolution."

(2) The poor do not know what is good for them; otherwise they

15

would not be poor. Only the experts know what the poor need to escape poverty—one school superintendent said of the poor: "If they had all their marbles, they wouldn't be poor!"

(3) What the poor need are jobs, not organizing into trouble-making groups.

(4) Citizen participation only stirs controversy, causes delay and polarizes the differences between the races and classes.

The Values of Citizen Participation

"Democracy," said Churchill, "is the worst possible form of government . . . except for all of the other forms."

Much the same could be said of Citizen Participation as an instrument for eliminating poverty. It is a concept which has been credited with duping the poor, fostering scandal and encouraging riot. Its evolution under the "maximum feasible participation" mandate of the Economic Opourtunity Act of 1964 has been a journalist's badlands, a social planner's disaster, and a politician's nightmare.

It is also expensive, time consuming and unpredictable in its results. Achieved in full measure, it is invisible. In the hands of demagogues and sensationalists, it is treacherous and often uncontrollable.

With all of its faults, it is indispensable to any real effort to eliminate poverty in America.

The values of citizen participation fall into three broad categories. It provides:

1. *A means of mobilizing unutilized resources*—a source of productivity and labor not otherwise tapped.
2. *A source of knowledge*—both corrective and creative—a means of securing feedback regarding policy and programs, and also a source of new, inventive and innovative approaches.
3. *An end in itself*—an affirmation of democracy and the elimination of alienation and withdrawal, of destructiveness, hostility, and lack of faith in relying on the people.

Participation by the poor as a means of mobilizing resources

The first value of citizen participation rests on the limitations inherent in democratic government—on the inability of any free government to survive without the consent and active support of its citizens. Short of total war, a free government is incompetent to marshal the full

16

resources of its people by compulsion. And the dimensions of poverty are such that anything short of full utilization of our human resources will be ineffective. But such a full utilization, in the absence of a totalitarian authority or an all-out war, depends on the will of the people themselves—in this case, on the active support of the citizens in poverty. It is to them that government must look for the motivation, the energy and the continued interest necessary to vitalize programs. Such motivation, in turn, depends on the relevance and self-interest bred only when the beneficiaries share responsibility in, and identify with, efforts affecting their conditions.

Citizen participation offers a means of so marshaling the poor, of converting them from passive consumers of the services of others into producers of those services. This can be a form of exploitation and manipulation; but it can equally be a way of subjecting demands of accreditation, testing and minimal educational requirements to the test of performance. By putting such traditional demands to the test of merit, citizen participation may demonstrate that we have unwittingly deprived ourselves—through disfunctional and artificial barriers to participation and contribution—of a vast manpower resource for the attainment of national goals.

Item 1

In Arizona, the donation of a 750-gallon tank and of a 1950 two-ton Chevrolet truck formed the nucleus for a volunteer fire department for Guadalupe.

The truck, a worn-out discard, was put back into running condition by the men of Guadalupe. They also patched, rustproofed and painted the tank, inside and out. The Guadalupe Organization, an OEO grantee, purchased a force pump and fifty feet of two-inch hose with fittings and fire nozzle.

A large number of members of the Guadalupe Organization agreed to serve as firemen and organized a volunteer fire brigade. About 40 of them took Red Cross lifesaving instruction and eight became qualified lifesaving instructors.

The organization has plans to build and equip an emergency service center which will provide fire-fighting service and emergency first aid service on a twenty-four hour basis.

One finds similar self-help efforts as a form of citizen participation in countless cooperatives and enterprises.

17

Item 2

Residents of a mountainous four-county area in Appalachia are doing something about their transportation nightmare. Representatives of several communities joined together, studied the problem and determined the costs of running their own minibus service—sliding payment scale or contribution of $3 a month for a family of 6. With a loan to make the down payment on several 12-passenger buses, the group is about to begin its own transportation services. The monthly contributions will pay off the loan and eventually pay for the buses.

Item 3

In the East Harlem Puerto Rican community, members of an organization called the Real Great Society can proudly point to "vest pocket" parks which have been fashioned out of former neighborhood garbage heaps. Now cleaned and smoothed out, they are furnished with ingenious playground equipment. That story is mirrored in countless cities across the country.

Item 4

In many forms, on the Navajo reservation, the difference in "doing it oneself" was pointedly made. Fire had levelled a structure which had housed a Headstart program run by the community for its children. Within hours, a community meeting had been convened in the chapter house, the decision made to convert the chapter house into a temporary facility, the material gathered, designs drawn up, workmanship executed—all as a volunteer effort on a crash basis. Twenty-four hours later, the chapter house had been converted into a usable facility and the program was maintained without break. The director of the poverty program pointed out that had that been a Bureau of Indian Affairs school, the people would have just stood, watched the fire, then turned and walked away. The difference was, this was their program. The responsibility was theirs for success, failure or impasse in the face of adversity.

Item 5

In Mingo County, W. Va., throughout Mississippi, and elsewhere, this story of support for Headstart Centers repeats itself, a story of clothes and furniture constructed or contributed by the poor, persons who gave what they could to a program they felt genuinely theirs to run, a program which offered the real possibility of giving their children the chance they had never had in life.

Item 6

In Newark, the BLAZER Youth Council canvassed the neighborhoods to raise enough money to start a planned work training program when OEO's delay in releasing a grant threatened to delay the opening of the center.*

One finds the self-help endeavor yielding remarkable productivity when it applies to services as well as to tangible goods. Medicare Alert was a particularly successful effort to mobilize the aged around the Medicare programs so that the deadline for eligibility for benefits could be met. In many respects the program had much in common with all the outreach efforts where individuals from the poverty group were employed to "reach out" to others, to bridge the communication gap and tell their friends and neighbors about a variety of government programs—i.e.: housing, welfare, food stamps, commodities, Headstart, job training, job corps and other programs. Messages can be most effectively carried by the poor to the poor.

Item 9

A social work aide, Mrs. Betty T. Smith, recounts her experience in a Headstart program administered by the Human Development Corporation of Columbia, Mo.:

"About one week after Headstart had begun last summer, I heard of a five-year-old boy who lived out in a rural area who really needed Headstart. I also heard that the old lady who was raising the child was awful hard to get along with and mean. When I went to visit, I was told that Mrs. Johnson was fishing with the little boy at a pond about half a mile from the house. So we walked down to the pond, and found them there fishing. I told Mrs. Johnson who I was and why I was there. And she started to take the poles out of the water. I told her to go ahead and fish. I would be glad to talk to her right there. I told her I had five boys

*Most of these examples are from *Communities in Action,* the CAP newsletter.

and one girl and that I was raising them alone, and how they like to fish and that I took them weekends when I didn't work. So we talked about fishing, and what kind of bait we used. Finally she acted like she didn't think I was so bad. Then I started talking to her about Headstart."

Mrs. Smith, with her own experience with poverty, welfare and Headstart, was able to help Mrs. Johnson overcome her fears, obtain clothes for Richard, and was able to help Richard make the big jump from isolation to Headstart group activities and the strangeness of fire engines and dentists. She goes on to say:

"Their home is small and they have very little, but Richard had love, I could see that. This old woman had a lot of love in her heart for this child. She was so proud of him. The school social worker said she thought they should take Richard out of that dirty mess. I just about flipped. I told her he might not have many clothes or the right kind of food to eat, but he was very fortunate. He had someone to love him and do her best for him. When Headstart was all over, I still went to see Mrs. Johnson and Richard, as I've tried to all the kids. Then it came time for school to start, Mrs. Johnson didn't have the money to send him. I asked her if she had ever tried to get welfare, and she said, yes, for three years, but she couldn't get it. She acted like she was afraid to go out there, so I said I'll go with you, I go out there all the time. So we went and Mrs. Johnson finally got her welfare."

There was a problem with bus transportation for Richard to get to school; with Mrs. Smith to act as liaison with the school people and Mrs. Johnson it was quickly resolved. Mrs. Smith concludes:

"She sends him every day now, and Richard really likes school. Since she got her welfare check, they have more to eat too. Mrs. Johnson came to two of our parent meetings for Headstart mothers. I go out and get her so she can come."

Public health nurses have found that they can provide more service to more people in shorter periods of time because of tasks carried out by non-professional aides.

Sanitarians found that they could communicate effectively for the first time with Puerto Rican tenants when they were accompanied by a Spanish-speaking Puerto Rican public health assistant.

Yet, even this outreach and informing function can spark controversy, precisely because it does produce unique results. Most controversial have been those groups which have vastly increased the impact of programs on the poor—by informing them of their rights. Those rights may be contained in housing codes. The results may be rent strikes which force landlords or city governments to make slum dwellings conform to building code standards.

Item 10

The Roanoke City Council voted for rigid enforcement of housing and hygiene ordinances enacted 18 months earlier, following a campaign waged by the members of the Southwest Community Center. In unanimous action, the Roanoke Council instructed the city manager to apply the code as written and adopted a set of regulations to guide enforcement.

The Southwest Community Center had appeared before the council requesting rigorous application of the ordinance and returned at a later meeting with pictures showing slum housing conditions. At the first meeting, the council instructed the city manager to investigate the enforcement of the housing code and to do something to rid the area of the snakes and rats infesting some of the houses.

As part of the campaign, the group began a voter registration drive to insure that all area residents would be eligible to vote in a coming election of councilmen.

Public education about rights may involve guarantees of adequate relocation under urban renewal programs—and this may spark city-wide controversies as it has in Camden, Newark and New Haven. Or they may involve welfare and related programs where citizen participation has resulted in a vast increase in the welfare rolls and higher levels of payments to individuals as a result of their receiving that which the law guarantees.

Item 11

Three welfare recipients' groups in the South Bronx focused on bringing clients up to the minimum standards set by the Welfare Department. In December, 1966, they obtained $8,000 in checks for winter coats, boots and necessary items, all of which they were eligible to receive but had been unable to obtain. Such participation has seldom been looked on with political favor.

In still other areas, spokesmen from the poor communities are disseminating a knowledge of the law and the rights guaranteed by

21

law. This has generated consumer boycotts of stores which over-charged the poor or charged usurious interest rates, boycotts which aroused the wrath of local Boards of Trade and Chambers of Commerce. But it has also instigated attempts to negotiate and resolve the problems.

Item 12

In New York, the Consumer Action Program of Bedford-Stuyvesant, Inc. (CABS) funded by OEO, has developed programs to deal coordinately with consumers and neighborhood merchants in interdependent economic and social problems.

Residents trained in consumer education and action have organized block committees in a 64-block target area to serve as units of consumer education and as forums to discuss and resolve consumer-retailer conflicts. They bring concerted action to bear on problems such as pricing, credit practices and consumer protection legislation. After the chief complaints of residents were determined, a comparison shopping survey was made.

Six residents submitted regular shopping lists of items, amounts and brand names together with the names of the chain stores where they regularly shopped. The lists were analyzed to determine a typical list of 20 items and five major chain stores.

Conducted on two separate days to determine the validity of complaints that prices were higher on welfare check days, the survey canvassed the five stores and one middle class store. In four of the five surveyed the Bed-Sty bills ranged from $.07 to $.78 higher than the middle class store on one day and from $.25 to $1.00 more on the other day. The fifth store which showed no discrepancy on the first day showed a variance of $.34 on the next.

This information is being used as a tool for negotiation and as a means of bridging the gap between consumer and business.

Similarly, efforts to involve parents in Headstart programs—and tutorial programs run by students for students—have manifested special promise in reaching the unreachable, in exciting tutor and pupil alike, in reshaping the parents' attitude toward the child and the school. But they have also generated demands, expectations, and have made the teacher and his school less a symbol of authority and of teaching purity. Often the educational system becomes recast in the

22

image of an institution of society which has failed to live up to the American promise of quality education for all. The poor, by participating as parent aides, lunch room aides and tutors have become less afraid and more prepared to speak of their dissatisfaction and disappointments.

Item 13

Community residents in a Teacher Aide Program in the Cardozo Area of Washington, D.C., provided services to teachers, children and parents.

One aide served in a welfare role for the school, distributing clothes, grocery shopping and taking children to clinics. She visited homes to encourage mothers to come to school and to participate in PTA, despite hostile or fearful feelings.

Another aide provided the bridge between parent and teacher. An angry mother, indignant that the teacher had called her child lazy, insisted that he just had 'tired blood' and that there was nothing that could be done about it. Her belligerence began to disappear when the aide confessed that she had a son who was lazy, but who had improved in school when she and the father began giving him some attention and help with his school work. Later, the mother admitted to the aide that her son threw his homework in the trash can. She began to encourage her son to do his work.

But residents in the school as aides can also cause controversy as they constitute an imagined or real threat to teachers and administrators.

Item 14

In Washington, D.C., Eastern High School, a group of young students, as a result of dissatisfaction with the school for offering no courses in black history or culture, spent a year planning, raising money and making arrangements for Freedom Annex, the first accredited student-run school in the country.

Teachers, hired by the students and accredited by the D.C. School Board, teach such courses as black history, Swahili, black philosophy, black literature, contemporary problems, economics, black art and drama and community organization.

With the sanction of the school system, students attending the

23

Freedom Annex go to regular classes at Eastern High for half a day and attend classes at the annex for the remainder of the day.

"Modern Strivers," the group which planned, organized, and is running the school, sought and obtained financing from foundations and private individuals. Major decisions are made by the students themselves. The first president of the board of directors was a 19 year old student.

The Assistant Superintendent for Secondary Schools, dubious at first, is now pleased and surprised at "the amount of interest shown by the students and the level of interchange between students and teachers . . . The school could be the beginning of a different kind of high school."

But politicians and educators alike have a difficult time appraising this kind of effort and distinguishing it from the kinds of concerns and demands which underlie the school decentralization controversies in the New York City public school system and which are spreading to other urban centers.

Such contributions are often accompanied by new demands. The very quality of contribution that is so unique is likely to stem from a sense of community, of esprit de corps, of mission which is impatient with obstacles. People engaged in such efforts sometimes cannot accept the ways of the past and the wisdom of the past as infallible. Their commitment is to move, from contribution to confrontation.

Moreover, once the poor become incorporated into the school system, the health system or the welfare system, that which yesterday seemed incomprehensible and inaccessible suddenly becomes part of their everyday world. The mystery disappears. The barriers—of accreditation, of the middle class schooling format which bears little relationship to performance or future realities—emerge as artificial means of discriminating, as ways to halt upward mobility, as ways of keeping the poor "in their place." It is this awareness which prompted a Negro sub-professional, when asked what term he preferred, "nonprofessional," "aide," "sub-professional" or "para-professional," to reply: "I'd rather be white."

Once the seemingly occult becomes comprehensible, these barriers to upward mobility are less comprehensible. The insistence that all decisions be made by the professionals, who themselves have had to turn to the poor for advice, is viewed with increased cynicism and anger.

Yet, given the shortage of trained professionals—and the capable,

24

critical contribution of the poor—it is no small tribute that a major portion of the new positions provided for in plans submitted under the Elementary and Secondary Education Act are for teacher's aides and non-professionals. These positions, in fact, exceed, in number the new accredited teacher positions requested in these plans.

Access into the system carries with it demands for full upward mobility. This controversy is already hitting construction unions where, under new programs, ghetto residents will be enlisted as trainees or advanced trainees. But the demand now is for some assurance that they will have the opportunity to obtain full apprenticeship and, later, journeyman status.

The unique contribution of the poor, the knowledge and special skills they bring to their efforts on behalf of one another, has ever present the potential for controversy and conflict. This potential rises first to the surface even more when we turn to the second distinctive asset of the poor—the knowledge they possess about the sources of failure in past efforts, accompanied by the creative, innovative approaches they offer to programming for the future.

Participation By The Poor as A Source Of Knowledge

It may be safe to assume that only the poor know the full dimensions of poverty. There are, of course, those who would cynically disclaim the knowledge a patient has when seeking treatments from a doctor, who would make a superior claim to the knowledge of poverty's symptoms—the aches and pains to which the poor fall heir by virtue of race, accident of birth, or region, age or occupation.

By virtue of this first expertise, the poor are heir to a second type of expertise. They hold a special knowledge of their benefactors' limitations and of the great deficiencies in the treatments "prescribed" for them.

The second major value of citizen participation lies in its power to inform and validate government efforts. It constitutes a source of special insight, of information, of knowledge and experience which cannot be ignored. Comprehensive action programs, devised by professionals and accepted by the dominant social, political, educational and economic institutions, represent from an empiricist's point of view merely a consensus, majority support for a given theory on the solution of social problems. The consumer perspective—the view of the person who must live day to day with the end results of those efforts—is a radically different perspective.

25

We have paid in the past for failure to take into account this source of corrective knowledge. The defects, inequities and false assumptions on which programs are based (and who can name a program free of such?) form an integral part of the design and redesign of these programs. Token approval, acquiescience and resignation have been eagerly equated with citizen participation. But in doing so, we as a society have deprived ourselves of the only form of validation yet devised for a majority consensus—critical scrutiny and dissent by those with a different perspective.

Item 1

Lorain, Ohio

In Skeels Alottment and McAlereth Park, impoverished families huddled in shacks and cabins. In wet weather they swept filth and excrement from their floors back into open sewerage ditches after each flooding. In dry spells, they grimly buried the small children burned to death in savage fires unchecked and uncontrollable in a community with no running water, no fire hydrants and no fire company.

Each house is supposed to have a water tank, with a capacity of hundreds of gallons of water. The water, however, costs money, which the poor do not always have. It is rare that a tank holds sufficient water to put out the fires which start each winter in the kerosene-lit, wood-burning, coal-cooking households. A retired railroad worker points to the charred skeleton of a cabin, and tells of a mother who went out to drink, leaving seven children locked up, five of whom died in the fire.

"She shouldn't drink, God knows, but it still ain't right that the kids should pay for her sins. If we could get some money to hire some old grannies to babysit while the mother's out, maybe we could talk the women into going after jobs, or back to school. Anything's better than seeing these kids getting killed every winter."

Where was the government? "Oh, this ain't a city ... it's just sort of county property. We get trustees appointed by the county who are supposed to be running things, but they're usually bankers from the city who don't come out here much."

There was a community action program, but it degenerated into a personal feud between a schoolteacher and an insurance executive and never got off the ground. "Programs of this sort can't be

26

left to people of no education," said the schoolteacher. "It takes experience in administration to set up these programs, and time," said the insurance executive, "You just can't rush into them . . . if you do, you will disappoint the poor by making them expect too much."

"Sure, we been to the community action meetings," said the housewife from Skeels Alottment, with a tired smile. "But all we see is these two men shouting and hollering at each other. If my children acted like that in public, I'd smack them good. But we thought they could get something done. Seems now if we want something done, we'll have to do it ourselves. But where we gonna get the money?"

The need to avail ourselves systematically of the views of the consumer of these programs, of the intended beneficiary—the need to promote and provide for the articulation of their needs, concerns and grievances—becomes all the more critical in the context of comprehensive planning. For here the commitment of resources is greater, the sources of dissent and criticism more readily muffled and ignored, and the scope of potential error increased many-fold.

The poor were aware of the differential standard of justice applied to them long before the legal profession or the U.S. Attorney General made this revelation.

Negroes always knew the stigma of inferiority which stems from segregation. The badge of slavery could be seen without a Supreme Court test case to reveal it.

The empty stomachs of the poor eloquently attested to the fact that food stamp prices were too high—though the Secretary of Agriculture in 1967 pointed to studies which showed prices were not too high. (A year later, he admitted that, on reexamination, those studies were methodologically unsound, and that they consistently over-estimated the amount the poor spent on food.)

Another foil to participation comes under the heading of "technical assistance." No one who has tried to remind the poor that they should be grateful for recent "progress," will deny that the complaints of the poor provide a new source of insight. For too often the "experts" are victims of their own propaganda; they begin to equate effort and sincerity with results.

Finally, the special expertise of the poor has utility beyond programs designed for the poor only. More acutely than others, the poor are fully cognizant of how all "citizen consumers" of government

27

services are shortchanged, victimized. Our entire society is plagued by government inadequacies in such areas as schooling, health service, housing, inflation, crime and pollution.

Many of these problems stem not from a lack of technical knowledge and experience, but rather from an inadequate distribution system which prevents certain individuals from reaping the maximum benefits from resources and knowledge already available.

Because the poor most acutely feel the shortage of trained teachers, lawyers, doctors, dentists, nurses—not to mention appliance, auto and household repairmen—they are more likely to demand vast revisions in the standards of mass production and distribution of goods and services than the middle class which only grumbles. The poor are less wedded to expanding the obsolescent systems of education, health or housing, as they know the systems will not work for them.

The poor knew that training programs do not necessarily lead to jobs—long before the experts began talking about "comprehensive" manpower programs.

Even the children of the poor surmised that their schooling did not equip them to compete successfully in the mainstream long before experts observed that preparation by a Headstart program was generally ineffective after the first six months of regular schooling.

In one of their displays of expertise, the poor demonstrated their astuteness about a new program, a pilot City Hall Complaint Center in the District of Columbia, by selecting the downtown City Hall Center, where they perceived power to lie in preference to the decentralized neighborhood complaint center located more conveniently in their own area. More revealing, the poorest of the poor declined to use the complaint center at all, partly due to a recognition that complaint mechanisms do not affect the fundamental disparities which reflect the deep cleavages of race and class in today's society.

To return to the patient-doctor metaphor, not only do the poor know what it feels like to be poor, but they also are the first to sense that the treatment prescribed is failing, even while they are being assured that the treatment will work if they give it a chance.

They know when old wine is being poured into new bottles, and old programs are being repackaged. In their terms, someone is "running a game on them." Consequently, they will temporize less than the rest of society—they are quicker to spot the ultimate futility of certain approaches to social change which they correctly perceive as simply more of the same.

In this respect, they make major contributions, not just to the design of efforts in their behalf, but in shaping attempts to reform our systems of education, justice, health, mass transportation, housing—all necessary elements of a just, compassionate and sane society. In short, the poor are the most likely to exclaim first that the emperor has no clothes.

Item 3

This has been known to occasion acute embarrassment. Dr. Robert Roessel, a nationally known expert in Indian education, told Congressional subcommittees of the understandable pride he had taken in having collected a galaxy of experts and superior professionals to staff a pilot community school at Rough Rock on a Navajo reservation. But the community school board rejected his choice of faculty.

They requested that a faculty be drawn principally from among Navajos who wished to help children bridge the gap between the worlds of whites and Indians, of home and boarding school, of traditional culture and formal education. Dr. Roessel had the vision and sensitivity to accept their judgment and to acknowledge subsequently that the community was right.

"The catastrophe I foresaw did not eventuate." In fact, in major differences between "expert" and "untutored" judgment, his records state that the "untutored" decisions have been right in at least twenty of the twenty-four most violent disagreements. Of the remaining four issues, he simply maintains that it is impossible to tell who was right.

Some professionals are not so tolerant—or willing to admit their own fallibility. In city battles now erupting nationally over new freeways, the poor are often alone in resisting the construction, knowing it will bring a greater rush of automobiles into city streets, greater air pollution, and that it may well mean being uprooted once again in the name of an illusory and destructive progress.

The battle over rising medical costs coupled with the increased lack of personal attention; the frustration of even the middle and upper class tenant with poor maintenance service by absentee, impersonal management corporations; the rise in divorce rates and suburban crime, and the newly discovered generation gap are all phenomena with which the poor have long been most familiar. If they do not have all the solutions, they at least know the needs and like Thomas Edison know of "999 things that do *not* work."

They know from experience that midwives can assist childbirth, that children can receive love from persons not experts in child psychology, that everyone suffers when those with minor scratches and those in serious condition are lumped together in one hospital waiting room. They know that teachers cannot teach, discipline and give individual attention simultaneously; that all marital disputes do not require a lawyer and that all neighborhood controversies do not have to be settled in court. They know, too, that the police cannot protect them from certain kinds of crime, that a different network of mutual protection for survival must be arranged and that punishment threatened by law has little deterrent effect on most criminals.

Item 4

Finally, they have suggestions—some simple, some complex. In Roxbury, a group of mothers told a team of medical "specialists" that the waiting room in a child's clinic should be equipped with rocking chairs instead of stationary, sanitary cribs because mothers want to hold and comfort a sick child and a well child should be free to play and explore.

Item 5

In public housing projects and private apartment complexes alike, they articulated the special need to housing "experts" for child day-care centers for working mothers.

Item 6

In the midst of riots, they have taught police that the unarmed youth, helmeted for identification, can often instill more trust, more cooperation to halt the looting and burning, than the billy club or tear gas grenade.

On those rare occasions when a lamb is slaughtered to eat on a Navajo reservation, when enough fish are caught and smoked to last the winter in Alaska—when beans and crusts of bread are passed around a migrant labor camp, the poor say "if one has, then all have, and if one goes hungry, then all go hungry." In practicing this they teach us the true meaning of humanity, a knowledge by which all men profit.

Participation As An End In Itself

The third and last asset of citizen participation springs from its own nature as an affirmative activity—the exercise of the very initiative, creativity and self-reliance that specific programs in education, job training, housing, urban renewal, health, consumer education and others seek to instill. Participation is, in fact, the active expression of our faith in the dignity and worth of the individual. To deny effective participation, including the opportunity to choose, to be heard, to discuss, to criticize, to protest and to challenge decisions regarding the most fundamental conditions of existence, is to deny the individual's own worth and to confirm his impotence and subservience. It is to render the citizen valueless in the state. Nor do such denials escape notice in the ghetto. There the message is read loud and clear. Ringing challenges to stand on one's own two feet, to pull oneself up by the bootstrap, to become self-sufficient, provoke only cynicism when officialdom, by acting unilaterally, effectively certifies its lask of trust in the capacity, intelligence and sensitivity of the individual.

Item 1

Bridgeton, New Jersey

For weeks, the city had been divided between black and white, poor and affluent, over the decision permitting low-income parents to conduct their own Headstart program rather than subcontract the program to the local school system, which at that time was undergoing internal stress and court proceedings centered on segregation. The school officials had issued an ultimatum—either the school ran the program or it would shut its doors and refuse use of its classrooms. The parents cast about for substitute facilities only to find room severely limited in the once prosperous farming center. Desperate, the parents invited the pastor of the city's leading church to attend a meeting and hear their plea for space.

At the meeting, the minister took the side of the school officials, firmly insisting that he felt the parents unqualified to conduct the program. The meeting came to a standstill; the room fell quiet with frustration.

In one corner sat an ageing black farmer, grandfather of several children eligible for the Headstart program, who had been quiet throughout the discussions. The man, whose father and grandfa-

31

ther before him had been local farmers, leaned across the table.

"Reverend" asked the farmer, "why do you say we are not qualified to run the program?"

The minister smiled. "Well," he replied, "no one doubts your good sense, but the fact is that to run the program qualified teachers must be hired, and it is obvious that the qualifications of such teachers can be judged best by people who are themselves educated and experienced in these matters."

"Reverend," rumbled the farmer, "you are wrong. When my grandchildren have to have their appendix taken out, or their teeth fixed, I am the one who must decide which doctor or dentist is best qualified to do the job, even though I don't know anything about medicine. And if I am qualified enough to decide on doctors and dentists, then why am I not qualifed to decide on teachers?"

The minister was graceful enough to concede logic when he saw it. He later championed the cause of the parents and was instrumental in securing the needed facilities for the program.

Not all confrontations are resolved so fortunately. And when, in larger cities in moments of high tensions, officials fail to see the other side or to recognize the logic of an opposing view, action often ensues.

In that context, protest is no blind fury exploding in sudden passion without direction or wit. It is an affirmation, a first step toward full citizenship for an electorate which before has spoken only in the language of withdrawal and alienation, of crime, of violence, of delinquency and dependency.

Citizens demanding and exercising a voice in their public affairs are no danger to a free state. They are the essence of its character.

The West Virginians who collected money among themselves to rent an office to dispense food stamps so that local residents wouldn't have to travel long distances over bad roads to get their stamps; the Iowans who developed a community task force from their activities as Headstart parents and, among other things, mobilized the town's resources to cope with the crisis of a major flood; the Californians and the New Yorkers who are working as teacher aides; the residents of Phoenix, Arizona, who agreed to assess themselves to pay for paving the streets in their part of town. Each one of them has made an investment in his country, each one of them has made a commitment to work responsibly to solve problems facing his community.

32

Poverty in this country is both relative and absolute. It is absolute when we speak of malnutrition so extreme that the protein deficiency thought to exist only in South America and Africa is equally severe in some areas of the United States. It is absolute when it causes thousands upon thousands of infant deaths. It is relative in that America's poverty seems better dressed and has a higher annual income and more years of formal education that that found abroad.

Nevertheless, participation for the poor, as an expression of personal dignity and of membership in this society, is indispensable. The poor must somehow find their way between the tantalizing cornucopia of commercial television and the taunting awareness of reality. It is not relevant that American poor people might appear better off than others of the world's poor. The fact is that they are not living in the rest of the world; they are living in the United States of America.

Our national wealth was founded on land from the Indian. Our industrial wealth, from coal, iron and steel, was cast at the cost of human life in the scarred mountains of Appalachia. Our cotton and textile industry was spun from black slavery. Our overwhelming agricultural yield is annually produced with the peonage of migrant workers. This land belongs to us all. If one must live in poverty, then participation as an assertion of citizenship, and an expression of dignity, may well be the only way to claim *a portion of that national heritage.* The citizen's right to participate might be the sole source of strength by which to face those countless tomorrows when change comes so slowly and imperceptibly as to seem non-existent. In the long run, we are all dead, said Kenynes. The poor add, "Amen."

Every ethnic group that has come to these shores clings to that sense of selfhood, of inherited identity and dignity, as he copes with the present in striving to build a different future. Whether it is black nationalism, strident Mexican-American chauvinism or the quiet consciousness of the Indian heritage, the expression of self—the assertion of identity through participation—has been indispensable for enduring the present and encountering the future.

How then does one weigh the values of participation against its risks and costs?

Based on the foregoing, one might reasonably conclude that the values outweigh the risks, the gains outweigh the costs. It seems reasonable to submit that the government must protect and foster participation as an essential element in the eradication of poverty.

Yet there are many who, for reasons deemed expedient or politically practical, stand unmoved, unpersuaded by this evaluation of the problems and values in participation.

The Necessity Of Citizen Participation

The three prime values of citizen participation are all affirmative—values which inherently add to the subject of their application. There is also a negative value, a prophylatic function placed on citizen participation which makes clear that officials dispense with meaningful citizen participation at their peril. This function is the final point in our analysis of the values of citizen participation.

The resources alloted to all programs are finite. Within the limitations of fiscal appropriations, priorities must be set, choices made and desirable projects sacrificed. Officials bear the responsibility for making those choices, based upon research, documentation and policy formulations. But they do not have to bear the burden of living with those choices, of directly experiencing the consequences.

People do not live happily with deprivations; but they can reconcile themselves to those scarcities, if they have had a say in choosing between X and Y, if the scarcity they must endure is at least partly of their own choosing. They may rail against such limitations, they may seek out other resources and other means; but ultimately they must live with them. In labor negotiations, the process of collective bargaining is specially protected on the basis that union members will live with a contract that their representatives have negotiated and they have ratified. They accept it even though it is less than they want (and it usually is), if they feel they have been fairly and adequately represented in a process where the terms of the contract are established by bargaining in good faith. The beneficiaries of social services programs must also live with a contract which gives them less than they want, (and often less by far than they need)—a social contract whose terms extend well beyond merely wages and hours and working conditions, whose terms comprehend the totality of opportunity, of education, of security and liberty and dignity for the individual and the group.

A willingness to abide by the terms of that contract will be founded upon whether those who negotiated that contract were viewed as genuine representatives who did their best and fought hard for the best terms they could get. Contracts negotiated by phony leaders, by sellouts, by puppets, by Uncle Toms, are as unlikely to win support from the poor as sweetheart contracts and company unions are to inspire workers.

We know what happens in the industrial order when people do not feel bound by the terms of the contract. It is called a wildcat strike. In our major cities we see also what happens when the terms of a social contract are imposed unilaterally and insensitively—a wildcat strike, not on the industrial order but on the entire social order.

We call it a riot.

And citizen participation—real, meaningful, genuine and total—is the only guarantee, frail as it may be, that people will be willing to endure the terms of social contract, and to have sufficient faith in the system to work within its limits. When such faith fails, citizen participation takes on a more sinister meaning—civil disorder. The participants call it rebellion.

Recent history suggests that we have no choice but to foster and promote participation. To attempt to undercut, undermine, bypass or eschew meaningful participation by the poor in governmental programs is tantamount to insuring failure.

The failure may take many forms. Some we may be prepared to live with—such as the 90% dropout rates in some Indian schools, the 30% dropout rate in our public school system nationwide, the mounting welfare rolls, the rising cost of crime, the increased deliquency, the growing evidence of malnutrition affecting tens of millions of Americans, the increased hostility between race and class that flares so continuously and so explosively. Perhaps government is prepared to do more of the same—to try a little harder, spend a little more, create a few more task forces and commissions, mount new interdepartmental efforts and to employ more experts to seek out the cause of riots, of violence, of third and fourth generation families on welfare. Even many of these questionable approaches cause politicians to react violently to the ingratitude of their supposed beneficiaries. They maintain that the pace of change must not come too swiftly or too expensively. For those who would so temporize, participation of the poor is not only unnecessary, it is distasteful and troublesome. They rationalize that experts, statesmanship and time will cure all. This position maintains that the militant poor must be silenced if "progress" is to continue, if "compassion" and "law and order" are to be made compatible.

But more and more money, more and more services, do not insure results.

35

The saturated services approach was tried in the now notorious Pruitt-Igoe Housing Project in St. Louis.

In a five-year period, July, 1962, through June, 1967, $5,816,520 was spent in 12 different programs under eight funding agencies for services to the residents of Pruitt-Igoe. The services were to benefit the members of 2,600 families living in the project, a total of 12,000 persons, 7,900 of them children. The median annual income for the families in 1962 was $1,712; 54% of the families received public assistance.

The goal of the program was that of the Joint Task Force which had selected Pruitt-Igoe as one of four demonstration projects to test the hypothesis that if all the services available to an area through federal sources were concentrated on a group of families, those families would demonstrate improved social behavior, reduced financial dependency and reduced delinquency, both adult and juvenile.

The programs made little impact on the people living in Pruitt-Igoe or on their lives. The efforts of the Task Force were directed at coordination between agencies and developing an awareness on the part of diverse agencies of the need for an integrated approach.

The emphasis on services could not, however, overcome such hurdles as the fact that at the time of the demonstration project at Pruitt-Igoe, welfare grants were about 50 percent of the minimum cost of subsistence. Services could not combat the effects of living in a housing project where the management was unable to provide minimum maintenance such as replacing broken glass in the middle of winter. Home Service Visitors for the housing management who made annual visits to each unit were required to report on poor housekeeping; but no provision was made for the reporting of absence of beds or bedding or lack of table and chairs or for doing anything about such lacks. In addition, harsh rent-collection procedures contributed to an atmosphere which services, even if adequate, could not have overcome.

The Joint Task Force from HEW and HUD concluded that:

". . . it is not possible to develop a sense of 'community' no matter how good the social services, as long as . . . management policies and practices make a sense of 'belonging' impossible and give no opportunity for residents to affect the way their homes are managed and maintained."

Item 2

The concerted services approach appears to reach the limits of absurdity on the Pine Ridge reservation in South Dakota where there is now a ratio of one "helping" person to every single Indian family.

Some 9,680 Oglala Sioux live on a reservation covering approximately 4,000 square miles in South Dakota. Annually, $17,639,365 is spent on the reservation, with $14,309,187 spent on services. There are 1,400 full-time officials and 425 part-time officials on the reservation. The average expenditure per household is $8,040 per year, and there is an average of one official for every household on the reservation.

Despite this concentration of money, personnel and services, the average household income is $3,050 and half the families live on less than $1,910 a year. In March, 1967, 1,022 persons, 34% of the available work force, were working full time. Of 1,917 housing units on the reservation, 1,041 are classified as so dilapidated they must be replaced. Over half the houses are tar paper shacks; 800 families are without individual housing.

The Oglala Sioux school dropout rate is 50% higher than the national average, resulting in an average school-year completion rate of 8.8, compared to the U.S. average for whites of 10.9 years. Only 20% of the Oglala Sioux complete high school; 4.2% go on to college and 1.2% graduate.

The average Oglala Sioux can expect to die when he is 43.8 years old, 20 years younger than the average age of death for the U.S. as a whole. Communicable diseases account for up to five times as many Oglala Sioux deaths as nationally. Barely a quarter of the Oglala Sioux have a safe water supply; sewage disposal is inadequate or non-existent; few toilet facilities are indoors; heating is crude and provides little protection from South Dakota winters.

Mental illness and alcoholism are most prevalent of all admissions to the nearest hospital. 11% are the result of violence, accidents, and poisonings; 25.6% of all Indian deaths are attributable to social disorganization—accidents, suicide, homicide and cirrhosis of the

37

liver. The national average for this category is 11%. The homicide rate is 2.6 times the national average. Suicide among the 15-19 year olds is 4.1 times the national average. It is probable that these rates for the Oglala Sioux hold for other Indians as well.

The statistics depersonalize the tragedy. On one visit, an OEO official was informed by a local priest that it was "commonplace" for young Indian girls to engage in prostitution. Their price: a bottle of beer.

The new industry—"The Care and Tending of the Poor Industry"— has a magnificent, in fact, infinite growth potential. But its benefit to the poor is dubious at best.

The poor have ways of frustrating superimposed professionalism.

In the now famous Ocean-Hill-Brownsville fight, the demand for accountability and community control brought the nation's largest public school system to halt for months. The poor have reached the point where they would rather do without education if there is to be no accountability and no effective participation.

Our nation's capital appears to offer more examples than any other city of the futility of superimposed programs. With Congress holding the purse strings, without home rule, with the collective power of both the executive and congressional federal bodies steering the community, the failures of the programs are overwhelming.

Item 3

A 330-acre tract in the northeast section of Washington, D. C., remains unutilized after residents successfully rebuffed a strong attempt by the Government Printing Office to use the site for a new plant. Plans purporting to use ordinary redevelopment techniques have met with such suspicion that a special advisory committee, Controlled Development Corporation, was created—directed at creating a new town within the city. The plan is still bogged down by controversy.

The burnt-out areas left by the April riots of 1968 remain unrebuilt. The community has successfully thwarted any plans to rebuild these sections despite offers of assistance, funds and subsidies from outside. The residents will not accede to terms dictated to them.

A similar standoff has materialized between the community and Congress over freeways. Congress and the city seem headed for a direct confrontation in the face of a congressional mandate to build freeways through the ghetto as the price to be exacted for commencing construction on a long overdue mass transit system. The residents simply refuse to permit such freeways.

A recent report issued by the Institute for Political Service to Society shows a marked increase in distrust by Washington's residents of any governmental programs for assistance. And as cited earlier, the Institute's own report on its experimental "City Hall Complaint Center" shows that by and large the poor abstained from using both the neighborhood center and the downtown center. Attitude studies conducted before and after the riots indicate that there has been a marked increase of those who believe that riots are an effective way of bringing about social change.

Dimensions of Citizen Participation

To date there have been two major methods of implementing citizen participation.

The first has involved representation of the poor on Boards of Directors and Advisory Boards of local poverty programs. The second has taken the form of employment of members of "the group to be served" in the program. They are usually called indigenous workers, sub-professionals or non-professionals.

Not only have efforts been limited primarily to these forms of participation, but more disturbingly, debate, discussion and examination have been circumscribed by preoccupation with these two modes.

Citizen participation cannot and should not be equated with efforts, of whatever scope, to provide employment for impoverished citizens in new job categories.

What citizen participation does mean is participation in every dimension of our culture, our political system, our decision-making processes. It means full enfranchisement with respect to the totality of society's activities. It does not mean the illusion of involvement, the opportunity to speak without being heard, the receipt of token benefits or the enjoyment of stop-gap, once-every-summer palliative measures.

We have not chosen to approach the question of participation in the terms of specific models, single suggestions or universal formats, but rather in terms of those values and rights which attempts to implement participation should emphasize.

Because of the magnitude of the task, any single effort or set of efforts will necessarily fall far short of establishing a sure guide for assuring citizen participation on its fullest scale. But at least such ef-

39

forts can begin, not piecemeal, but with an appreciation of the many forms, aspects and implications of citizen participation.

In that view, seven dimensions of participation appear distinguishable. They are related, complementary and perhaps, to a certain extent, overlapping. Yet each dimension can be seen as a distinct right, akin to those inalienable rights which stem from a commitment to the democratic credo. They include:

---the right of effective speech
---the right to be wrong
---the right to be different
---the right to influence decision-making
---the right to contribute
---the right to consume, with dignity
---the right to a continuing share in this society's burdens and benefits

The rights should be kept in clear sight as an overview—because officials, in seeking to function well under often trying circumstances, can and do lose sight of the totality of the problems they confront. In attempting to define what can be done, they often accept the constraint of the politically feasible, without relating their immediate activity to the overall objective.

It is not unfair to suggest that officials, in their preoccupation with today's slogans and battles, may overlook certain possibilities which lie outside present controversy, and which can be effectuated pragmatically without being caught up in the rigid, often irrelevant, terms of the ongoing political debate. Because we believe that something is gained by distinguishing the individually distinctive aspects of citizen participation, we have chosen to explore each such aspect with a specific example, illustration or new story and a more general and abstract statement of principles. *The illustrations or examples do not represent models.* They offer only a context within which the implications of the more general propositions can be explored and tested.

The Right of Effective Speech

Item 1

In Newark, New Jersey, the mayor proposed clearing 45 acres of slum property in order to build a complex of medical school buildings which will provide expanded health facilities for the city and suburbs, and which also are expected to generate jobs and business revenue. The slum clearance will be accompanied, it is said, by extensive relocation efforts, together with the widening of thoroughfares to provide ready access from all parts of the city and suburbs to the medical center. Advisers in the Governor's office reportedly favored the plan because of the difficulty of attracting business into the ghetto and because they believe that the human services sector of the economy (in particular as exemplified by sub-professional jobs) will provide a major new source of employment opportunity for the surrounding community.

In the community, there is considerable opposition to these plans. Neighborhood groups charged that this is one more instance of Negro removal in the name of supposed progress; that far more acreage is being cleared than is needed for the plan; that past assurances to provide adequate relocation for the displaced have never been honored; that the hospital will only be a source of menial, dead-end, low-paying jobs; that the whole project is a cover for a racially motivated refusal to seek to attract business and industry; that the widened thoroughfares (with no pedestrian crosswalks or overpasses) are a means of physical containment of the Negro population; that what is needed is a good mass-transit system so that ghetto dwellers can seek jobs in the suburbs, together with a rehabilitation home-ownership loan program within the reach of low-income residents.

Under a foundation grant, a law student with training in city planning offers his services to the community groups as an "advocate planner" to help them design an alternative redevelopment plan for the neighborhood. He is being assisted in this effort by VISTA workers, paid with government funds, who are helping to organize neighborhood groups which will fight the city's redevelopment plan. Federal, state and local officials enter into negotiations with the community's leaders.

After the riots ended, an effort to find the causes was undertaken. Officials then learned, in a city now palled by tragedy, of the need felt in the black community for better mass-transit facilities, for home rehabilitation loans and most of all, for the need to eliminate unilateral decisions about the clearing of "rundown Negro neighborhoods."

By year's end, the New York Times had dropped the story to page 39, a considerable distance from the page-one pictures of angry flames

41

and overturned cars. The headline ran: "College cuts size of site in Newark . . . it acts to ease relocation problem in Central Ward."

"City officials," noted the Times, "immediately hailed" the change in plans.

Speech is the most basic element of democracy. But it is a right belonging to the listener as well as to the speaker—to the community as an audience as well as to the individual or group as proponent or advocate.

For the listener—for the community as audience—free speech is vitally necessary to reach an informed decision. The listener needs the opportunity to hear all sides, to elicit further information to weigh all positions. As part of this right, he needs an atmosphere, a setting, a forum which leaves him free to consider, to ponder and to draw his own conclusions.

For the individual or group as speaker, speech is necessary to persuade others, to test one's own views in open debate, to enjoy the dignity of self-expression, to experience the opportunity to participate. And none of these are possible unless the speaker has the freedom to define issues on his own terms, to appeal to broader audiences, to reply to critics. And in the last resort to challenge the fairness of traditional forums and to bypass methods of appeal which have been tried and found wanting and which are deservedly suspect as false, as manipulative, as diversionary.

Item 2

In Dayton, Ohio, the advent of summer led, as in too many other cities, to a rise in racial tensions and a last-minute, frenzied release of federal funds for temporary summer programs. As a concession to demands for citizen participation, power was given to citizen review committees from the target areas to decide on what programs were to be undertaken or supported with the federal funds.

The city's recreation department applied to one citizen review committee for allocation of the funds, to be used to supplement an ongoing city program which was suffering from financial anemia.

The citizens' committee said no, summing up its rejection in one sentence: "If the city has enough money to buy tanks and tear gas, they don't need our money."

In Washington, D. C., after detailed planning, the community action agency applied for and was granted federal funds with which to carry out a planned parenthood program.

As a concession to political sensitivity, a condition was attached to the grant prohibiting the use of program facilities or the furnishing of program benefits to unwed mothers.

The communities, debating the program, decided to reject the grant outright rather than accept a condition which would prevent the program from giving aid to those who, in the opinion of the community, most needed it.

Effective speech requires more than offical protection, more than lip service and more than mere toleration. It requires an active appreciation so that it may be most prized even when its exercise is most offensive and disturbing.

If these rights are vouchsafed to the citizen as an aspect of participation, it is wise to remember that the official has a special interest in seeing that both the listener and the speaker are secure in their right to effective speech. In a democracy free speech is the part of the political process which has the special function of both enabling and compelling officials to be responsive and accountable to the people.

There must be inducement, amounting even to compulsion, for an official to listen to all points of view. Officials, too, are both speakers and listeners—sharing the same rights and the same needs as others—but laboring under the special burden that they must distinguish dialogue from offical pronouncements. With that goes a corollary duty to make known which statements are official decisions and statements of policy so that their response can be broadly known and performance broadly judged. Thus, for officials, the right of effective speech entails an obligation to disclose promptly when a position or a decision has or has not been reached—either by choice or by default.

To do otherwise, is, in effect, to convert speech into an exercise in futility—for both the listener and the speaker. When policy has been made, the real world has changed, and speech which has been precluded from addressing itself to that new world—because it cannot—is not speech at all, only sound and fury.

The Right To Be Wrong

The price of free speech is the protection of dissent. But today, meaningful citizen participation encompasses more than the protection of mere dissent. It entails the right of a group or a people to risk choosing wrongly where they and not others will bear the primary consequence of that choice.

Our tradition of local self-government is based upon the notion that groups, communities and geographic areas ought to be permitted, so far as feasible, to chart their own courses, to live their own lives. The same principle goes for the poor and for minority groups—for every area, group, neighborhood and town is, in the larger context, a minority.

When we speak of citizen participation, we are really talking about participation by the poor and by minority groups. The more affluent portions of society already participate—not fully enough to be sure— but the option is always there. And it is because citizen participation really is a euphemism for participation by poor people, by Negroes, Puerto Ricans, Mexican-Americans, urban newcomers from Appalachia or the deep South, that we must reassert the right to be wrong which lies at the heart of local government, state government and our entire federal system.

Item 1

The Boston neighborhood of Roxbury-North Dorchester, in fact and in common knowledge, is not one neighborhood at all, but two. One (North Dorchester) is Irish, employed and strongly supportive of school segregationist Louise Day Hicks. The other is a black, out-of-work, crime-infested area where the dismal ruins of old wooden houses are relieved only by the red scars of bulldozed blocks from which thousands of black families have been, in local parlance, "urban renewed." Unfortunately, the city's urban renewal authority chose to consider Roxbury-North Dorchester as a single major area, and the proverty program, in haste to secure funds, adopted the same definition.

So it was that when the black citizens in Roxbury demanded and won the right to hold elections to elect representatives to the city-wide anti-poverty board from the "target area" they found themselves in a heated contest with residents of North Dorchester who at first contested the election, then ignored it, and finally decided to try their luck in court to bring it to a halt.

The election was to be conducted by a loose assortment of black Roxburians known as the Ad Hoc Committee. The committee, working with little political and less administrative experience, went about finding candidates, devising procedures, securing polling places, advertising the election in stores and schools and generally trying to insure that the poor would have an effective say in who might represent them.

On the eve of the election members of the Ad Hoc Committee gathered in their storefront headquarters, where they were informed that a court order had been obtained by the North Dorchesterians prohibiting the Committee and its members from proceeding with the election.

It became evident to the group that they could not hope to have the order lifted in time for the 10 a. m. opening of the polls. It became evident also that further delay and debate would effectively kill the neighborhood's chances of having any election at all, as the poor had already become thoroughly confused over the election as a result of earlier maneuvers by the North Dorchesterians. At length, acting with no legal advice, the committee came to a decision that a vote was in order on whether the election should be called off, or on whether it should be held even in the face of the court order.

Each voter knew that his vote was, in effect, his own arrest warrant. The matter had come to a tie when the last member was polled—an old blind man who had earned a living by working on re-upholstering automobiles. He hesitated, to ask a question about the effect of a vote to hold the election on the arrest of committee members not present. "It's not right," he said, "to vote somebody else into trouble, although I'm willing myself to go."

He was assured that the committee would exempt those absent from its motion, whereupon he voted to proceed with the election. By unexpected good fortune, the court lifted its injunction early the next day, presumably in ignorance of the act of courage and sensitivity it had evoked.

The right to be wrong, let there be no mistake about it, requires opportunity to learn from the trials and errors of others. It is not necessary that each community or group reinvent the wheel, go through the whole period of tortured evolution and experimentation, repeat the process of error and suffering of others. It is not a mandate to begin from ignorance. But if there is not to be such a mandate, then the right to be wrong carries with it a corollary

45

obligation—that society must furnish the expertise, the knowledge, the technical assistance necessary to enable people to choose in an informed fashion when they take upon themselves the risk of error.

The right to err includes the right to acknowledge a mistake. The right to be wrong means freedom from retaliation—freedom from being punished for trying. There must be no penalty for choosing wrong, other than those consequences which flow directly and necessarily from that decision. Rights and wrongs are difficult to distinguish; today's orthodoxies were yesterday's heresies. And what we call wrong may be merely what people prefer to live with—just as what we call right is only what we prefer to live with, irrational though it may be.

Finally, the right to be wrong does not release the majority from its responsibility to do right as it is given to see the right.

The Right To Be Different

Item 1

"In most states, the schools are actually mandated by law to make English the language of instruction. An appropriate comment on this type of law was forthcoming recently from Charles Olstad, Assistant Professor of Romance Languages at the University of Arizona: 'I had always thought such a law archaic, a carry-over from early days of benighted ethnocentrism, a distorted form of superpatriotism which saw anything non-English as a threat to the nation.'

In some schools the speaking of Spanish is forbidden both in classrooms and on the playground, except, of course, in classes where Spanish is taught. Not infrequently students have been punished for lapsing into Spanish. This has even extended to corporal punishment. A member of our Survey team tells of one school at which such punishment was dealt out to children who lapsed into Spanish despite the fact that 99 percent of the school's enrollment was Mexican-American!

The obvious theory is that a child will learn English if he is required to speak English and nothing but English, at least during those hours of the day when he is in school. "If you want to be American, speak American," he is admonished over and again."*

---

* *The Invisible Minority* .. Pero No Vencibles, Report of the NEA-Tucson Survey On the Teaching of Spanish to the Spanish-Speaking. Published by Department of Rural Education, National Education Association, 1201 Sixteenth Street, N.W., Washington, D.C. 20036.

The right to be different could logically be classed with the right to be wrong—were it not that the purpose of articulating this right distinctly is to free difference from the taint of inferiority.

In a society of mixed races, nationalities, cultures and religions, and in an era of racial turmoil, it is important to emancipate difference from the stigma of ethnic or cultural paternalism.

What does the right to be different mean in specific, practical terms? It means, of course, the right to be oneself, to take pride in one's heritage.

Item 2.

On the Navajo reservation the first school owned and operated by the Navajo nation opened a little over two years ago. Prior to that time, all schools had been run by the Bureau of Indian Affairs with strict credentials required, with children being allowed to return home only twice a year during the school year, with English being the required language taught—and with a constant problem of runaways, dropouts and poor academic performance.

In the new school, parents chosen by the community served as the dormitory staff; the faculty included silversmiths, basket weavers, rug weavers, pottery makers, moccasin makers. The children were taught Indian lore, not by a Ph.D. anthropologist, but by old men and women of the tribe who spoke from memories passed down from generation to generation.

Children were allowed to return home each weekend, classes were conducted in English—but English itself was taught as a second language—and some of the instruction, including cartoons and stories on closed-circuit TV, was in the Navajo language.

A board chosen by the community ran the school and exercised decision-making and hiring power. On a dozen occasions a year the board aimed at decisions over the vehement objections of the director. The director reports that for each of those times he was overruled the board was later vindicated in its judgment. There has not been a single runaway child since the school opened and academic performance is superior by all objective tests that have been applied to date.

It means, too, the right to have that heritage presented, respected and transmitted positively, not just to one's own group but to the entire society. It means taking all possible consideration, allowance

47

and accommodation for rhythms of life and styles of decision-making that are not those of the dominant society or the governing elite. It includes the right to contribute, to have that contribution respected and, also, the right to abstain from contributing on other people's terms without paying a penalty.

Item 3.

The Yakima Valley in the State of Washington is apple-growing country, a prosperous land noted for a variety of crops. It is, as are so many of America's farming regions, a place in which migrant workers find themselves much in demand, but only on the growers' terms.

In Athenum, which is a migrant labor camp built by the federal government in depression days and now serving out its time as a county operation, a federal program operates for the farmworkers. In its early stages, the program was a subject of much dispute between a statewide migrant affairs group (which cared much for migrants but knew little of their problems) and a local community action group heavily representative of local farmers, which knew much about migrant needs but, in the eyes of the farmworkers, cared little.

In the tug of war that ensued, the statewide group and the local group found themselves competing on the basis of which could do more for the migrants. At Athenum, the migrants came up with their own ideas, and proceeded, by juggling their support between the two groups, to win a large degree of autonomy in running their own programs.

At a meeting one night, the farmworkers discussed their program with a visitor. They were asked what they could do in running a program which was different from what others could do.

The difference, they replied, was not in anyone's ability to administer a program, but in their ability to see the unique needs of farmworkers which grew out of their very mobility.

"Take for instance," commented one weatherbeaten man in bluejeans, a man who might have stepped straight from Steinbeck's notes, "the beans and root problem."

"Usually a family gets here in the middle of the day, often with no money for beans or shelter. He has no way of knowing where to go to get work, so he has to wait till next morning to go to the employment office. But the employment office don't open

48

till 8:30, and farmers do their hiring by sunup. So they usually can't get on a list until the afternoon, and then it's for work the next day, which means he can't make any money until almost two days after he gets here. No big money, we don't mean: just a few bucks for beans and a cabin.

"So, we decided to set up our own program. We got some money from the government and set up an employment center, which is mostly a telephone and a bulletin board. Then we asked all the farmers to call us as soon as they knew how many pickers they need. Now, a man comes in with his family, we can be pretty sure of getting him to work first thing in the morning. Last week, we had a family come in with six kids and no money at all, and we got them a job right off that very night setting out smudge pots."

The right to be different does not mean that the dominant society is entitled to abandon or lessen its concern for the needs of a minority, or neglect to take actions, or support programs which provide promise of filling the needs of a culturally, socially or economically distinct group.

It only means that the thrust and direction of such programs and activities undertaken to fulfill those needs must preferably come from the group itself, no matter how weakly, falteringly, tentatively or even hastily at first.

The Right To Influence Decision-Making

Item 1.

On June 27, 1967, the New York State Board of Welfare, in an unprecedented move, announced that it would hold public hearings on a proposed set of rules governing the hearing procedures to be established for the benefit of persons applying for and those receiving public assistance.

The proposed regulations were (comparatively speaking) enlightened.

But it became clear at the hearing—because of the concerns expressed by persons on welfare, because of the analysis prepared by the lawyers from the Columbia Center on Social Welfare Policy and Law, and from the statements of various persons—including the Borough President of Manhattan—that the proposed rules were deficient in certain respects and could be improved by

— the provision of hearings *before* cut-off

— the provision of prompt hearings on the standards applied and the conditions of payment

— provision of emergency aid pending the hearing and decision on applications or requests for increased aid

— provision of shortened time limits and an overall time limit

— provision for retroactive payment to the date of instituting the request

— provision of access to welfare clients to see their own case records

— provision of free legal assistance

— provision of free copies of all welfare rules for client groups and in all welfare centers

— exclusion of illegally obtained evidence

— access to previously rendered decisions

As a consequence of these hearings, some of the proposed regulations were modified to accede to the demands of those who would have to live under them—and to incorporate the recommendations of experts who had prepared a critique of the regulations as advocates, "rule drafters," for welfare rights groups. But the full significance of the event came not from the changes that actually occurred but from the process itself. As Richard Boone, then Director of the Citizens' Crusade Against Poverty observed:

"These rules are a kind of legislation. The State Board of Welfare is the State Legislature on Welfare issues. The rules they make are the law for welfare recipients. And the significant thing about today is that, for the first time, this legislature, the State Board of Welfare, is letting democracy work where it really counts. The big laws are fine. But the little laws can be far more important. And the democratic process has something special to say about how all laws should be passed, big or little . . . For the first time, we are injecting democracy, injecting the political process into rule-making, lawmaking at the level where it really counts."

In a democracy, the grant of a voice to the citizen is not a license to play jester in the king's court. The right to participate in decision-making must confer power wherever decisions are made that shape this society. And, particularly, it must confer the power to affect decision-making proportionately to that stake which one has in the outcome.

The right to influence decision-making is a form of enfranchisement. But enfranchisement must take as many forms as decision-making takes—legislative, executive, administrative, and even judicial.

Citizenship goes beyond the formal ballot, beyond the vote, beyond electoral reapportionment, beyond numerical representation: it is a mandate to proliferate the format of representation.

Wherever there is any form of representation—on boards, through employment of staff, elections, public meetings, volunteer service, in the day-to-day administration, through complaint bureaus, grievance procedures or adversary contests—there must be access to knowledge and to the resources necessary to present the best possible case for the position taken.

The right to influence decision-making is complicated by the necessity of delegating that function to others—and equally by the fact that the most important decisions are not necessarily made by governing boards and councils, but on a day-to-day level by staff.

In consequence, meaningful representation must take place both on the formal and on the operating level.

Where representation is to take place at the formal level, it is clear that those represented should have the controlling voice in nomination, selection and recall.

Where representation takes place through staff positions, the interests of the employer in performance and the interests of those represented in advocacy may conflict. And, consequently, where representation is effected through a staff position, the power to fire and hire will usually reside with the employer. But failure to be responsive to the concern of those represented should then be made a

51

cause for dismissal as a form of lack of performance. Service not accompanied by empathy and advocacy does not provide representation—even if staff functions are performed efficiently.

Item 2.

West Virginia's Mingo county is coal country, a drab and gloomy collection of hills, hollows, and shacks slumbering through the twilight of an Appalachian winter. The big coal mine operators have broken the back of the United Mine Workers Union, partly through mechanization, partly through the use of subcontracting dodges exploiting the independence of the West Virginian, and partly through relentless opposition to the concept of organized labor.

With the gutting of the union locals, the men of Mingo county have split into five major occupational groups. The smallest and luckiest group are those who remain employed in modern, largely mechanized captive mines owned by big companies. A larger, exploited group of miners grub out in existence as "independent contractors" running unsafe and primitive "truck mines." There is some lumber and mill work for about 6% of the men. The largest occupational group is the unemployed, disabled or occasional miners. The last group, inevitable in the mountain counties, is the men working for the county or townships.

The statistics are as dismal as the grimy mine entrances. Ranked against the rest of the country, Mingo County has a higher rate of unemployment than 99% of the 3,135 counties in the U.S. The median family income is $4,440 as of 1966—lower than 66% of other U.S. counties. The county is rural to an extensive degree, its chief community of Williamstown having a population of slightly more than 6,000, and some 84% of its citizens living in communities of less than 2,500.

And, to decrease even the present dim chances for economic health, the county is losing its people. In the past six years more than 18,000 people were lost through the adverse mathematics of migration—a loss of over 7% of the county population. It is, of course, the young who are leaving, as shown by a steady rise in the median age.

Poverty in the county is severe by any standards. More than one in three families fall below the OEO poverty income cutoff. The median school level for the county is more than one full year less than the national average. Nearly 13% have had less than four years of school, a fact reflected rather precisely in a 13% unemployment rate.

Underlying the statistics are the political relationships in the county. Where jobs are scarce, patronage assumes a disproportionate role, and jobs as school bus drivers become as important in the life of the county as sub-cabinet posts in the national capital. Corruption and exploitation are commonplace, and opposition to the courthouse politicians is usually a sure road to unemployment.

Woven into the life of the county are the wishes of the mine owners, who are dependent on a docile labor force and a surplus of available men. The location of new industries, the establishment of job training for non-mine work and similar efforts are paid lip service by all, but are the dream of few in power.

Federal monies, as they became available in the past, came quickly to be recognized as a supplement to local patronage operations, a new source of favors and rewards available to the courthouse for its own preservation.

With the passage and implementation of the Economic Opportunity Act, local politicians became alarmed at the success of their neighboring county in securing fresh funds, and moved speedily to establish a community action agency.

Within three years, the community action agency, named the Mingo County Economic Opportunity Commission, was to be successful in attracting more than a million dollars in federal programs for the conduct of a variety of programs aimed at the elimination of poverty.

By June, 1965, it had secured $18,000 from OEO for development of programs. Six months later it received nearly a quarter-million dollars to run a Neighborhood Youth Corps program, later $8,000 for Medicare Alert, $120,000 for central administration and a home improvement program, more funds still later for Headstart programs, legal services and Nelson Amendment activities.

As the federal dollars began to flow in, the county politicians might well have felt themselves satisfied at the success of their creature. Unfortunately, they were to suffer some rather severe political indigestion as well.

In its initial stages, the county commissioners invited all local organizations to send representatives to an organizational meeting

53

to implement the poverty program. A board of directors was formed, composed of the key leaders and representatives of agencies and groups in the county.

An executive director was selected, some staff personnel were employed and the program began to take shape. Conflicts began quickly to develop between some of the county leaders and the EOC around the concept of community organization and the composition of the board.

Poor people were added to the board, replacing some of the initial members and expanding the total size of the board.

With the funding of a Headstart program, more conflicts developed. Although the program was delegated to the county board of education for operation, the EOC wanted the power to hire sub-professionals for the program. When the educators proved intractable, the EOC developed a Headstart program which was to be operated by the EOC itself year round.

In July, 1966, the Appalachian summer volunteers began operation in Mingo County. Within a year, they were able to stimulate large-scale grass roots involvement of persons who wanted to focus their own efforts on the resolution of their problems through political education. These persons began to develop countywide issue groups around such problems as fair elections, education, roads, taxes, etc. The first such group developed was the Education Committee, stimulated by the experience of staff and board members in confronting the educational establishment on the Headstart issue.

In August, 1967, five low-income volunteers formed a task force to educate the local community action groups on the election process. Out of this grew a widespread interest in the issues of political reform, and ultimately a Fair Elections Committee took shape.

At this stage the work of the poverty program and the efforts of the low-income citizens began to diverge. Soon county officials, seeking increasing amounts of federal patronage, realized that the EOC, their creature initially, was less interested in securing more political patronage than in achieving some vital reforms in the ongoing political world. The struggle was reflected in a fight for the chairmanship of the Economic Opportunity Commission. A chairman sympathetic to the need for political reform was elected, and the EOC's bylaws were amended to provide more effective grass-roots representation.

With the increased representation from low-income citizens, the EOC moved to the left. In December, 1967, an issues council of the EOC was formed, to handle the work of the Fair Elections Committee.

Two months later, a Political Action League (PAL) was formed as an autonomous spin-off group of the local community action groups. Formulation of PAL permitted the poor citizens, active in the local community action groups, to organize themselves for partisan poltical involvement, which they could not do directly as members of the EOC. Thus PAL developed its own platform and governing structure.

County reaction was swift and clear. Operating under the new provisions of the Green Amendment to the Economic Opportunity Act, the county commissioners, in March, 1968, applied to OEO to implement the first stage of development required to divest the EOC of its status as the official community action agency, and to transfer the functions of the EOC to the county commission.

The poor demonstrated in opposition to the move of the county commission, with an organized effort led by the Economic Opportunity Commission.

OEO, confronted by conflicting applicants and caught between the mandate of the Green Amendment and the mandate of maximum feasible participation embodied in the original legislation, conducted an extensive evaluation of the operations of the program. The findings of the evaluators are, in part, descriptive of the process of citizen participation itself:

"In the case of Mingo County, the evaluation team finds . . . that the EOC is clearly charted on a single-purpose course of community organization of and by and for the poor exclusively, for the purpose of political and institutional change.

. . . it had not thought through the intervening steps for pursuing this goal

. . . it uses information of crisis as the primary tool for reaching this goal

. . . it has not focused on any other long-range goals."

The report pointed out the inconsistency of fighting for political change at the expense of the major weapon in the fight: the viability of the organization itself. Yet, in analyzing the performance of the agency from the standpoint of *its own perceived goals,* the evaluators conceded, with an inconsistency of their own:

"Within the agency's perceived objective of community organization there is a highly sophisticated linkage between all the programs and activities directly or indirectly associated with the EOC."

The Right To Contribute

Item 1.

In its issue of May 22, 1967, *Newsweek* stated:

"The Department of Health Education and Welfare will provide a $238,000 grant this summer to the unofficial Community Alert Patrol in Watts. Suspected as troublemakers and harassed at first by police, CAP's neighborhood volunteers have helped avert several potential riots in past months. Privately, Los Angeles police now admit they are pleased that the grant will permit expansion of the volunteer patrol as well as introduction of a CAP auto-maintenance training clinic for jobless young men."

Automobiles will be prepared for patrol, and patrol operations will begin. A base, equipped with a two-way radio, will serve as a dispatching center.

The Patrol assembles at a stated time each evening for a briefing and assignment of a patrol area. Cars are plainly marked with signs identifying "Community Alert Patrol." Disturbances of any sort are reported immediately to the base.

It is in this capacity that members of the Patrol attempt to use verbal persuasion in preventing disturbances from breaking out either as a result of the behavior of citizens or the police. The Patrol members are instructed to observe police activities in the area, but are not allowed to interfere or become directly involved in law enforcement activities. Their principal role is to help citizens of the community observe the law and avoid conflict with the police. It is felt that through this means a measure of informal community control can be established. In addition to the patrol service they proposed to run a car repair center with the dual function of servicing the cars used by patrol members and providing training for youngsters interested in learning to repair automobiles.

Funding for the action phase of the program was subsequently denied because of police opposition and political pressure. A compromise alternative was finally designed and funded—a Community Justice Center program to insure that arrested Watts residents would be released promptly, if they had bail and if one could substantiate the information they gave to the police. The members of the center were trained to contact families and employers, to search records and to develop the information required by the police. They are linked to the police stations by telephones and use their own cars in tracking down the necessary information.

The right to contribute is as elemental as the urge to feel needed, useful, significant and unique. Each individual has something special to contribute—a unique knowledge of his own conditions, desires, needs, misfortunes and frustrations.

The concept of participation carries with it a recognition that all have something to contribute, that our social problems are in part the product of forced non-contribution— of barriers to participation. In this society, not only does non-contribution deny the individual an opportunity for expression but stigmatizes the individual as dependent and inferior.

Yet, notwithstanding our work ethic, many people are consigned to idleness by a network of policies and simultaneously penalized for being non-productive.

Among these barriers are the monopoly power and restrictive practices of professionals, public officials and unions. Then there are the artificial barriers of accreditation, standardization, over-specialization and unrealistically high or non-functional entry and employment standards.

Citizen participation requires that this society acknowledge as productive work such socially essential activity as child-rearing, job retraining and other service activities.

The elderly are driven from the labor market, stigmatized as useless, prevented from making a continued contribution and forced to bear disproportionately the burdens of inflation and change.

The young are kept from the marketplace by more and more extensive requirements as they are simultaneously branded useless, dependent, irresponsible, irrational and dangerous. Males in our society are required to provide adequately for their families—yet, when the victims of circumstances, they are prevented from remaining with their families and therefore cannot keep them together as units.

Women in our society are expected to rear their children properly,

57

yet are often denied support if they are seen in the company of a male.

If citizen participation is to be given real meaning it will call for redefinition of work, a redesigning of useful roles, and an abolition of artificial barriers to productivity and contribution by all.

Item 2.

Close to the Mississippi River in the Delta, the heart of Mississippi's black belt, is a collection of houses and small stores, the homes and businesses of about 300 people, 200 who are black, 100 white. This is Glen Allan, pleasant iñ appearance under its great shade trees. But behind the pleasant facade are the hard facts of life for the Negroes who live there—houses which are splintered shacks with neither running water nor plumbing, wages of $2 to $3 a day when there is work, and the fear that comes with living in a center of Ku Klux Klan activity and knowing that terror can strike anytime the white man pleases.

Ignorant and often illiterate Negroes, caught in a society of forms and rules controlled by whites, can become overwhelmed by a feeling of helplessness. In Glen Allan, "Hoplessness and diet deficiencies sapped their energies and their community grew more slovenly. Out of degradation comes apathy and, naturally, doubt of one's own worth and even humanity."

Jake Ayers refused to be caught in the traps of fear, helplessness or hopelessness. He registered to vote in 1958, an act so unprecedented it was treated as a joke. In 1963 he went to the white owners of the community well and managed to get a pipe installed from the well to the Negro section. In 1965 he heard of CDGM's efforts to start Headstart programs and decided that the children of Glen Allan should have this opportunity.

The empty school buildings seemed a natural facility for the summer program. The residents of Glen Allan wrote and signed a petition to the School Board requesting permission to use the buildings. The fact that everyone signed the petition was surprising in itself: "They had never done such a thing but this was a real chance to lift their children and they were willing to take the risk." The response to the petition was an instruction to appear before the Board in the county seat 30 miles away. The instruction effectively baffled them. "We were so ignorant," says Ayers, "that we didn't know who the Board members were or where they met and no one would tell us."

Instead they turned to St. Mark's Baptist Church, and despite its ramshackle appearance and slantwise tilt, refurbished it for the Headstart classes. A local board was formed to operate the program and the Glen Allan Headstart Center opened in mid-July, 1965. Within a few days it was over-enrolled by 50%.

Local women taught in the center, in sufficient number to insure that each child received individual attention and affection. It was the salaries of the teachers, up to 82 dollars a week, which began waves unexpected from a nursery school for children. For the first time there was money coming into the community which was not controlled by white people. This fact outraged the Glen Allan whites. They drove by and glared at the church. The insurance policy on the building was cancelled. A building inspector ordered the church closed. Ayers managed to hold him off until the close of the seven-week program.

The program had not only affected the children—turning shy, frightened youngsters into bright-eyed, playful, eager learners—it had affected the adults of the community as well. "It was a huge success . . . There was a by-product for the community, a new pride. The people had accomplished something independently. They had brought in money. They had the beginning of organization and strength."

A new spirit infused the community; its residents began doing things they never would have dared before. They boycotted a white attempt to have liquor sold only in white stores; they enrolled their children in the white school when the county passed a freedom-of-choice plan.

The reaction of the whites was swift and decisive: a cross was burned in Ayers' yard, an armed calvacade paraded threateningly through town, Ayers was fired from his job, followed by police, jailed for a minor traffic violation, cursed and threatened by whites. This reaction was taking place all across the state as whites sensed a change in Negro attitudes. It led to pressure on OEO, through Senator John Stennis, and an effort to block all further funding to the CDGM program.

While the refunding fight was going on in Washington, Ayers raised $500 in Glen Allan for the installation of plumbing in an old house which had been purchased on a $1000 note. Volunteers patched and painted the walls, inside and out, and created play equipment from scraps and junk so that the building would be ready

59

as soon as the funds came through. After a stormy meeting at OEO, word came that the program was to be refunded. Glen Allan embarked on a six-month Headstart program. And the adults continued their new activities—they began to register to vote. The white children were withdrawn and bussed to nearby white schools. Although still segregated, the Negro children have better facilities without a long bus ride to reach school. At the end of the six-month funded program, the Glen Allan Center scraped along for five months, running its program without any funds from OEO while the CDGM battle was fought out in Washington.

"CDGM itself may well not survive, but the sense of success in Glen Allan seems too deeply engraved to die. The center bulges with children being given a future . . . The change in the adults is just as remarkable. Confidence continues to spread. There is more money. Salaries at the Center spread through the community in ripples of increasing prosperity. This in turn has driven up the salaries white people pay. A maid in Glen Allan makes $4 a day now, and a tractor driver may make $6." Families are eating more and better food, they're cautiously beginning to buy what they have always wanted—an electric fan, washing machine, in one instance, a house.

Through their Headstart program the adults of Glen Allan have developed a new pride which has now taken on its own momentum and leads to continuing improvements in their lives, their homes and their community.

The Right To Consume With Dignity

Item 1.

"Sammy Smith just got busted again. Sammy is 13 and he hates cops who keep picking him up, even if they aren't able to make a case. That particular night, he happened to be in a High's ice cream store when police arrived after getting a call that some teenagers had robbed or were about to rob the store.

"The boy had been through this sort of thing often enough that it didn't particularly bother him. In fact, he didn't even stop drinking the bottle of grape soda he had with him. Once in the patrol wagon, Sammy . . . set the soda bottle down on the floor between his feet. The cop who was to ride with him to the station, got in, took a long drag on his cigarette and with elaborate nonchalance, dropped the butt into Sammy's half-full soda bottle . . ."

Item 2.

Port Norris, New Jersey, is a once-prosperous oyster port nestled far down the Delaware Bay. It is a town whose houses were built and lived in when the Civil War was a fresh memory, and much of its racial views are of the same era.

The town itself is largely white. A mile from the town, located a few yards from the large shellfish houses still operating, is the tiny town of Shellpile, an all-black community. It is distinguished chiefly by its reputation among the State Police as "the roughest goddamn place on Saturday night this side of Mexico." The community has no running water, nor sewers, nor fire protection, nor most of the other modern conveniences.

Midway between Shellpile and Port Norris lies the "black school"—a dry, dangerous old building in which the toilet facilities, although located indoors, consist of a board running across a waste pit. The board has four holes cut in it; two for the boys and two for the girls.

After examining the school, a local poverty official sought to win the consent of the school board to permit a Headstart program for the Shellpile youngsters to be conducted in a newly erected modern school in Port Norris proper. The school board, incensed at the prospect of allowing Negroes to conduct their own program in any situation, refused. In the words of one member of the school board, delivered with heat at a regular meeting, "there ain't no use letting them niggers use flush toilets. They don't know how to. They will go behind them, on the sides of them, and every place but in them. The only way them niggers know how to use a flush toilet would be if you put wine in them, and then they'd use it as a drinking fountain."

The citizen is a consumer—not just of material goods—but also of the services and products of our government and of our culture. He is the consumer of our police systems' protection (or lack of it), our welfare systems' social services (or lack of them), our school systems' education achievments (or lack of them)—as well as of defective cars, radioactive TV sets, inflammable garments and polluted air and water.

The consumer needs protection. Consumer protection starts with consumer power, knowledge and choice. The ability to make an informed choice is the ability to reward or to sanction. It needs to rest firmly with the consumer and the regulatory instrumentalities that genuinely represent the consumer.

61

The consumer's interest can be advanced by group representation. But persons suffer as individuals. They thus need power as a group and protection as individuals.

The right to consume—with dignity—includes:

— adequate representation for consumer interests

— a meaningful choice among goods and services to fill needs

— knowledge and disclosure with respect to goods and services

— penalties against misconduct by producers and suppliers who do not perform adequately or who supply harmfully inadequate services

— indemnity for those who are injured by providing an adequate remedy

— dignity of treatment through entitlement

— grievance, settlement and arbitration procedures

— surveillance by the government as protector of the consumer interest.

In the final analysis, the right to consume in dignity is an extension of that most comprehensive of all rights—the right not to consume, the right to abstain, the right of privilege, the right to be left alone.

The Right To a Continuing Share In This Society's Benefits and Burdens

Item 1.

In its final report the McCone Commission, which for two years was the chief "watchdog agency" on remedial activities growing out of the Watts riot of August, 1965, noted that "inadequate and costly transportation currently existing throughout the Los Angeles area seriously restricts the residents of such disadvantaged areas as south central Los Angeles."

Bus service in Watts has been expanded with the help of federal subsidies. However, residents feel it has not been very beneficial, and the cost is beyond their means.

Now bus riders of the poverty-stricken area are faced with a possible curtailment of existing services. Last week the Brotherhood of Railroad Trainmen warned that unless its drivers were provided with the protection of "shotgun riders," its members would refuse to operate buses in the southern, southeastern and southwestern sections of Los Angeles.

Thomas Ryan, associate director of NEGRO (National Economic Growth and Reconstruction Organization) said:

"Right now one-way bus fare costs a resident of Watts at least 35 cents if his place of employment is within the two-and-one-half square mile area of Watts. If it is outside the area, one way costs 90 cents and hours of lost travel time.

"The Blue and White bus (a division of NEGRO), when it goes into operation, will undercut any existing public transportation rate. We will not use union drivers or mechanics, so our operating costs will be less. We will not be paying union wages."

"Our average one-way fare from home to place of business within Watts will be 20 cents. For residents working outside of Watts the cost will be about 40 cents."

"The bus company is being paid for at a cost of $100,000 by NEGRO bonds, which are sold in denominations ranging from 50 cents to $10,000."

New York Times, November 12, 1967, Pg. 49

* * * * *

Participation means in effect, an ownership share in society. Wages are payment for what the society defines as work—as useful tasks. But the demand for participation does not stop with a demand for wages or even a guaranteed minimum income. As the saying goes in Harlem, "we had full employment on the plantation."

Citizenship entails an equal stake in society. And ownership rights go beyond a right to wages. They confer a share in profits, in growth, in change. The citizen in a democracy wants a participating share in the economy and the society—for better and for worse. We will take the risks inherent in ownership, in full citizenship. Taxes, war, pollution, crime, urban sprawl and decay, epidemics, depletion of natural resources are borne by all. But citizenship also demands a share in prosperity, a share in the growth section of the society—particularly as the poor are a central reason for that growth, the market for radical expansion in goods and services, programs and institutions in which both the public and private sector participate and profit.

Item 2.

The Albina Corporation is a black-owned, black-managed wood and metal fabrication plant in the state of Oregon. Capital for the corporation was made available through grants from the Office of Economic Development, the Small Business Administration, the Economic Development Administration, the Department of Labor and the Office of Economic Opportunity, through the Albina Investment Trust. The initial Board of Trustees has nine members, three selected by the Albina Citizens War on Poverty, three by active community organizations and three from outside the community. The trust is borrowing funds to purchase stocks from the Albina Corporation on behalf of the employees in investments and investment management, stimulating expanded economic development, and administering the project.

The idea for Albina was initiated by a white businessman, Louis Neidermeyer, who had been impressed by the plants being set up in Watts. At the beginning the plans were kept from the community, primarily because of bidding competition for the building which he wanted to use for the factory. Once OEO became seriously involved in the project, pressure was exerted to involve the community in developing the plans for the company.

There was considerable trepidation on the part of the "experts" involved, as members of the community were asked to participate in decision-making which would determine the future of a business.

Meetings were begun with a community action advisory group, and the experts were thoroughly surprised by the degree of sophistication revealed in questions about and discussions of stock and profit-sharing plans.

The residents knew many business procedures and demonstrated good understanding of technical business matters. What they did not already know they were quick to learn.

The experts were particularly impressed by the way in which decisions were reached by the group. Thorough discussion and thoughtful examination of alternatives laid the groundwork for decision-making. Areas in which the citizens made decisions in-

64

cluded stock distribution, organization and establishment, and ways of presenting the corporation to the entire community.

In determining the employment guidelines, the residents were particularly concerned with obtaining a realistic balance which would provide jobs for members of the community, regardless of skills, and would provide enough skilled people to get the company on its feet and to train the others. The experts had also been worried about the relationship between the man whose idea it had been and the group who would be working in and eventually running the plant. He was white and affluent; they were black and poor.

A relationship based on mutual respect has developed in which Mr. Neidermeyer serves as a senior consultant, bringing tangible skills and services to the company.

Within the first months of operation the Albina Corporation successfully bid on a number of contracts totaling approximately $250,000. Through the employee's ownership of the stock in the company, profits will remain in the community, providing a base for continuing economic growth and development of the area.

The citizen—particularly those from poor and minority groups— wants ownership rights and ownership prerogatives. He will bear risk and loss and even deferred enjoyment of income to invest in the future. But he will no longer be relegated to sharing the risks while watching others exclude him from a share in the profits, the jobs, the opportunities for advancement and status.

This last dimension of citizen participation is at once most revolutionary and most conservative. It does not seek to destroy but rather to build and to share. And if society can respond positively to that demand, it may have found an answer to the warning de Tocqueville issued over a century ago:

"By this system, the people shake off their state of dependence just long enough to select their master, and then relapse into it again."

"It must not be forgotten that it is especially dangerous to enslave men in the minor details of life. For my own part, I should be inclined to think freedom less necessary in great things than in little ones, if it were possible to be secure of the one without possessing the other.

"Subjection in minor affairs breaks out every day, and is felt by the whole community indiscriminately. It does not drive men to resistance, but it crosses them at every turn, till they are led to surrender the exercise of their own will. Thus their spirit is gradually broken and their character enervated . . .

* * *

"To manage those minor affairs in which good sense is all that is wanted, the people are held to be unequal to the task; but when the government of the country is at stake, the people are invested with immense powers; they are alternately made the playthings of their ruler, and his masters, more than kings and less than men.

"It is, indeed, difficult to conceive how men who have entirely given up the habit of self-government should succeed in making a proper choice of those by whom they are to be governed; and no one will ever believe that a liberal, wise and energetic government can spring from a suffrages of a subservient people."

Part II

**GENERAL CONCERNS REGARDING
CITIZENS PARTICIPATION**

EIGHT RUNGS ON THE LADDER OF CITIZEN PARTICIPATION

by: Sherry R. Arnstein

Editor's Note:

For the past six years Sherry Arnstein has been a consultant to most of the (non-OEO) Federal agencies wrestling with new strategies for citizen participation: HUD, HEW, Labor, Justice. She was chief citizen participation advisor to the Model Cities Administration and is now director of community development studies for the Commons, an institute supported by church groups.

Her monograph, which appears also in the July, 1969, issue of the Journal of the American Institute of Planners, presents a deliberately "provocative typology" of citizen participation. She herself raises many of the questions which a trainer would ask.

Mrs. Arnstein, who has a B.A. from UCLA and an M.A. from American University, was Staff Consultant to the President's Committee on Juvenile Delinquency, Washington Editor of Current Magazine; *and has worked in the probation and hospital fields.*

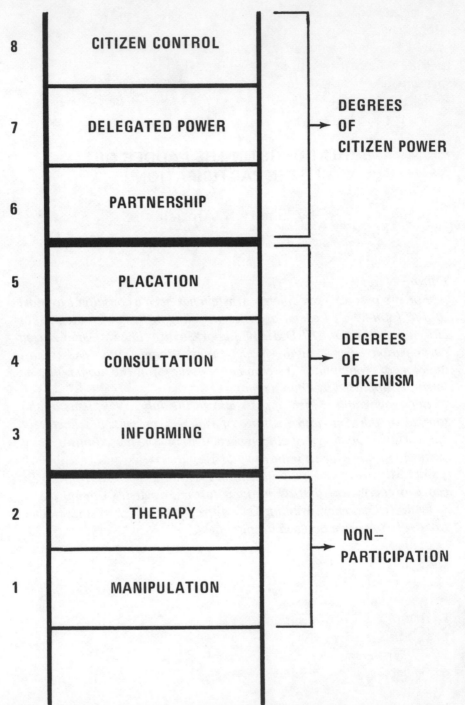

EIGHT RUNGS ON THE LADDER OF CITIZEN PARTICIPATION
By Sherry R. Arnstein

The heated controversy over "citizen participation," "citizen control," and "maximum feasible involvement of the poor," has been waged largely in terms of exacerbated rhetoric and misleading euphemisms. To encourage a more enlightened dialogue, a typology of citizen participation is offered using examples from three federal social programs: urban renewal, antipoverty and Model Cities. The typology, which is designed to be provocative, is arranged in a ladder pattern with each rung corresponding to the extent of citizens' power in determining the plan and/or program.

The idea of citizen participation is a little like eating spinach: no one is against it in principle because it is good for you. Participation of the governed in their government is, in theory, the cornerstone of democracy—a revered idea that is vigorously applauded by virtually everyone. The applause is reduced to polite handclaps, however, when this principle is advocated by the have-not blacks, Mexican-Americans, Puerto Ricans, Indians, Eskimos and whites. And when the have-nots define participation as redistribution of power, the American consensus on the fundamental principle explodes into many shades of outright racial, ethnic, ideological, and political opposition.

There have been many recent speeches, articles and books[1] which explore in detail *who* are the have-nots of our time. There has been much recent documentation of *why* the have-nots have become so offended and embittered by their powerlessness to deal with the profound inequities and injustices pervading their daily lives. But there has been very little analysis of the content of the current controversial slogan: "citizen participation" or "maximum feasible participation." In short: *What* is citizen participation and what is its relationship to the social imperatives of our time?

Because the question has been a bone of political contention, most of the answers have been purposely buried in euphemisms like "self-help" or "citizen involvement." Still others have been embellished with misleading rhetoric like "absolute control" which is something no one—including the President of the United States—has or can have. Between euphemisms and rhetoric, even scholars have found it difficult to follow the controversy. To the headline reading public, it is simply bewildering.

My answer to the critical *what* question is simply that citizen participation is a categorical term for citizen power. It is the redistribution of power that enables the have-not citizens, presently excluded from the political and economic processes, to be deliberately

71

included in the future. It is the strategy by which the have-nots join in determining how information is shared, goals and policies are set, tax resources are allocated, programs are operated and benefits like contracts and patronage are parceled out. In short, it is the means by which they can induce significant social reform which enables them to share in the benefits of the affluent society.

There is a critical difference between going through the empty ritual of participation and having the real power needed to affect the outcome of the process. This difference was brilliantly capsulized in a poster painted in spring, 1968, by the French students to explain the student-worker rebellion:[2]

Je participe	I participate
Tu participes	You participate
Il participe	He, she, or it participates
Nous participons	We participate
Vous participez	You participate (plural form)
Ils profitent	*They profit*

The poster highlights the fundamental point that participation without redistribution of Power is an empty and frustrating process for the powerless. It allows the powerholders to claim that all sides were considered, but makes it possible for only some of those sides to benefit. It maintains the status quo. Essentially, it is what has been happening in most of the 1,000 Community Action Programs, and what promises to be repeated in the vast majority of the 150 Model Cities programs.

In an attempt to cut across both the euphemisms and the rhetoric of citizen participation, this typology substitutes eight different levels of participation in planning and operating public programs. For illustrative purposes the eight types are arranged in a ladder pattern with each rung corresponding to the extent of citizens' power in determining the end product."[3] (See Figure 1.)

The bottom rungs of the ladder are (1) *Manipulation* and (2) *Therapy*. These two rungs describe levels of "nonparticipation" that have been contrived by some to substitute for genuine participation. Their real objective is not to enable people to participate in planning or conducting programs, but to enable powerholders to "educate" or "cure" the participants. Rungs 3 and 4 progress to levels of "tokenism" that allow the have-nots to hear and to have a voice: (3) *Informing* and (4) *Consultation.* When they are proffered by powerholders as the total extent of participation, citizens may indeed hear and be heard. But under these conditions they lack the power to insure that their views will be *heeded* by the powerful. When participation is restricted to these levels, there is no followthrough, no "muscle," hence no assurance of changing the status quo. Rung (5) *Placation,* is simply a higher level tokenism because the groundrules allow have-nots to advise, but retain for the powerholders the continued right to decide.

Further up the ladder are levels of citizen power with increasing degrees of decision-making clout. Citizens can enter into a (6) *Partnership* that enables them to negotiate and engage in trade-offs with traditional powerholders. At the topmost rungs, (7) *Delegated Power* and (8) *Citizen Control,* have-not citizens obtain the majority of decision-making seats, or full managerial power.

Obviously, the eight-rung ladder is a simplification, but it helps to illustrate the point that so many have missed—that there are significant gradations of citizen participation. Knowing these gradations makes it possible to cut through the hyperbole to understand the increasingly strident demands for participation from the have-nots as well as the gamut of confusing responses from the powerholders.

Though the typology uses examples from federal programs such as urban renewal, antipoverty, and Model Cities, it could just as easily be illustrated in the church, currently facing demands for power from priests and laymen who seek to change its mission; colleges and universities which in some cases have become literal battlegrounds over the issue of student power; or public schools, city halls, and police departments (or big business which is likely to be next on the expanding list of targets). The underlying issues are essentially the same—"nobodies" in several arenas are trying to become "somebodies" with enough power to make the target institutions responsive to their views, aspirations and needs.

The ladder juxtaposes powerless citizens with the powerful in order to highlight the fundamental divisions between them. In actuality, neither the have-nots nor the powerholders are homogeneous blocs. Each group encompasses a host of divergent points of view, significant cleavages, competing vested interests, and splintered subgroups. The justification for using such simplistic abstractions is that in most cases

73

the have-nots really do perceive the powerful as a monolithic "system," and powerholders actually do view the have-nots as a sea of "those people," with little comprehension of the class and caste differences among them.

It should be noted that the typology does not include an analysis of the most significant roadblocks to achieving genuine levels of participation. These roadblocks lie on both sides of the simplistic fence. On the powerholders' side, they include racism, paternalism, and resistance to power redistribution. On the have-nots' side, they include inadequacies of the poor community's political and socioeconomic infrastructure and knowledge-base, plus difficulties of organizing a representative and accountable citizens' group in the face of futility, alienation, and distrust.

Another caution about the eight separate rungs on the ladder: In the real world of people and programs, there might be 150 rungs with less sharp and "pure" distinctions among them. Furthermore, some of the characteristics used to illustrate each of the eight types might be applicable to other rungs. For example, employment of the have-nots in a program or on a planning staff could occur at any of the eight rungs and could represent either a legitimate or illegitimate characteristic of citizen participation. Depending on their motives, powerholders can hire poor people to coopt them, to placate them or to utilize the have-nots' special skills and insights.[4] Some mayors, in private, actually boast of their strategy in hiring militant black leaders to muzzle them while destroying their credibility in the black community.

It is in this context of power and powerlessness that the characteristics of the eight rungs are illustrated by examples from current federal social programs.

1. MANIPULATION

In the name of citizen participation, people are placed on rubber-stamp advisory committees or advisory boards for the express purpose of "educating" them or engineering their support. Instead of genuine citizen participation, the bottom rung of the ladder signifies the distortion of participation into a public relations vehicle by powerholders.

This illusory form of "participation" initially came into vogue with urban renewal when the socially elite were invited by city housing officials to serve on Citizen Advisory Committees (CACs). Another target of manipulation were the CAC subcommittees on minority groups, which in theory were to protect the rights of Negroes in the renewal program. In practice, these subcommittees, like their parent CACs, functioned mostly as letterheads, trotted forward at appropriate times to promote urban renewal plans (in recent years known as Negro removal plans).

At meetings of the Citizen *Advisory* Committees, it was the officials who educated, persuaded, and advised the citizens, not the reverse. Federal guidelines for the renewal programs legitimized the manipulative agenda by emphasizing the terms "information-gathering," "public relations," and "support" as the explicit functions of the committees.[5]

This style of nonparticipation has since been applied to other programs encompassing the poor. Examples of this are seen in Community Action Agencies (CAAs) which have created structures called "neighborhood councils" or "neighborhood advisory groups." These bodies frequently have no legitimate function or power.[6] The CAA's use then to "prove" that "grassroots people" are involved in the program. But the program may not have been discussed with "the people." Or it may have been described at a meeting in the most general terms: "We need your signatures on this proposal for a multiservice center which will house, under one roof, doctors from the health department, workers from the welfare department and specialists from the employment service."

The signators are not informed that the $2 million-per-year center will only refer residents to the same old waiting lines at the same old agencies across town. No one is asked if such a referral center is really needed in his neighborhood. No one realizes that the contractor for the building is the mayor's brother-in-law, or that the new director of the center will be the same old community organization specialist from the urban renewal agency.

After signing their names, the proud grassrooters dutifully spread the word that they have "participated" in bringing a new and wonderful center to the neighborhood to provide people with drastically needed jobs and health and welfare services. Only after the ribbon-cutting ceremony do the members of the neighborhood council realize that they didn't ask the important questions, and that they had no technical advisors of their own to help them grasp the fine legal print. The new center, which is open 9 to 5 on weekdays only, actually adds to their problems. Now the old agencies across town won't talk with them unless they have a pink paper slip to prove that they have been referred

75

by "their" shiny new neighborhood center.

Unfortunately, this chicanery is not a unique example. Instead it is almost typical of what has been perpetrated in the name of high-sounding rhetoric like "grass-roots participation." This sham lies at the heart of the deep-seated exasperation and hostility of the have-nots toward the powerholders.

One hopeful note is that, having been so grossly affronted, some citizens have learned the Mickey Mouse game, and now they too know how to play. As a result of this knowledge, they are demanding genuine levels of participation to assure them that public programs are relevant to their needs and responsive to their priorities.

2. THERAPY

In some respects group therapy, masked as citizen participation, should be on the lowest rung of the ladder because it is both dishonest and arrogant. Its administrators—mental health experts from social workers to psychiatrists—assume that powerlessness is synonymous with mental illness. On this assumption, under a masquerade of involving citizens in planning, the experts subject the citizens to clinical group therapy. What makes this form of "participation" so invidious is that citizens are engaged in extensive activity, but the focus of it is on curing them of their "pathology" rather than changing the racism and victimization that create their "pathologies."

Consider an incident that occurred in Pennsylvania less than one year ago. When a father took his seriously ill baby to the emergency clinic of a local hospital, a young resident physician on duty instructed him to take the baby home and feed it sugar water. The baby died that afternoon of pneumonia and dehydration. The overwrought father complained to the board of the local Community Action Agency. Instead of launching an investigation of the hospital to determine what changes would prevent similar deaths or other forms of malpractice, the board invited the father to attend the CAA's (therapy) child-care sessions for parents, and promised him that someone would "telephone the hospital director to see that it never happens again."

Less dramatic, but more common examples of therapy, masquerading as citizen participation, may be seen in public housing programs where tenant groups are used as vehicles for promoting control-your-child or cleanup campaigns. The tenants are brought together to help them "adjust their values and attitudes to those of the larger society."

76

Under these groundrules, they are diverted from dealing with such important matters as: arbitrary evictions; segregation of the housing project; or why it takes three months to get a broken window replaced in winter.

The complexity of the concept of mental illness in our time can be seen in the experiences of black and white students who served as civil rights workers in the South. They soon learned that it was not abnormal for their fears to verge on paranoia. There were brutal forces in the South using guns, whips and other forms of terror to maintain the status quo. To be horribly afraid of such fearful forces was normal. Fortunately, two socially attuned psychiatrists helped the students understand that one man's "mental illness" was another's decency. The students were therefore able to deal with their fears without being diverted from the objective that had first brought them to the civil rights movement.[7]

3. INFORMING

Informing citizens of their rights, responsibilities, and options can be the most important first step toward legitimate citizen participation. However, too frequently the emphasis is placed on a one-way flow of information—from officials to citizens—with no channel provided for feedback and no power for negotiation. Under these conditions, particularly when information is provided at a late stage in planning, people have little opportunity to influence the program designed "for their benefit." The most frequent tools used for such one-way communication are the news media, pamphlets, posters, and responses to inquiries.

Meetings can also be turned into vehicles for one-way communication by the simple device of providing superficial information, discouraging questions or giving irrelevant answers. At a recent Model Cities citizen planning meeting in Providence, R.I., the topic was "tot-lots." A group of elected citizen representatives, almost all of whom were attending three to five meetings a week, devoted an hour to a discussion of the placement of six tot-lots. The neighborhood is half black, half white. Several of the black representatives noted that four tot-lots were proposed for the white district and only two for the black. The city official responded with a lengthy, highly technical explanation about costs per square foot and available property. It was clear that most of the residents did not understand his explanation. And it was clear to observors from the Office of Economic Opportunity that other options did exist which, considering available funds, would have brought about a more equitable distribution of facilities. Intimidated by legalistic jargon and the prestige of the official, the citizens accepted the "information" and endorsed the agency's proposal to place four lots in the white neighborhood.[8]

4. CONSULTATION

Inviting citizens' opinions, like informing them, can be a legitimate step toward their full participation. But if consulting them is not combined with other modes of participation, this rung of the ladder is still a sham since it offers no assurance that citizen concerns and ideas will be taken into account. The most frequent methods used for consulting people are attitude surveys, neighborhood meetings, and public hearings.

When powerholders restrict the input of citizens' ideas solely to this level, participation remains just a window-dressing ritual. People are primarily perceived as statistical abstractions, and participation is measured by how many come to meetings, take brochures home, or answer a questionnaire. What citizens achieve in all this activity is that they have "participated in participation." And what powerholders achieve is the evidence that they have gone through the required motions of involving "those people."

Attitude surveys have become a particular bone of contention in ghetto neighborhoods. Residents are increasingly unhappy about the number of times per week they are surveyed about their problems and hopes. As one woman put it: "Nothing ever happens with those damned questions, except the surveyer gets $3 an hour, and my washing doesn't get done that day." In some communities, residents are so annoyed that they are demanding a fee for research interviews.

Attitude surveys are not very valid indicators of community opinion when used without other input from citizens. Survey after survey (paid for out of antipoverty funds) has "documented" that poor housewives most want tot-lots in their neighborhood where young children can play safely. But most of the women answered those questionnaires without knowing what their options were. They assumed that if they asked for something small, they might just get something useful in the neighborhood. Had the mothers known that a free prepaid health insurance plan was a possible option, they might not have put tot-lots

78

so high on their wish lists.

A classic misuse of the consultation rung occurred at a New Haven, Connecticut, community meeting held to consult citizens on a proposed Model Cities grant. James V. Cunningham, in an unpublished report to the Ford Foundation, described the crowd as large and "mostly hostile:"[9]

Members of The Hill Parents Association demanded to know why residents had not participated in drawing up the proposal. CAA director Spitz explained that it was merely a proposal for seeking Federal planning funds—that once funds were obtained, residents would be deeply involved in the planning. An outside observer who sat in the audience described the meeting this way:

"The city officials ran the meeting on their own. No representatives of a Hill group moderated or even sat on the stage. Spitz told the 300 residents that this huge meeting was an example of 'participation in planning.' To prove this, since there was a lot of dissatisfaction in the audience, he called for a 'vote' on each component of the proposal. The vote took this form: 'Can I see the hands of all those in favor of a health clinic? All those opposed?' It was a little like asking who favors motherhood."

It was a combination of the deep suspicion aroused at this meeting and a long history of similar forms of "window-dressing participation" that led New Haven residents to demand control of the program.

By way of contrast, it is useful to look at Denver where technicians learned that even the best intentioned among them are often unfamiliar with, and even insensitive to, the problems and aspirations of the poor. The technical director of the Model Cities program has described the way professional planners assumed that the residents, victimized by high-priced local storekeepers, "badly needed consumer education."[10]

The residents, on the other hand, pointed out that the local storekeepers performed a valuable function. Although they over-charged, they also gave credit, offered advice and frequently were the only neighborhood place to cash welfare or salary checks. As a result of this consultation, technicians and residents agreed to substitute the creation of needed credit institutions in the neighborhood for a consumer education program.

5. PLACATION

It is at this level that citizens begin to have some degree of influence though tokenism is still apparent. An example of placation strategy is to place a few hand-picked "worthy" poor on boards of Community Action Agencies or on public bodies like the board of education, police commission or housing authority. If they are not accountable to a constituency in the community and if the traditional power elite hold the majority of seats, the have-nots can be easily outvoted and outfoxed. Another example is the Model Cities advisory and planning committees. They allow citizens to advise or plan ad infinitum but retain for powerholders the right to judge the legitimacy or feasibility of the advice. The degree to which citizens are actually placated, of course, depends largely on two factors: the quality of technical assistance they have in articulating their priorities; and the extent to which the community has been organized to press for those priorities.

It is not surprising that the level of citizen participation in the vast majority of Model Cities programs is at the placation rung of the ladder or below. Policy-makers at the Department of Housing and Urban Development (HUD) were determined to return the genie of citizen power to the bottle from which it had escaped (in a few cities) as a result of the provision stipulating "maximum feasible participation" in poverty programs. Therefore, HUD channeled its physical-social-economic rejuvenation approach for blighted neighborhoods through city hall. It drafted legislation requiring that all Model Cities' money flow to a local City Demonstration Agency (CDA) through the elected city council. As enacted by Congress, this gave local city councils final veto power over planning and programming and ruled out any direct funding relationship between community groups and HUD.

HUD required the CDA's to create coalition, policy-making boards that would include necessary local powerholders to create a comprehensive physical-social plan during the first year. The plan was to be carried out in a subsequent five-year action phase. HUD, unlike OEO, did not require that have-not citizens be included on the CDA decision-making boards. HUD's Performance Standards for Citizen Participation only demanded that "citizens have clear and direct access to the decision-making process."

Accordingly, the CDAs structured their policy-making boards to include some combination of elected officials; school representatives; housing, health and welfare officials; employment and police department representatives; and various civic, labor and business leaders. Some CDAs included citizens from the neighborhood. Many mayors correctly interpreted the HUD provision for "access to the decision-making process" as the escape hatch they sought to relegate citizens to the traditional advisory role.

Most CDAs created residents' advisory committees. An alarmingly significant number created citizens' policy boards and citizen's policy committees which are totally misnamed as they have either no policy-making function or only a very limited authority. Almost every CDA created about a dozen planning committees or task forces on functional lines: health, welfare, education, housing, and unemployment. In most cases, have-not citizens were invited to serve on these committees along with technicians from relevant public agencies. Some CDAs, on the other hand, structured planning committees of technicians and parallel committees of citizens.

Variations on the theme are almost infinite because HUD encouraged the CDAs to experiment with administrative and policy mechanisms. The structural role for have-not citizens may show similar and related variations, but in most cases their power in the Model Cities planning process remains strictly advisory or deliberately ill-defined.

In most Model Cities programs, endless time has been spent fashioning complicated board, committee, and task force structures for the planning year. But the rights and responsibilities of the various elements of those structures are not defined and are ambiguous. Such ambiguity is likely to cause considerable conflict at the end of the one-year planning process. For at this point, citizens may realize that they have once again extensively "participated" but have not profited beyond the extent the powerholders decide to placate them.

Results of a staff study (conducted in the summer of 1968 before the second round of seventy-five planning grants were awarded) were released in a December, 1968 HUD bulletin.[11] Though this public document uses much more delicate and diplomatic language, it attests to the already cited criticisms of non-policy-making policy boards and ambiguous complicated structures, in addition to the following findings:

1. Most CDAs did not negotiate citizen participation requirements with residents.

2. Citizens, drawing on past negative experiences with local powerholders, were extremely suspicious of this new panacea program. They were legitimately distrustful of city hall's motives.

3. Most CDAs were not working with citizens' groups that were genuinely representative of model neighborhoods and accountable to neighborhood constituencies. As in so many of the poverty programs,

those who were involved were more representative of the upwardly mobile working-class. Thus their acquiescence to plans prepared by city agencies was not likely to reflect the views of the unemployed, the young, the more militant residents, and the hard-core poor.

4. Residents who were participating in as many as three to five meetings per week were unaware of their minimum rights, responsibilities and the options available to them under the program. For example, they did not realize that they were not required to accept technical help from city technicians they distrusted.

5. Most of the technical assistance provided by CDAs and city agencies was of third-rate quality, paternalistic, and condescending. Agency technicians did not suggest innovative options. They reacted bureaucratically when the residents pressed for innovative approaches. The vested interests of the old-line city agencies were a major— albeit hidden—agenda.

6. Most CDAs were not engaged in planning that was comprehensive enough to expose and deal with the roots of urban decay. They engaged in "meetingitis" and were supporting strategies that resulted in "projectitis," the outcome of which was a "laundry list" of traditional programs to be conducted by traditional agencies in the traditional manner under which slums emerged in the first place.

7. Residents were not getting enough information from CDAs to enable them to review CDA developed plans or to initiate plans of their own as required by HUD. At best, they were getting superficial information. At worst, they were not even getting copies of official HUD materials.

8. Most residents were unaware of their rights to be reimbursed for expenses incurred because of participation—babysitting, transportation costs, and so on.

9. The training of residents, which would enable them to understand the labyrinthe of the federal-state-city systems and networks of subsystems, was an item that most CDAs did not even consider.

These findings led to a new public interpretation of HUD's approach to citizen participation. Though the requirements for the seventy-five "second-round" Model City grantees were not changed, HUD's twenty-seven page technical bulletin on citizen participation repeatedly advocated that cities share power with residents. It also urged CDAs to experiment with subcontracts under which the residents' groups could hire their own trusted technicians.

A more recent evaluation was circulated in February, 1969, by OSTI, a private firm that entered into a contract with OEO to provide technical assistance and training to citizens involved in Model Cities programs in the northeast region of the country. OSTI's report to OEO corroborates the earlier study. In addition it states:[12]

In practically no Model Cities structure does citizen participation mean truly shared decision-making, such that citizens might view themselves as "the partners in this program. . . ."

In general, citizens are finding it impossible to have a significant impact on the comprehensive planning which is going on. In most cases the staff planners of the CDA and the planners of existing agencies are carrying out the actual planning with citizens having a peripheral role of watchdog and, ultimately, the "rubber stamp" of the plan generated. In cases where citizens have the direct responsibility for generating program plans, the time period allowed and the independent technical resources being made available to them are not adequate to allow them to do anything more than generate very traditional approaches to the problems they are attempting to solve.

In general, little or no thought has been given to the means of insuring continued citizen participation during the stage of implementation. In most cases, traditional agencies are envisaged as the implementors of Model Cities programs and few mechanisms have been developed for encouraging organizational change or change in the method of program delivery within these agencies or for insuring that citizens will have some influence over these agencies as they implement Model Cities programs. . . .

By and large, people are once again being planned for. In most situations the major planning decisions are being made by CDA staff and approved in a formalistic way by policy boards.

6. PARTNERSHIP

At this rung of the ladder, power is in fact redistributed through negotiation between citizens and powerholders. They agree to share planning and decision-making responsibilities through such structures as joint policy boards, planning committees and mechanisms for resolving impasses. After the ground rules have been established through some form of give-and-take, they are not subject to unilateral change.

Partnership can work most effectively when there is an organized power-base in the community to which the citizen leaders are accountable; when the citizens group has the financial resources to pay its leaders reasonable honoraria for their time- consuming efforts; and when the group has the resources to hire (and fire) its own technicians, lawyers and community organizers. With these ingredients, citizens have some genuine bargaining influence over the outcome of the plan (as long as both parties find it useful to maintain the partnership). One community leader described it "like coming to city hall with hat on head instead of in hand."

In the Model Cities program only about 15 of the so-called first generation of 75 cities have reached some significant degree of power-sharing with residents. In all but one of those cities, it was angry citizen demands, rather than city initiative, that led to the negotiated sharing of power.[13] The negotiations were triggered by citizens who had been enraged by previous forms of alleged participation. They were both angry and sophisticated enough to refuse to be "conned" again. They threatened to oppose the awarding of a planning grant to the city. They sent delegations to HUD in Washington. They used abrasive language. Negotiation took place under a cloud of suspicion and rancor.

In most cases where power has come to be shared it was *taken by the citizens,* not given by the city. There is nothing new about that process. Since those who have power normally want to hang onto it, historically it has had to be wrested by the powerless rather than proffered by the powerful.

Such a working partnership was negotiated by the residents in the Philadelphia model neighborhood. Like most applicants for a Model Cities grant, Philadelphia wrote its more than 400 page application and waved it at a hastily called meeting of community leaders. When those present were asked for an endorsement, they angrily protested the city's failure to consult them on preparation of the extensive application. A community spokesman threatened to mobilize a neighborhood protest *against* the application unless the city agreed to give the citizens a couple of weeks to review the application and recommend changes. The officials agreed.

At their next meeting, citizens handed the city officials a substitute citizen participation section that changed the ground rules from a weak citizens' advisory role to a strong shared power agreement. Philadelphia's application to HUD included the citizens' substitution word for word. (It also included a new citizen-prepared introductory chapter that changed the city's description of the model neighborhood from a paternalistic description of problems to a realistic analysis of its strengths, weaknesses, and potentials.)

Consequently, the proposed policy-making committee of the Philadelphia CDA was revamped to give five out of eleven seats to the
residents' organization, which is called the Area Wide Council (AWC).
The AWC obtained a subcontract from the CDA for more than $20,000
per month, which it used to maintain the neighborhood organization,
to pay citizen leaders $7 per meeting for their planning services, and to
pay the salaries of a staff of community organizers, planners and other
technicians. AWC has the power to initiate plans of its own, to engage
in joint planning with CDA committees and to review plans initiated by
city agencies. It has a veto power in that no plans may be submitted by
the CDA to the City Council until they have been reviewed, and any
differences of opinion have been successfully negotiated with the AWC.
Representatives of the AWC (which is a federation of neighborhood
organizations grouped into sixteen neighborhood "hubs") may attend
all meetings of CDA task forces, planning committees, or subcommittees.

Though the City Council has final veto power over the plan (by
federal law), the AWC believes it has a neighborhood constituency that
is strong enough to negotiate any eleventh-hour objections the City
Council might raise when it considers such AWC proposed innovations
as an AWC Land Bank, an AWC Economic Development Corporation,
and an experimental income maintenance program for 900 poor
families.

7. DELEGATED POWER

Negotiations between citizens and public officials can also result in
citizens achieving dominant decision-making authority over a particular
plan or program. Model City policy boards or CAA delegate agencies on
which citizens have a clear majority of seats and genuine specified
powers are typical examples. At this level, the ladder has been scaled to
the point where citizens hold the significant cards to assure accountability of the program to them. To resolve differences, powerholders
need to start the bargaining process rather than respond to pressure
from the other end.

Such a dominant decision-making role has been attained by residents
in a handful of Model Cities including Cambridge, Mass.; Dayton, and
Columbus, Ohio; Minneapolis, Minn.; St. Louis, Mo.; and Hartford and
New Haven, Conn.

In New Haven, residents of the Hill neighborhood have created a corporation that has been delegated the power to prepare the entire Model Cities plan. The city, which received a $117,000 planning grant from HUD, has subcontracted $110,000 of it to the neighborhood corporation to hire its own planning staff and consultants. The Hill Neighborhood Corporation has 11 representatives on the 21 member CDA board which assures it a majority voice when its proposed plan is reviewed by the CDA.

Another model of delegated power is that of separate and parallel groups of citizens and powerholders, with provision for citizen veto if differences of opinion cannot be resolved through negotiation. This is a particularly interesting coexistence model for hostile citizen groups too embittered toward city hall—as a result of past "collaborative efforts"—to engage in joint planning.

Since all Model Cities programs require approval by the city council before HUD will fund them, city councils have final veto powers even when citizens have the majority of seats on the CDA Board. In Richmond, Calif., the City Council agreed to a citizens' counter-veto, but the details of that agreement are ambiguous and have not been tested.

Various delegated power arrangements are also emerging in the Community Action Program as a result of demands from the neighborhoods and OEO's most recent instruction guidelines which urged CAAs "to exceed (the) basic requirements" for resident participation.[14] In some cities, CAAs have issued subcontracts to resident dominated groups to plan and/or operate one or more decentralized neighborhood program components like a multipurpose service center or a Headstart program. These contracts usually include an agreed upon line-by-line budget and program specifications. They also usually include a specific statement of the significant powers that have been delegated, for example: policy making; hiring and firing; issuing subcontracts for building, buying, or leasing. (Some of the subcontracts are so broad that they verge on models for citizen control.)

8. CITIZEN CONTROL

Demands for community controlled schools, black control and neighborhood control are on the increase. People are simply demanding that degree of power (or control) which guarantees that participants or residents can govern a program or an institution, be in full charge of policy and managerial aspects and be able to negotiate the conditions under which "outsiders" may change them.

A neighborhood corporation with no intermediaries between it and the source of funds is the model most frequently advocated. A small number of such experimental corporations are already producing goods and/or social services. Several others are reportedly in the development stage, and new models for control will undoubtedly emerge as the have-nots continue to press for greater degrees of power over their lives.

Though the bitter struggle for community control of the Ocean Hill-Brownsville schools in New York City has aroused great fear in the headline reading public, less publicized experiments are demonstrating that the have-nots can indeed improve their lot by handling the entire job of planning, policy making and managing a program. Some are even demonstrating that they can do all this with just one arm because they are forced to use their other one to deal with a continuing barrage of local opposition triggered by the announcement that a federal grant has been given to a community group or an all-black group.

Most of these experimental programs have been capitalized with research and demonstration funds from the Office of Economic Opportunity in cooperation with other federal agencies. Examples include:

1. A $1.8 million grant was awarded to the Hough Area Development Corporation in Cleveland to plan economic development programs in the ghetto and to develop a series of economic enterprises ranging from a novel combination shopping-center-public-housing project to a loan guarantee program for local building contractors. The membership and board of the non-profit corporation is composed of leaders of major community organizations in the black neighborhood.

2. Approximately $1 million ($595,751 for the second year) was awarded to the Southwest Alabama Farmers Cooperative Association (SWAFCA) in Selma, Alabama, for a ten-county marketing cooperative for food and livestock. Despite local attempts to intimidate the co-op (which included the use of force to stop trucks on the way to market), first year membership grew to 1,150 farmers who earned $52,000 on the sale of their new crops. The elected co-op board is composed of two poor black farmers from each of the ten economically depressed counties. (See Zimmerman, above)

3. Approximately $600,000 ($300,000 in a supplemental grant) was granted to the Albina Corporation and the Albina Investment Trust to

create a black-operated, black- owned manufacturing concern using inexperienced management and unskilled minority group people from the Albina district. The profit-making wool and metal fabrication plant will be owned by its employees through a deferred compensation trust plan.

4. Approximately $800,000 ($400,000 for the second year) was awarded to the Harlem Commonwealth Council to demonstrate that a community-based development corporation can catalyze and implement an economic development program with broad community support and participation. After only eighteen months of program development and negotiation, the council will soon launch several large-scale ventures including operation of two supermarkets, an auto service and repair center (with built-in manpower training program), a finance company for families earning less than $4,000 per year, and a data processing company. The all black Harlem-based board is already managing a metal castings foundry.

Though several citizen groups (and their mayors) use the rhetoric of citizen control, no Model City can meet the criteria of citizen control since final approval power and accountability rest with the city council.

Daniel P. Moynihan argues that city councils are representative of the community, but Adam Walinsky illustrates the nonrepresentativeness of this kind of representation:[15]

Who . . . exercises "control" through the representative process? In the Bedford-Stuyvesant ghetto of New York there are 450,000 people—as many as in the entire city of Cincinnati, more than in the entire state of Vermont. Yet the area has only one high school, and 80 per cent of its teen-agers are dropouts; the infant mortality rate is twice the national average; there are over 8000 buildings abandoned by everyone but the rats, yet the area received not one dollar of urban renewal funds during the entire first 15 years of that program's operation; the unemployment rate is known only to God.

Clearly, Bedford-Stuyvesant has some special needs; yet it has always been lost in the midst of the city's eight million. In fact, it took a lawsuit to win for this vast area, in the year 1968, its first Congressman. In what sense can the representative system be said to have "spoken for" this community, during the long years of neglect and decay?

Walinsky's point on Bedford-Stuyvesant has general applicability to the ghettos from coast to coast. It is therefore likely that in those ghettos where residents have achieved a significant degree of power in the Model Cities planning process, the first-year action plans will call for the creation of some new community institutions entirely governed by residents with a specified sum of money contracted to them. If the ground-rules for these programs are clear and if citizens understand that achieving a genuine place in the pluralistic scene subjects them to its legitimate forms of give-and-take, then these kinds of programs might begin to demonstrate how to counteract the various corrosive political and socioeconomic forces that plague the poor.

In cities likely to become predominantly black through population growth, it is unlikely that strident citizens' groups like AWC of Philadelphia will eventually demand legal power for neighborhood self-government. Their grand design is more likely to call for a black city hall, achieved by the elective process. In cities destined to remain predominantly white for the foreseeable future, it is quite likely that counterpart groups to AWC will press for separatist forms of neighborhood government that can create and control decentralized public services such as police protection, education systems, and health facilities. Much may depend on the willingness of city governments to entertain demands for resource allocation weighted in favor of the poor, reversing gross imbalances of the past.

Among the arguments against community control are: it supports separatism; it creates balkanization of public services; it is more costly and less efficient; it enables minority group "hustlers" to be just as opportunistic and disdainful of the have-nots as their white predecessors; it is incompatible with merit systems and professionalism; and ironically enough, it can turn out to be a new Mickey Mouse game for the have-nots by allowing them to gain control but not allowing them sufficient dollar resources to succeed.[16] These arguments are not to be taken lightly. But neither can we take lightly the arguments of embittered advocates of community control—that every other means of trying to end their victimization has failed.

NOTES

[1] The literature on poverty and discrimination and their effects on people is extensive. As an introduction, the following will be helpful: B. H. Bagdikian, *In the Midst of Plenty: The Powerful America* (New York: Beacon, 1961); David T. Bazelon. "The Brutalizing of America," *Dissent,* XI (Autumn 1964); Stokely Carmichael and Charles V. Hamilton, *Black Power: The Politics of Liberation in America* (New York: Random House, 1964); Eldridge Cleaver, *Soul on Ice* (New York: McGraw-Hill, 1968); L. J. Duhl, *The Urban Condition: People*

89

and Policy in the Metropolis (New York: Basic Books, 1963); William H. Grier and P. M. Cobbs, *Black Rage* (New York: Basic Books, 1968); Michael Harington, *The Other America: Poverty in the United States* (New York: Macmillan, 1962); Peter Marris and Martin Rein, *Dilemmas of Social Reform: Poverty and Community Action in the United States* (New York: Atherton Press, 1967); Mollie Orshansky, "Who's Who Among the Poor: A Demographic View of Poverty," *Social Security Bulletin,* XXVII (July 1965); and Richard T. Titmuss, *Essays on the Welfare State* (New Haven: Yale University Press, 1968).

[2] The poster is one of about 350 produced in May or June, 1968 at Atelier Populaire, a graphics center launched by students from the Sorbonne's Ecole des Beaux Arts and Ecole des Arts Decoratifs.

[3] This typology is an outgrowth of a cruder typology I circulated in March, 1967 in a HUD staff discussion paper titled "Rhetoric and Reality." The earlier typology consisted of eight levels that were less discrete types and did not necessarily suggest a chronological progression: Inform, Consult, Joint Planning, Negotiate, Decide, Delegate, Advocate Planning and Neighborhood Control.

[4] For an article of some possible employment strategies, see, Edmund M. Burke, "Citizen Participation Strategies," *Journal of the American Institute of Planners,* XXXVIV, No. 5 (September 1968), 290–1.

[5] U.S., Department of Housing and Urban Development, *Workable Program for Community Improvement, Answers on Citizen Participation,* Program Guide 7, February, 1966, pp. 1 and 6.

[6] David Austin, "Study of Resident Participants in Twenty Community Action Agencies," CAP Grant 9499.

[7] Robert Coles, "Social Struggle and Weariness," *Psychiatry,* XXVII (November 1964), 305–15. I am also indebted to Daniel M. Fox of Harvard University for some of his general insights into therapy being used as a diversion from genuine citizen participation.

[8] See, Gordon Fellman, "Neighborhood Protest of an Urban Highway," *Journal of the American Institute of Planners,* XXXV, No. 2 (March 1969), 118–22.

[9] James V. Cunningham, "Resident Participation," Unpublished Report prepared for the Ford Foundation, August, 1967, p. 54.

[10] Interview with Maxine Kurtz, Technical Director, Denver CDA.

[11] U.S., Department of Housing and Urban Development, "Citizen Participation in Model Cities," *Technical Assistance Bulletin,* No. 3 (December 1968).

[12] Organization for Social and Technical Innovation, *Six-Month Progress Report to Office of Economic Opportunity, Region 1,* February 1, 1969, pp. 27, 28, and 35.

[13] In Cambridge, Massachusetts, city hall offered to share power with residents and anticipated the need for a period in which a representative citizens group could be engaged, and the ambiguities of authority, structure, and process would be resolved. At the request of the mayor, HUD allowed the city to spend several months of Model Cities planning funds for community organization activities. During these months, staff from the city manager's office also helped the residents draft a city ordinance that created a CDA composed of sixteen elected residents and eight appointed public and private agency representatives. This resident-dominated body has the power to hire and fire CDA staff, approve all

plans, review all model city budgets and contracts, set policy, and so forth. The ordinance, which was unanimously passed by the City Council also includes a requirement that all Model City plans must be approved by a majority of residents in the neighborhood through a referendum. Final approval power rests with the city council by federal statute.

[14] U.S., Office of Economic Opportunity, *OEO Instruction, Participation of the Poor in the Planning, Conduct and Evaluation of Community Action Programs* (Washington, DC; December 1, 1968), pp. 1–2.

[15] Adam Walinsky, "Review of *Maximum Feasible Misunderstanding*" by Daniel P. Moynihan, New York Times *Book Review,* February 2, 1969.

[16] For thoughtful academic analyses of some of the potentials and pitfalls of emerging neighborhood control models, see, Alan Altshuler. "The Demand For Participation in Large American Cities," An Unpublished Paper prepared for the Urban Institute, December, 1968; and Hans B. C. Spiegel and Stephen D. Mittenthal, "Neighborhood Power and Control, Implications for Urban Planning." A Report prepared for the Department of Housing and Urban Development, November, 1968.

WHICH CITIZENS TO PARTICIPATE IN WHAT?

by: Irving Lazar

Editor's note:

Irving Lazar provides a common-sense grounding on the sociology of groups in the American experience. He defines some characteristics of participation and proceeds to evaluate OEO's ground rules for participation by those criteria. His emphasis on strategies for participation dovetails with Arnstein's and provides a broader context for Saliterman's description of citizen participation in educational institutions.

Some questions:
1) Is Lazar's conception of OEO strategy the same as the Cahn's?
2) Is "town meeting romanticism" at the heart of much of the Federal emphasis on participation? What are "communities" in huge urban areas? In spread out rural areas?
3) Are there valid examples of creation of communities through Federal programs, with needs surveys and training built in to assist the growth of participation?

Now Director of Child Development for the Appalachian Regional Commission, Washington, D.C., Dr. Lazar has been responsible for the development of some 60 community organizations in the past 20 years. He is a social psychologist, an expert in community mental health, a former intern at the Menninger Clinic and former director of the Neumeyer Foundation. He received his Ph.D from Columbia University.

De Tocqueville noted that Americans were joiners, and that American communities teemed with organizations and clubs. Let a problem rear its head, and at least one committee will be formed. Leave ten people alone in a room and they'll pick a chairman, select a by-laws committee and argue about the name of their newborn group.

Usually the committee or club has a purpose. Usually it has members whose interests and skills are relevant to that purpose. And usually it will seek out people who can fill its gaps of knowledge or skills so that the job it has set for itself can be done well. Thus do Americans participate, and thus have we transformed a cultural idiosyncracy into a national norm, prescribed for all our people -- rich or poor, introversive or extraversive, social or reclusive. This prescription pervades our architecture (which permits doors for only the most private of functions), our psychiatry (which sees a desire for solitary contemplation as schizophrenic) and our education (which insists that the students in a classroom be as diverse a group in intelligence and culture as the community can possibly assemble). And so it should be no surprise that in our anti-poverty programs, we ask recipients as part of their emergence from poverty to learn to behave like people in the majority culture and to "participate" for its own sake.

It is this last point -- that participation is somehow good for all people and all purposes -- which lies at the heart of some of the strange and sometimes destructive things that have happened in the name of participation.

Before examining citizen participation in the War on Poverty, I wish to review, in abbreviated form, some of the usual ways in which citizens participate, and how individual citizens learn the complex of organizational skills that lie at the heart of community organization. At each stage of this description I will suggest a comparison with both Community Action Agencies and with Headstart programs. These are "suggestions" because of the diversity of those programs and because, although I have visited CAAs and Headstart centers throughout the United States, hard data are hard to come by. Later in this paper I will focus, in detail, on the nature and meaning of citizen participation in these programs as I have seen them in operation.

A. THE COMMUNITY ORGANIZATION

1. The Group

Most groups form around a common purpose. Needs for communication between businessmen produce a Rotary Club; needs to promote business, a Chamber of Commerce; needs to prevent a new highway from fragmenting a neighborhood, a taxpayers' association. Church-related organizations will promote sectarian solidarity, bridge clubs an assurance that bridge hobbyists can find partners.

Supplementary purposes may attach to a group, thus increasing its size and stability and meeting multiple needs: the Rotary Club organizes family picnics, the church group provides a setting for single people to meet and seek mates.

In time, the association of members may lead to friendships and to cooperative action for purposes distant from or entirely separate from the group's original goals. The members of a PTA may support a new bond issue or a school-board candidate, or may form a committee on adolescents' use of drugs.

Because most groups organize around a set of common needs, their memberships are likely to be quite homogeneous. Members of a community group will usually have similar incomes, levels of education, vocations and styles of life. Typically they will be run by the older members and will have a fairly well-defined route for promotion of members to leadership.

How does this compare with CAA boards and Headstart committees? The CAA and Headstart groups were created by fiat. Extra-community decision-makers determined that they should exist. The motivation offered was "control" of Federal moneys. The composition of the group was determined first by agency regulation and later by federal law. "Reducing poverty" was so ill defined -- as were such terms as "community"[1] -- that the only real motives offered for group organization were the promise of federal funds and whatever fantasies of power, patronage and personal wealth individuals may have projected onto OEO's press releases. The artificial structure of CAA boards set the stage for conflicts, for confusion and often for inane compromise. To such boards came agency officials paid to sit on them, who were experienced in maneuvering and who had a vested interest in protecting and expanding their fiefdoms. Alongside them sat community influentials: the people who had worked their way up through organization subcommittees and committees to offi-

94

cerships and board memberships. These veterans of the community's organizations already knew the agency officials, and had available both their experience and a network of influence to move the CAA in the directions they felt made sense. And then there were the "representatives" of the poor. Even if they were in fact poor, they were both outnumbered and outclassed on the board. Not having served the prior apprenticeship of the other board members, they could only feel inept and angry -- and could only lose, for even their nominal victories were by sufferance of the rest of the board. If they were simply the ethnic politicians, as was often the case, then the notion of representativeness was largely a farce.

In the case of Headstart, the issue was different. Service to preschool children is a concrete and comprehensible basis for group organization. Headstart supplied fairly explicit budgeting and staffing guides, provided staff orientation and training and, building on the long-established profession of nursery education, pretty much pre-packaged Headstart programs in Washington.

Thus, the Headstart advisory groups and boards were not initially confronted by the issue of program content and could cope instead with staff and site selection. Once these battles were fought and resolved, they discovered the uncertainty and unpredictability of OEO's refunding procedures, and could find in this uncertainty a common cause -- or at least a common enemy. On such an issue the poor parent could join cause with the agency official or professional on the board and, although the chronic problem remained of whether to hire untrained people as head teachers or administrators solely on a racial or ethnic basis, participation could be easily shared around issues essentially peripheral to program content. Nonetheless, these Headstart Boards remained essentially artificial groups. Except in small towns, I have yet to hear of a Headstart Board with diverse membership that developed strong secondary goals or cross-class social bonds. If Headstart disappeared tomorrow, I would predict that most of these "non-groups" would promptly dissolve; their primary bond is federal money.

2. The Purpose of a Group

As was indicated above, groups generally form around a central goal and, as they grow and age, acquire secondary and supplementary goals to meet additional needs of the membership. The acceptance of such secondary goals may come about without much conscious awareness, as long as the group does not divert time or resources from the primary goal. An example of this is the dating and mating functions which attach to many church groups which are organized for other reasons. When the secondary function does require diversion of resources, then, typically, it is adopted only after a hard fight among the members, the committees and the officers of the organization. New goals are added slowly, and one at a time. At each stage, the group's priorities are redefined and these priorities directly reflected in budget and staffing decisions. In the course of time, goals may change and priorities switch, but always a step at a time. If changes happen too quickly or without consensus, members may leave or the group may split or dissolve. When a member goes through this process, he knows he has participated -- and quits if he feels "railroaded."

How does this apply to CAA and Headstart programs? The goals of OEO have never been defined in any way that would lead to a set of priorities -- because in order to avoid influencing communities, OEO essentially treated all strategies as having equal priority at one time or another. Champions of each strategy were issuing conflicting guidelines and peacekeepers were trying to incorporate all of them in each program. Three major strategies emerged, and three separate wars on poverty have been waged:

(1) A Service Strategy — This is based on the belief that OEO could best help the poor by providing services they had been denied, to help them bridge the gap to full use of their talents. Legal and Health service programs are examples of such programs. These programs see the major portion of the poor as "damaged."

(2) A Jobs Strategy — This position says that the best way to help people out of poverty is to give them jobs, and that the place to start is with OEO programs. Here the priority is not service; it's jobs. The "client" is the worker, and the poor are seen as competent but "deprived" of opportunity. An example of this strategy is the Neighborhood Aides program.

(3) Institutional or Social Change Strategy. This approach sees the poor as "downtrodden," and states that the best way to help the poor is to organize them so that they can use their political potential to gain their rights and to force concessions from the larger society. It is argued that once they have power the poor will be able to make relevant choices of services and jobs.

96

It is not the purpose of this paper to select one of these strategies -- all are different and all have different implications for citizen participation.

The point is that OEO never did arrive at a firm set of priorities. In its effort to be noncommittal OEO arrived at the classical bureaucratic solution: namely to try to include all three strategies simultaneously in each program. Headstart was thus to provide services to children, to give jobs to their parents (whose lack of skill in child-rearing may have made the Headstart program necessary in the first place) and somehow to serve as a base for social change and community organization. Each OEO project was to fight out its own priorities among these.

3. Members of a Group

In a later portion of this paper we will explore why people join groups and how they function in them. In this portion we seek simply to remember that, in most groups, people have joined voluntarily -- that is, the pressures are informal or are not directly related to the group -- and have stayed because they feel a community of purpose and congeniality with the other members. These purposes are never explicitly financial; membership in that kind of group is called a "job" or a "partnership." As a result, most groups are quite homogeneous along several dimensions, and the points of similarity are borne proudly.

Memberships in most OEO-sponsored groups are all too often fiscal, are rarely homogeneous and the points of similarity -- poverty, ignorance, low status - are not borne proudly in our still-Calvinistic society. The viable groups that have grown out of OEO programs seem to have become viable for other reasons, such as ethnic pride, economic pressure and political party organization. These reasons for viable groups are the ones that OEO discourages, for they tend to get OEO in trouble![2] Suffice it to say, most of the rapidly organized OEO groups can hardly be considered as viable: none had time enough to grow in stable ways, and all were mandated by the utopian regulations of young bureaucrats, largely inexperienced and situated far from the program sites.

B. THE SETTING

Groups don't originate in vacuums; they emerge from cultural contexts, from the Zeitgeist, the mood of a community, and from complex sets of traditions.

Usually they form and grow around an issue -- sometimes a social issue ("Let's stop the pollution of our river"), sometimes a personal one ("If I join the Kiwanis Club I'll make good business contacts"). Usually both kinds of issues or motives are present to some degree. When the group forms around a social issue it does so because the members have reason to believe that their unity will give them strength, that their membership can mobilize public opinion and that together they can influence social decisions. Middle-class people hold these beliefs because they have been validated in the past. In psychological terms, such behavior has been reinforced.

Is it any wonder, then, that the really poor rarely organize? What in their history can even suggest that they could rationally hold such beliefs and expectations? Indeed, poor people have learned that their power is minimal and their groups ineffective. The only mass action by the poor that we have reinforced has been riots. But mobs are not groups, and participation in looting is not what most anti-poverty warriors have in mind.[3]

If citizen participation is to be an effective way of improving the lot of the poor, then considerable preliminary work must be done in the larger community to prepare fertile soil for such a novel -- and fragile -- plant.

C. THE INDIVIDUAL

Who joins the groups -- and why? In a study[4] of the composition of committees and boards of voluntary organizations[5] in a large metropolitan area, the author of the report was able to draw several generalizations about the concentrations of membership in service-oriented and issue-oriented groups, as follows:

a) Adolescents join groups -- out of a mixture of idealism and a need for useful and focused activity, and as a social experience.

b) Married women in their early thirties join groups -- as a stimulating variation from their child rearing and housekeeping routines, as a way of having a "job" and status in a society which does not highly value homemaking as a career, as a way of enhancing their husbands' positions in the community, and, not the least, as a way of finding social stimulation and friends.

c) Single people of all ages join groups -- because Americans abhor "loneliness."

d) Men just starting in their business or profession join groups -- for obvious reasons. But I have observed that the most ardent members of male groups tend to be in their mid-forties -- a time when vocational mobility has slowed down and feelings of inadequacy tend to creep into the normal man's self-image.

To be sure, people of all ages are to be found in groups of all kinds. These generalizations refer to concentrations of active members.

In addition to the motives summarized above and corporate and peer-group expectations, which are quite influential, people join a specific group because they *believe* in the goals and philosophy of the group.

To believe -- to invest feelings and time and money -- implies either (1) that the individual has surpluses in these areas that he can invest in extra-personal activities because his own needs are sufficiently met or (2) that his needs are unusual, and he needs or expects the group to fulfill them. In a sense, the active participant is often making a trade. In exchange for this time, energy and money, he receives recognition, status or power from the group. Even this trade implies that basic material and nutritive needs are not paramount in his life.

What does all this mean for citizen participation among the poor? From my visits to community groups I draw two sets of generalizations:

First: the most active participants in community groups are not the poorest people in their communities; they tend to be upward mobile people, with middle-class (economic) expectations, who *can* invest in issues other than the daily struggle for sheer survival that plagues and drains the energies and perspectives of the very poor.

Second: it appears unrealistic to expect widespread participation among the very poor until their basic economic and health needs are met. It is the daily struggle and pressure that makes the normal time-lag between an idea and action, which is built into the democractic process, so frustrating to the very poor. In fact, few poor people do actually participate -- even in Headstart, which goes to unusual lengths to encourage parental participation. For example, in one recent study[6] of an active countywide Headstart program, it was learned that 35 percent of the parents had never been to a formal Headstart meeting and only 7 percent had been to more than one formal meeting.

The reader has noted that we are focusing on the *joiner's* reasons for joining, and not the social engineer's reasons for wanting people to join. (Participation as a strategy of change is ably discussed by Edmund M. Burke.)[7]

Once in a group, the member moves in ways well described in the extensive literature on group behavior. He modifies his expectations to the group norm, learns the group's tempo, accepts initial "apprenticeship" assignments, moves through its committee structure, modifies his role in response to group requirements and *learns* from his contacts with other, older members how to act and how to get things done. For middle-class people, the basic learning starts early. In addition to having the example of his parents, he is enrolled in scout troops, church groups, clubs and committees from an early age. By the time he is an adult, he knows an enormous amount about how to participate.

Most poor people have not had this informal curriculum of the middle class. As a result, even if a poor person is somehow motivated to go to a meeting he is totally unprepared for the complex mores of group behavior. Some anti-poverty programs have made real attempts to provide training for poor new members (such as the group training guides and charts prepared by the New Jersey Community Action Training Institute); however, these attempts seem to be exceptions. We will discuss the effects of this lack later in this paper.

D. TYPES OF PARTICIPATION

One of the characteristics of most voluntary organizations is that in a sense a member has a choice as to the extent to which he will participate, and may stay at a given level of progress if he chooses. One such system of choices looks like this:

Level

1. Pays dues, attends meetings rarely.
2. Attends meetings regularly, passively.
3. Is very active and vocal at meetings.
4. Undertakes committee work.
5. Becomes committee chairman.
6. Becomes an officer.
7. Becomes president.
8. Becomes board member.

Only rarely does a member become a staff member. Separation of staff and membership is usually quite complete. As a result each member -- and each staff employee -- knows the structure and his choices.

No such structure is characteristic of most anti-poverty projects. There is no progression, and therefore no opportunity for training. Members become staff, newcomers are elected directly to boards, membership is relatively meaningless, and so there is little choice of level of participation or reward for participation. For the poor person, a staff appointment is more desirable than an officership; the political results (and the weakness of the board) or its domination by the non-poor are clearly predictable.

E. STRATEGIES OF PARTICIPATION

It having been decided for one reason or another[8] that citizen participation is important, the techniques for achieving such participation have been well known for many decades. Identifying group needs and readiness through random-sample surveys, creating needs through advertising, co-opting influentials and other respected figures, providing group settings, reinforcement devices, etc., have all been described.

A few examples are presented here because they will help point up the contrast between the usual, successful, "traditional" approaches of social scientists, and the very different approaches of the non-professionals (in social science) who constructed OEO's participation "strategies."

Despite Dr. Moynihan's assertions,[9] social scientists have had virtually no involvement in OEO policy-making. At the time the bill was being written a few social scientists, including Dr. Moynihan and Dr. Frank Riessman, were consulted; however, no social scientist with field experience has ever served in any major policy-making role in OEO, and virtually none has served at any other level at headquarters. Even "Sandy" Kravitz, the beloved "Dr. Strangegrant" of the early demonstration projects, is a social worker -- not a social scientist in the usual meaning of that term. Kravitz was also one of the few people in OEO who had had rich field experience working in poor communities. Most OEO headquarters policy makers have been -- and are -- lawyers, newspapermen and politicians. Most junior-level people seem to come from the humanities and fine arts. Some are social workers, ministers or former law enforcement personnel. Dr. Robert Levine, former Chief of Research, Program Planning and Evaluation, is the only social scientist in a major (third-level) position in the agency[10] who comes to mind.

Example I: In 1933 when the New Deal established the then radical innovation of a planned national crop -- through subsidies, production and acreage quotas and other federal devices for control of the farm

101

economy -- it was felt necessary to involve farmers in the process of making these and other innovative decisions. Because at the time only the wealthier farm owners were organized, and no mechanism existed for representation or involvement of the smaller and poorest farmers, the Department of Agriculture turned to social scientists for help. Using what were then the most sophisticated survey techniques available, stratified random samples of farmers were interviewed, their responses used as a basis for policy-making and the farmer-respondents shown this connection. The department demonstrated its seriousness in seeking and using the advice of small farmers; it established real and useful liaison through a revitalized Farm Agent program and an extensive program of out-stationed rural sociologists. Poor farmers were therefore willing to risk going to meetings, forming caucuses, pushing for legislation and finally constructing a set of organizations whose present political strength far outshadows their actual numbers.

Note that this approach used professionals (farm extension agents) for technical assistance and information-giving, involved the opinions of even the most reticent farmers through the use of public opinion surveys, delivered what it did promise -- and didn't imply promises it could not deliver -- and assisted the sensible, long-term development of what are now quite hardy, powerful and permanent organizations of farm groups.[11]

Example II: More than twenty-five years ago the Commission on Community Interrelations of the American Jewish Congress demonstrated an effective approach to the fact that most Americans denied the extent to which prejudice was endemic in the country (Sounds familiar, doesn't it?).

Using a technique called "the Community Self-Survey," teams of influentials and ordinary citizens were organized and, with the help of a professional, were shown how to build and field-test surveys, draw samples, interview people, codify and count their responses and interpret their findings. Because they did it themselves, they could not reject the findings. Because they talked to the people and knew that the sample was representative, they had to deal with their own emotional reactions to the realities of prejudice.[12]

With this basis, people were willing to act. They "sold themselves."

In the use of this same technique to identify program priorities in two communities, the results were similar. Political battles over program priorities were avoided, a base for communication was established and the surveys opened the door for beginnings of attendance at community meetings. Poor people, rich people and professionals found in the self-survey process a way to keep working together because all discovered, together, what the voice of the people was saying.

F. OEO'S STRATEGIES FOR PARTICIPATION

The word "strategy" implies planning, and in all fairness the author points out that he is unaware that there was ever a formal prior "strategy" for participation. Instead, there was an implicit assumption that the poor were straining at the bit to join boards and plan programs; -- that once Washington fired the starting gun a mad scramble would ensue, leaders would come out of their shacks and tenements and Town Hall democracy would reign.[13]

The "strategy" outlined here is derived by deduction from what seems to have happened. It had four main thrusts (arranged in approximate historical order):

1. Membership of the poor on boards
2. Employment of the poor in projects
3. Community meetings
4. Elections of board members

1. Membership of the Poor on Boards

The initial mad rush did not occur. It turned out that indigenous organizations were scarce; those that did exist were dominated by the middle-class substructure of the poor neighborhood: the ministers, landlords, businessmen, teachers and social workers.

The "representatives of the poor" often turned out to be middle-class neighborhood politicans or their carefully selected, docile followers, most of whose identifications were upward bound. Some cities had not even such token representatives, and more than one mayor proclaimed that he, as the elected head of the city, was the representative of the poor.

Many poor people would not participate because they weren't being paid, or couldn't afford either the time or the expenses of babysitters and car fare.[14]

Art Buchwald, in an article written during the early days of OEO, fantasizes a poor man who agrees to serve on a neighborhood board if he is paid for this time, the way the agency representatives are paid. Asked what was the first thing he would do on the board, if he were paid, the imaginary man replies, "Why, move out of the neighborhood, of course."

Those who did join faced the problems mentioned before of lack of skills. Not knowing the ways of boards, or Robert's Rules, they were often swamped, outmaneuvered, condescended to, and indeed were very bad advocates of the poor.

2. Employment of the Poor in Projects

A second strategy was to provide staff jobs to poor people in the belief that their presence and presumed special knowledge of poverty would provide a policy-influencing input into agencies. Here again, naivete (mine, too) failed to anticipate the obvious problems of such a policy. The problems were:

a) Countless observations in other settings had told social scientists that the oppressed tend to identify with their oppressors. Many of the poor, achieving status as staff and assurance of their own economic stability, became harsh, punitive and authoritarian in their treatment of poor people.

b) Many were seen -- accurately -- as having "joined the establishment," and so were seen in a new and negative light by their less fortunate and often envious neighbors.

c) In at least one city, where control of the new "indigenous non-professionals" remained centralized in the CAA, workers were told that their function was to serve as "sand in the machinery" of the agencies they were assigned to. As a result, those who took the instruction seriously were quickly isolated by the agencies. Those who could be co-opted were, of course, accepted.

d) Having little or no orientation to the world of work in agencies, the relationships between board and staff, the policy-making process, and the supervisory structure of agencies, and having received only sketchy introductions to their new and often make-work assignments, these new workers quickly got into trouble, got frustrated, and got either very angry or further convinced of the accuracy of their feelings of inadequacy.

e) The new jobs were often dead ends. Workers entered at minimum wages and had nowhere to move -- either vertically or laterally. The initial notion that they would prove so valuable that agencies would absorb them into their own payrolls was patently silly. What local public or private agency has expanding sources of local money?

Most of the jobs have remained dead ends. The yeoman efforts of such people as Frank Riessman aside, only a tiny percentage of Scheuer Amendment money has actually created real career ladders. Riessman's work in Newark's public schools has been widely reported. But rarely copied. Indeed the only large-scale career ladder this author knows of was created entirely outside of OEO, by the Illinois State Department of Mental Hygiene. There a person with no formal education can, through time and by taking the courses provided, rise to a $15,000-a-year administrative post. The ladder he is on is not a separate ladder for the poor, it's the same ladder everyone climbs, although trained people enter at higher rungs.

Not only is there little opportunity or training for upward mobility, but no provision for lateral mobility exists. A Headstart assistant teacher in one agency cannot transfer to another Headstart agency in another community, and often not even to another neighborhood in the same community.

With no structured way to advance within the agency and no credentials to move to another agency, the worker is vocationally immobilized and is dependent on the refunding of that agency or the retention of its supervisors and board (who hired him). Having no comparable vocational options he is in a trap. "Participation" in such a setting can only take the form of political in-fighting to prevent changes in the status quo -- except to advance one's friends.

Such a "strategy" is simply cruel. Pointing to exceptions or good intentions doesn't change its cruelty. Headstart, at least, is serious about the problem of mobility. Few other programs even give lip service to this problem.

3. Community Meetings

The romantic fantasy of the Town Hall meeting was the paradigm of this approach to citizen participation. Well, as I read my history, it was the landed gentry who came to Town Hall. The ghetto equivalents are the upward-mobile, power-seeking, politically ambitious and angry people who come to community meetings.

Most very poor people don't belong to groups, don't go to meetings, don't express themselves in public. Before meaningful attendance can occur, many other things have to happen. At the minimum, preparatory steps which could lead to meetings could be taken (and occasionally have been taken).

105

For example, in one community a drop-in sewing center was established across the street from the neighborhood supermarket. Free and low cost fabrics, sewing machines, instruction and child-care were available. Counting on the regularity of the shopping day, we found that indeed the same women tended to drop in at the same times each week. Built around sewing instruction, conversations could be led to meetings and finally, into group formation.

Similar paving blocks could be built for men, with repair facilities, and for teen-agers.

Then meetings can become meaningful sites for participation.

4. Elections of Board Members

The election of CAP "poor" representatives by public election procedures is another example of expecting people to start out doing what we hope they will want to do if the program is successful.

—Individuals in poverty have changed. New leadership has emerged, and people are vocal. Because OEO has failed to teach people effective ways of channelling their energies and concerns, the strategic repertoire of the poor remains primitive and narrow. Demonstrations and confrontations are childish techniques, no longer effective. But no one has really taught the new leadership the other "roads to Allah."

This has been due in part to OEO's real reluctance to intervene, but it is also in part a reflection of the amateur status of most of OEO's field staff: young, bright, idealistic, energetic people out of the humanities and other non-relevant areas of training. OEO's own training staff has always been too small to do the job, and the decision to give universities grants and responsibility for training CAA staffs assured that the job would not be done well. It is hard to think of any social institution less involved in the problems of poverty and community than the university. The argument that these piddling grants would change the universities is silly; it's like trying to bring General Motors to its knees with a one-quarter million dollar manpower program.

The other overall effects of the current participation programs are, it seems to me, less defensible. The effects include:

The middle-class volunteers have been driven out of most city programs; their skills, their contacts and their decision-affecting power has thus been largely lost to the poor who need their collaboration.

City halls have either been alienated from or have simply taken over control of CAA's. I cannot believe that either of these reactions serves the best interests of the poor.

106

The generally low turnout at such elections raises another, larger issue: why should any poor person participate in a CAA or neighborhood board? The members of most other kinds of boards have power:

They determine programs

They set policies

They hire and fire people

They determine budgets

Telling the poor that they have such power on a CAP Board is simply not telling the truth. OEO headquarters and regional offices and city halls usually determine priorities, push for programs and determine hiring and spending procedures. Refunding has always been so sluggish that projects typically experience three-month anxiety attacks each year. Given the realities of a board's power, the ambiguity of program goals and the confusions of authority, it is little wonder that few participate.

When program goals are clear, when membership is meaningful and when activities correspond to felt needs, then we can expect that an informed electorate will begin to appear at polls.

G. WHAT'S HAPPENED?

To summarize the gloomy picture painted above is to point out that not all is gloom.

--Organizations now exist that might never have come into existence without the impetus of OEO. These are new organizations -- not funded by OEO but originally organized in response to issues created by OEO programs.

--The Zeitgeist -- the atmosphere and mood of the ghetto -- has changed, and is not likely to regress to its former apathy and resignation. OEO's focus has undoubtedly contributed to these real changes.

Most seriously, the lack of structure and clarity of purpose has produced hostilities which have, I feel certain, played a significant role in the polarization of racial antagonisms. The cause of integration has been virtually destroyed and the cause of inter class collaboration which lay at the heart of the CAA concept has been seriously damaged.

If one of the goals of the CAA was to train poor people to compete successfully as board members and organizers in our complicated and competitive pluralistic society, then the process used could only have been selected out of ignorance of how community decisions are made

107

or out of a romantic delusion that such skills are inherited rather than learned, or out of a desire to see the experiment fail.

What was set as a goal of the CAP -- effective participation -- became a prerequisite of the program. How one could expect people to exercise the skills at the beginning of a program which purported to help them acquire those skills as an end-product has remained a source of wonderment to me since the requirements and definitions were first issued.

H. WHERE DO WE GO FROM HERE?

First of all, participation is clearly here to stay. To make it effective requires that we use some knowledge and accept some basic principles. I suggest these:

1. The kind and amount of participation desirable in a program can only be defined in terms of the specific goals of the program, the community in which it will be carried out and the stage of readiness of its population. The role of a citizen is less central in a surgical team than it is in a rent strike -- or ought to be less if the surgeons are to do their job well. Effective membership on a board requires training and experience, which needs to be provided in advance.

2. Village democracy is a meaningless model in megalopolis, where even the mayor is powerless in many critical areas. If village democracy is what we want, then let's build villages.

3. The idealistic federal bureaucrat is really no better judge of need than was the old-style do-gooder club lady. If we want meaningful programs, let us start with where the people who need the programs are at this moment.

— We know how to conduct surveys to identify needs.
— We can design programs around such needs -- including the concrete design of helpful levels of participation.
— We can *train* participants, so that they don't need to reinvent the wheel but can benefit from our unique human ability to pass knowledge and the results of experience on to each other.
— We can provide varieties of settings attractive to people to encourage group formation.
— We can keep alert for new issues around which groups can mobilize, and show them how to act effectively in dealing with those issues.
— We can stop labelling and sloganeering and getting sold on our own public relations.

The youngsters want us to "tell it like it is" -- all of it, not just

108

the frosting and fantasies. That's good for oldsters, too. And finally, if we want people to join in the decision-making process, we need to stop thinking of them as a homogenous mass.

People differ; communities differ; and participation is not an end in itself. Participation is a constantly changing process which is one of many means to larger social ends.

NOTES

1. For example, the notion that more than 100 named areas which comprise Los Angeles County could be considered as a single "community" stretches the meaning of that word beyond any utility.
2. It is fairly simple—really, unfairly simple— to select particular OEO grants as examples of any point of view. Probably, some of virtually every kind of program option exists somewhere in the 1,100 CAAs and 12,000 Headstart sites in the U.S. The author knows of specific exceptions to all of the generalizations he offers here.
3. However, systematic looting *is* a faster road to riches than most of our funded community action programs provide most poor people.
4. Unpublished. Such sociometric and demographic studies are a standard procedure among social scientists seeking to establish new programs in communities, and the findings discussed here are not at all unusual.
5. We are purposely omitting groups organized primarily for social reasons, only because such groups are not central to this discussion.
6. Feagen, J.R., "The Parents in Riverside County Head Start Programs: An Evaluative Study of Their Characterisitcs, Perspectives, Reactions and Participation," University of California, November, 1968.
7 Burke, Edmund M., "Citizen Participation Strategies", J. American Institute of Planners, September, 1968, pp. 287-294.
8. This is not said with tongue in cheek. There are many very different reasons why policy-makers may want to have citizen participation; see Edmund M. Burke, op. cit.
9. Moynihan, D.P., *Maximum Feasible Misunderstanding*, The Free Press, 1969.
10. This is not the situation in Operation Headstart, not housed in headquarters, which has always included a wide variety of relevant professionals in its staff. Although neither Director of Headstart came from a child-development discipline, each has used professionals extensively in policy making roles.
11. *cf.* "Farmers In A Changing World," *Yearbook of Agriculture,* Sup't. of Documents, 1940.
12. Wormser and Sellitz, *How to Conduct a Community Self-Survey of Civil Rights—A Manual Based on the Northtown Method*, Commission on Community Interrelations of the American Jewish Congress, New York, 1943.
13. These comments, and their tone, are not made from the comfortable vantage of hindsight. As an editor of this volume remembers, they represent views expressed by the author prior to the onset of CAP programs.
14. Expenses were authorized later by OEO.

HEALTH CARE AND POOR PEOPLE

by: Wendy Goepel Brooks

Editor's Note:

Wendy Goepel Brooks argues that not only the poor, but the vast majority of other citizens as well, have been barred from actual participation and influence in the field of health care. The poor suffer more—more get sick because they are poor, and more get poorer because they are sick. Mrs. Brooks cites the major reasons and goes on to assess the new trends of participation by the poor.

The poor have begun to benefit from new jobs. More important, OEO has asked of the poor something unprecedented in American medicine: to help design health care centers of their own.

Mrs. Brooks has done graduate study in medical sociology at Stanford University and has worked extensively in the field of community health. She is a former staff member of the California Department of Public Health and of the United Farm Workers Organizing Committee, AFL-CIO. In 1967 she helped develop rural health centers for OEO in Alabama, West Virginia and California. She is now on the staff of a community health clinic in Woodville, California, where her husband, an internist, practices medicine.

Some questions:

1) How could citizens prevent a national health insurance system, such as that advocated by Mrs. Brooks, from becoming a bureaucratic mechanism, indifferent to the people it serves?

2) Do institutions now exist through which the poor might coalesce with the new forces for reform in medicine, such as socially concerned young doctors?

3) Are there specific kinds of training which might help the poor compete (and/or cooperate) more effectively with medical professionals in the management of health centers?

INTRODUCTION

A lot of people get sick because they are poor.

People who work by the hour don't want to lose money to see a doctor.

Children who live in crowded quarters get TB more; children who drink impure water get diarrhea more; children left at home alone get hurt more.

Women saving money by delaying pre-natal care lose more babies and have smaller, weaker babies and have poorer health themselves.

Kids who can't keep up in school becuase they don't know the language or there's no place at home to study or they don't have the clothes to keep up with other kids become behavior problems or mental health problems or get classified as emotionally disturbed and are sent to special schools for the retarded.

Fathers who can't keep up with the bills or give their kids what the TV commercials say they need become behavior problems and they try to forget with a bottle or they leave.

Poor people live in out-of-the-way places and think health care is sitting on a wooden bench all day and then listening to five minutes of big words and getting some pill.

A lot of people get poorer because they are sick.

If a child is sick and his working mother gives up her job to care for him, there just isn't enough food for the family or money left over for the rent and the gas.

If a father gets sick and there are no disability insurance benefits and no workmen's compensation benefits, then the wife goes out and tries to find a job and leaves the children or the oldest boy quits school and becomes a young man too soon.

People with the most demanding labor jobs are not only most likely to "break down" in middle age, but are also least likely to be retrained for less arduous work so they can keep on living.

"Examined farm worker with early congestive heart failure this day. Patient advised to seek less arduous work." . . . Patient reported to Department of Rehabilitation and was refused as "poor investment." Patient then returned to job of swamping grapes. "Daughter reports patient carried into county hospital emergency room. Prognosis poor."

So the poor get sick and the sick get poorer. There are three basic parts to this investigation. The first looks at some of the reasons why health care and health systems for the poor have lagged so far behind other areas. The second looks at how poor people are participating in the health field today. The third attempts to see how they and others might work for a better future.

I. SOURCE OF THE PROBLEM

Health care has lagged, both as a concern and as a reality, behind other fields. We accept the fact that all children should go to elementary schools in their neighborhood, but we do not give medical care to our children in their community.

There are reasons why this problem came about and continues with us: the attitude of the medical profession, the experience of poor people with medical care and the more general problem of why it is hard to organize people to talk about their health care.

A. The Role of Medical Education

A boy entering medical school has only a vague and generally inaccurate idea about what a doctor is and does. His professional future is molded carefully by his years in training.

Medical school faculties have, as a rule, very little contact with a cross-section of sick people, with medicine in communities and with the realities of financing medical care. Physicians on the faculty, on the other hand, have the best equipped physical plants in which to practice medicine, the nation's sickest patients (referred from the community physician to the local hospital and on to the medical center) and a budget heavily supported by federal grants to engage in basic research.

The orientation of the medical school is toward academic discovery. It is toward learning to use and to rely on the broadest and newest range of diagnostic tools. It is toward learning to specialize and sub-specialize with the aim of proficiency in some small part of a burgeoning scientific disipline. Status within the medical center is awarded to those who discover syndromes, perform heroic surgery, devise new treatments. It is in this atmosphere, far away from the reality of the family physician, the common cold and the routine pre-natal workup, that the future doctor begins his training. It is no surprise then, that fewer and fewer medical school graduates talk about going into family practice. Students are told that it is bad medicine to practice alone, to practice general medicine or to practice very far from a medical research center.

Admission is so competitive that discrimination naturally occurs against those applicants—the rural people, the minority groups, the low-income student—who come from, and who would be most likely to return to, rural and urban ghetto family practice. Discrimination also occurs against those students whose motivation for entering medicine is a strong desire to work with people rather than an aspiration to scientific brilliance. The four classes at UCLA in 1969 contained one black student, a junior. UCLA's admission committee has found that there is no correlation between college grades in science and overall grades in medical school. It is also known that there is no correlation between grades in medical school and quality of practice after graduation.

During his post-graduate period of internship, residency and military service, the physician usually works very long hours for low pay and practices his out-patient medicine in a hospital clinic setting where there is no continuity in the relationship between one doctor and one patient. Small wonder that, when they finish their training, so few elect to work on county hospital staffs, in ghetto practices or rural solo practice.

B. Where Policy is Set

Physicians, through the American Medical Association, have one of the nation's strongest lobbies. The AMA has historically been a champion of free enterprise, and still succeeds to a large extent in keeping government out of medicine. The AMA successfully protects the high

113

income of physicians by controlling the number of new physicians trained; there are no federal scholarships for medical students, although a medical sociologist can get a full scholarship and living allowance from the National Institutes of Health. It contributes to the manpower shortage by focusing on "quality control" and prohibiting the use of subprofessional aides to the physician. Because the lobby continues to prevent any national health insurance program, this country lags behind "less-developed" countries by many years in basic health status. Because the only sizeable federal grants to medical schools are for basic research, the orientation of the schools has been more and more deflected away from teaching. AMA's power protects sacred concepts like private practice and fee-for-service and thereby perpetuates an inferior health status for those citizens who do not have access to a private practitioner and/or cannot afford the fee for the services. The AMA's general position is that everyone who wants health care can get it and that if there are problems, then doctors can solve them alone. Only the recent competition from universities and OEO is beginning to break the monopoly in American medicine.

C. What the Poor See in Medical Care

The theory of rising expectations says that people who have a little bit of something good want a lot more and will go after it or, being denied it, will feel slighted and fight for it. Maybe the problem with health is that the poor don't have the idea that there is something good out there to get—because they haven't seen much of it yet.

Their contact with doctors and medicine has been limited in many cases to charity or county hospital services or to public health services. They feel that the care rendered at county clinics is impersonal, degrading and inconvenient. They know county hospitals are training grounds for young physicians and that they will be used as teaching patients if they become in-patients. The county hospital has a fixed budget, which is usually low compared to other hospitals, and a chief of hospitals who is appointed at the pleasure of elected county officials. Even if poor people haven't seen what good care is, they know this is poor care; so they don't use it as much as they "should" and when they do go, they are sicker than they "should" be and are less likely to recover.

The public health departments, though they give the poor more personal attention, have a lot less to offer. The departments are charged with protecting the health of the general public; but that still means detecting and preventing communicable disease or inspecting houses and restaurants. Poor people can get immunizations, health checkups, pre and post-natal checkups—and a lot of words about what they should do. But they see the public health workers as people who tell them more than they want to know about relatively unimportant things. Public health doctors can screen for illness, but they can't treat illness or pay for the treatment; they revoke midwives' licenses, but can't provide hospital deliveries; they must screen people and plug them into "categorical programs" for which public health is responsible, and turn away the people whose problems can't be properly classified. Since public health officials are usually appointed by elected county officials, they aren't likely to pursue the health of the poor public when it involves a confrontation with the local powers.

D. Why People Don't Get Organized Around Health

The health field is difficult for community organizers. The medical needs of people are sporadic, not continuing. A target area for organizing people should be easily understood and continually visible. When the roof leaks and people are out of work, those who are well don't think about being sick and the problems it will create. People see getting sick as something that comes and goes away. It is hard to sit with people and talk about a problem that may exist only in the future.

The medical problems of poor people are frequently emergencies. An organizer of an organization cannot develop membership, do community education, plan a confrontation and when all is ready, plan an emergency. When illness strikes, each family must deal with it then— there's no time to organize.

The medical problems of the poor are very often the result of a more visible, more important problem: mine accidents are the result of poor mine inspection and bad working conditions; pesticide poisoning of farm workers is the result of untested sprays; worms grow in kids who don't have toilets to use. Those are the issues around which people want to organize.

Sick people don't all live on the same block or in the same housing project. People with the same disease or the same clinic appointment don't usually know one another or see one another or have any easy way of getting together to help themselves. The people who get sick most often—women, little children and old people— are generally less involved in any kind of community organizing drives than are teenagers

115

and men who don't feel the problem as heavily.

It is also hard to organize people for better health because of the respect and fear which people have for doctors. People usually see the doctor as overworked and "doing the best that he can." They hesitate to critize him or his system. It is also very true that people are afraid to criticize doctors because first, they have told the doctor things in confidence that they feel he could divulge if they crossed him, and second, they think they might need the doctor in an emergency and would be denied care if they had said anything against him.

Finally, health care is a hard place to organize because the whole system is so complex and so invisible. A person never sees a doctor-patient relationship in the office or hospital room or surgery suite unless he is the patient. He doesn't understand the words or have the knowledge to refute a medical judgment or know what the standards are. He sees a huge building, a lot of staff and a lot of machinery and feels very small and very dependent.

Perhaps the basis of the entire problem, among both doctors and poor people, is that they still think of health care as a privilege and not a right. A couple of years ago, people at OEO started saying that poor people have a right to be healthy—and this was a new idea to a lot of people.

Western European countries have national health insurance; socialist countries have decentralized free health care; Mexico requires its physicians to spend two years in the rural villages curing the sick. But this country is clinging stubbornly to fee-for-service and "free choice of physician" concepts, which discriminate against the poor. We have two classes of care: private doctors and private hospitals for those who can pay; charity or county hospitals and clinics for those who cannot.

II. PARTICIPATION OF THE POOR

There are two important areas where poor people participate directly in health care issues. The first is where poor people are involved as employees of health care agencies; the second is where poor people are being asked, as consumers, to help design and direct OEO community health centers.

A. Jobs

When we talk about jobs for the poor in health care, we are talking mainly about *new* kinds of jobs for people who *were* poor before they got the job. We are talking about people without credentials being let in on a piece of the action in health.

There have, of course, always been a lot of poor people working in hospitals as orderlies, aides, custodians, etc. In some places, such as mental hospitals, these employees probably have more contact with the patients than have all the "trained" people. It wouldn't be fair to talk about new careers in health for the poor without stopping first to say that most poor people employed in deadend menial hospital jobs are the invisible working poor—poor because they draw very low pay and have no union. Perhaps it is very significant that today's health and poverty thinking runs toward creating new jobs for the unemployed and fails to put more emphasis on organizing the working poor into a union.*

When most people discuss health roles for the poor, they are thinking about the "new careers" in health which have been created for the poor to fill. These are of two basic kinds: technician aides and community health aides.

1. Technician Aides

This new job set is a function of the rapid growth of the health care industry. The idea behind this development came from the realization that highly trained people were spending much time doing non-professional tasks, that job components could be factored out and the skill required for each determined and that the less-skilled components could be regrouped into a job for an "aide"—lab aide, home health aide, nurse's aide, social work aide, etc.

The merits of this job program are that the professional has more time for direct patient contact, that steady employment in an expanding field is created for large numbers of poor people and that technical skills are transmitted to those who supposedly lack the education to learn these skills. The disadvantages of this new job program are that the jobs for which the poor are trained generally are dead-end jobs; that the aide training programs are frequently carried on within the

*There is evidence of a new emphasis on organizing such workers into unions. In New York City, Local 1199 of the International Drug and Hospital Workers Union has waged a militant campaign to represent the underpaid in the health care field, and won important gains in wages and working conditions. In Charleston, S.C., black hospital workers striking in 1969 for recognition of their union became the focus for temporary revitalization of the old labor and civil rights coalition.

institution in which the person is to be employed and other institutions have shown little interest in hiring them; and that these jobs usually involve a direct, sometimes deprecatory relationship between aide and professional in which the aide is told to do those things which the professional doesn't want to do.

The nationalization of health insurance for the aged and some poor has increased the demand for health services rapidly, and the presence of OEO and MDTA funds and incentives for creating jobs for the poor has successfully "demonstrated" to most major health centers that aide jobs have an important role.

The important reforms that must be fought now are for the creation of an "industrial model" rather than a professional model within the health field, so that a person's skills and formal training within a program of one name can be assigned some worth as that person seeks a higher rung on the health professional ladder. Thus North Carolina's experiment says that medical corpsmen who have treated frontline casualties for years should be able to learn a little additional theory and then work as physician's assistants. The California Committee on Health Manpower says that nurses' aides who have passed chemistry, anatomy and physiology courses ought not to have to repeat these if they want to enroll in an RN program later on. This industrial mobility model ought to have a chance, but health professional organizations are staunchly opposing any efforts in this direction. When Philip Lee, then Assistant Secretary of HEW, told a California committee that Indian women, trained to fill teeth, had had their work judged superior to that of an equal number of licensed dentists by a panel of *dentists*, the president of the California Dental Association walked out of the meeting. When Lee was being considered for the job of Chancellor of the University of California Medical Center in San Francisco, as a known advocate of developing the industrial model in health professional training, his appointment was strongly opposed by the San Francisco Medical Society.

The aides owe their jobs to the institution in which they are trained. They have little horizontal mobility, but they have not said much yet about their own aspirations and dissatisfactions.

2. Community Health Aides

This new career is built around the realization that the communication gap between the health professional and the patient might be overcome by the employment of an intermediary from the cultural, social or economic group of the patient. It formalizes the customary practice of taking your friend or relative with you to drive the car, hold the children, translate or give you courage when you go for medical care.

The community aide program began experimentally in the 1950's with the Indian Health service, but became more widespread and more popular with the passage of the Migrant Health Act of 1963. In this program, health aides were widely used as assistants to nurses and health educators who worked among migrant farm workers. The aide program was multiplied many times over with the advent of the OEO Neighborhood Health Centers. The use of community aides, unlike that of the technical aide group, has not really extended beyond the corridors of federally financed operations.

The effect of having aides in an agency is that it retrains the professionals as well as employs the poor. The aides force awareness of the social setting in which health care is given because they are asked to "deliver the patient" and must therefore cope with many "irrelevant" but real obstacles. They transmit the patients' whole set of problems to the professional. The aides can move easily into the rural or urban ghetto and are verbally and culturally more adept at delivering the message, they do increase health utilization figures for their employers. The health aides in the community also get caught in the inter-relationship of health, welfare, education, probation and legal problems of their clients and, when they are selfconfident enough, can transmit this to their more insulated superiors. The problem of the aides' independence and judgment is a difficult one. The technician aide is physically close and there can be supervision. The community aide is out in people's homes, usually alone; she is representing an official agency, and being asked regularly to make judgments about health and medical matters. It is unrealistic to expect that all aides will or could refer every question to a professional, yet aides are seldom trained to make professional judgments.

Another problem is their identity. They are asked to come on as regular salaried members of a professional team, with job security, contacts and some future, yet they are required to continue to think and act and respond "poor" and to maintain their identity as members of the poor community, if they are to fulfill their liaison function successfully. This causes many hangups for the aide so employed. There are two escape avenues. The first and most common is that the aide

119

become increasingly middle class like her work associates. She naturally wants and can now afford to dress like them, learns to talk like them (the key transition is when the aide starts calling the poor "they" or "these people"), can afford to move to a new neighborhood (and why shouldn't she). Her role, as far as many in her agency are concerned, is one of explaining why people don't do right. By instruction and experience, she gradually learns always to do right. Among the poor, the idea quickly and legitimately spreads that the aide is no longer "one of us," that she is paid money to make us try and adopt her style but we aren't given the money and experience to do it. The aide in one health center recently told me: "Well, I don't have to use the health center. I have my own family physician."

The other escape is for the aide to retain her identity as one of the poor. By calling things as she sees them, by pointing up the bureaucratic entanglements, inconsistencies and major gaps in services, she becomes an advocate for the problems of the poor, but will then have trouble walking her clients through the morass of half-way services. She may become a liability to her employer at the point that she becomes an effective spokesman. The aides that do stay on the job and don't fall into one of these two escape routes are most often those who work with a fairly large group of other aides in the same job category, who have a formal training period as a group and thereby establish a group identity, who are seeking the respect of their economic level rather than the approval of their superiors and who are part of an agency which is out to adjust agency style to accommodate the clientele. This would be most likely to happen in one of the few health programs which are actually controlled by the poor themselves.

In many OEO centers the role of community aide is changing. Where good, convenient medical care is provided, the need to persuade people to come in has largely disappeared. With a bi-lingual facility open in the evenings when the car is home, the aide's role of translating, bussing and babysitting disappears. But by being around poor patients and being obliged to keep busy, health aides have picked up on a whole new array of problem areas. In many instances they are assuming the position of patient-advocate. They are becoming ombudsmen, and this is probably good community health.

B. The Poor as Directors of Health Care Systems

OEO asked poor people to help design health care centers for themselves. This is something that private practitioners have not asked of

120

their patients, nor unions of their members, nor insurance companies of their policy-holders. Just because this mandate was given, the health centers are very important. So even though the citizens' actual role in designing and running the centers has been disappointingly limited in most cases, it is important to see what the potential was and is.

OEO's Neighborhood Health Centers began as part of the Community Action Program and were therefore charged with creating "maximum feasible participation" in planning, implementation and direction of health care services they funded. This meant that there had to be community people on a board of directors before a Neighborhood Health Center began operation.

Even the worst OEO health centers are probably a lot better than county hospital clinics. But it is hard to say whether this is because the poor people themselves came up with the new ideas or because the professionals knew all along how to improve things, but hadn't had a strong incentive to do this any earlier—namely OEO money earmarked to do things differently.

The strengths of the health centers lie in their coordination of different agency services under one roof, their simultaneous concern with preventive medicine (or public health problems) and medical care and rehabilitation, their policy of training and hiring community people at many levels, their policies on hours, languages and attitude toward patients, their attempt to provide continuity of care between one family and one doctor-nurse-aide team, their location in neighborhoods where the poor live.

It is important that the professional staff, at least in theory, work for a community-based board of directors which includes consumers of the health center's care. The consumer boards have not dictated how doctors practice medicine or overstepped their competence boundaries. The biggest problem is that the community people have not exercised strong leadership. Perhaps the poor in the target communities don't have confidence or competence yet, maybe control of the centers is based much more in Washington or existing medical centers. But since this is the only large scale alternative to an old, bad system, we should look at the poor people's leadership role, see where it has failed and how it might be different.

The general failure of the poor to provide strong direction to the health centers is explained in much the same way that the poor have failed to exert leadership in the Community Action Agency Boards of Directors: the poor often represent only themselves while the other

121

representatives are truly representative of established and influential county agencies; the poor have no background in formal organizations and cannot compete in formulations and making decisions; the poor do not speak the language or have the conceptual background of other board members, the poor board members come from dispersed places within a city or county and do not have the regular contact with one another through which they might develop a block vote; the poor put on boards often represent the middle-class aspiring group of the poor.

In the particular case of health boards, there is a vast and highly complex system of medical knowledge that cannot be learned well, quickly, by anybody. It is also true that the OEO health center program was an unusually large and complex program in that it set the goal of providing complete care to 10-30,000 people in a new facility within a year at the cost of some $1 million per year, per center. This scope made meaningful involvement of the poor most difficult. In addition, OEO had trouble selling the health center concept initially to community-based groups and ended up making most of its grants to university medical centers which would reach out from their established compelxes into the ghetto. The people in these university medical centers had not traditionally been involved in either community medicine or work with low-income people as partners. The involvement ended up being very token in many cases, as in the much-repeated rocking chair story: the story of a poor board member who suggested using rocking chairs instead of straight backs in the health center waiting room, and how this shows that the poor can make meaningful contributions.

If community power is to be exercised on the development and operation of health centers, then there are certain steps which can make this more of a reality than it is now:

1. Health centers should be located in areas where an organized group of poor people want neighborhood-level health care, not where an organized professional group wants to develop a program.

2. The poor people's organization should receive intense training in the components of health care systems, the pros and cons of various methods of approach, the successes and failures of existing health centers from the viewpoint of the poor involved in these now.

3. Components of the health care package should be delineated, and control over certain of these should be given to the poor—transportation system, recruitment and selection of aides, the number and type of staff who will make home visits and their relationships with one another and with the patients; locating, renovating, decorating and

122

maintenance of the health facility itself, personnel policy (at all levels in a center with strong community involvement, and limited to the aide positions above in a weak one); public information and education about the center, grievance policy and implementation eligibility (i.e. implementation of OEO guidelines for admission). What is important initially is that there are some components, some specific tasks which the local people can perform adequately, or even better than can trained professionals. The converse of this is that certain components of the health package must be delineated and assigned to the health professional sponsor or staff for development and control.

4. A clear relationship between community people who serve on the board of directors and those who serve as staff must be maintained. The people in a community who are interested in starting a center will want jobs when it opens. They, unlike others, will be volunteering time until the grant is actually made. But it is crucial to begin plans with people who want board positions and do not want employment because it is this group who should know the most about the full operation and scope of the center if they are to exercise wise leadership over the others. If this is not done, then the community people on the staff have more knowledge and more skill than those technically responsible for directing them in their work, and the staff tend to run the center. Either the board must be continually educated and informed about how the center is going and how problems might be resolved, or it tends to become an inactive figurehead.

5. If community power is to become a reality, the sponsoring group must want to make it happen. There are two dimensions to this which must be considered.

a. Basic Organizational Structure

Three kinds of structures have emerged in health centers, sometimes by design and sometimes by default. The first is that in which a strong poor people's board has control over the entire operation and has a health professional advisory team. This can come about only when a professional group—medical society, university department, group practice—is willing to accept professional responsibility yet delegate full control to the poor people's board. In this structure, the medical director walks a thin line, being responsible to the poor but also implicitly to his peers in the professional group. This structure hands the entire package to the poor and attracts only those health professionals who

123

are willing to really live with local control. In Alviso, Calif., an established organization of the poor turned a small-scale voluntary health clinic into an OEO Neighborhood Health Center with the advice and assistance of Stanford University. A five-man community board accepts the OEO funds directly and runs the program.

The second structural model is that of dual control. Again, the community board has fiscal control: here it includes health professionals and the poor. The poor run certain departments and the health professionals accept responsibility for others. This balance of power structure is similar to that of many hospitals where the "professional" and the "administrative" responsibilities are clearly delineated. The importance of giving some responsibility and control to the poor and thereby forcing an organization of equals, interacting, may be more significant than the structural problems inherent in this model.

The third structural model, probably the most common, results when the grant is made to a medical center and power is therefore concentrated there; community people here serve as an advisory board to the professionals and in many subprofessional training slots. In cases where the health center is an outreach project of a major medical center, it is hard to create anything other than this structure—and the ability of people in the community to really exercise control is very minimal.

b. Professional Staff Loyalties

Professional staff play a key role in the operation of any health center. Somewhat independent of the basic structure of the center, these individuals may do much to advance or hinder community control. Professionals who work full-time for the center are more susceptible to community control than those who are part-time or rotating. If the center's purpose is to develop an ongoing relationship with the community, it cannot also train faculty or residents in community medicine by rotating them through health centers. If the physicians employed continue to maintain their regular practice of middle-class clients, the special services due the poor under the OEO grant and the different orientation of special interests of the poor board are only a part of the man's interest and due only a part of his attention. Many times compromises must be made by health center boards because of the physician shortage, but accepting part-time physicians, faculty-assigned rotating physicians or services from a pre-existing middle-class panel of physicians sharply compromises the power that the community board, staff and patients can exercise over the man's practice of medicine. Ideally then, there must be full-time primary physicians staffing the center on a long-term basis.

The ultimate power of the community board of a health center depends then on whether it actually represents an organized group of poor people, how well trained its members are, how much fiscal and personnel control actually resides in the community and how much the health professionals allied with the center want community control.

The irony of community control is that the poor are being asked to pioneer a new institutional structure for health consumers of the nation at large. OEO's health centers are suggesting that the health consumer should have a say over how much of what kind of service he receives for a fixed amount of money. Consumer rights are now being demanded by middle-class patients who purchase care in the open market but find that that market lacks variety, compassion and economy. The California Council for Health Care Alternatives is a new joint effort by unions in the state to get some control over the health care their members get. This whole trend, begun by OEO, bears close attention.

III. THE HEALTH FUTURE OF POOR PEOPLE

We want to outline the main areas of action for the next decade and see both what the poor can do and what others should do if the poor are to be brought into the mainstream of health care.

A. Action for Improved Medical Education

The reform movement in medical education is one of the encouraging things about American medicine today. It began at the University of Southern California Medical School in 1965 when medical students protested the scientific emphasis in their training and the total lack of concern with the community. The students then began by volunteering to work in nearby ghettos, involving themselves in health care, youth education and organizing health clinics for out-patients. In four years, the work and concerns of these students have spread to more than 70 other medical, dental and nursing school campuses. A national organization of medical students, the Student Health Organization, works to educate students about community problems and responsibilities, to press for curriculum reform and to build a new image for themselves as

125

America's future physicians. The organization has inevitably sparked controversy within medical schools and has led, in some instances, to meaningful curriculum changes.

Students at many schools now assist physicians and public health personnel during a "community medicine" rotation in their training. Beginning last year, pressures were exerted on admissions committees with the aim of enrolling some minority students in medical schools. At UC Medical Center in San Francisco, black hospital staff members have threatened a walkout if black student demands for the training of more black doctors are not met.

Some student physicians argue that they should be permitted to serve the poor in this country as an alternative to serving war casualties in Viet Nam.

At one hospital in New York, interns have urged clinic patients not to pay for second-class service and to send back their bills. In others, they are working to organize employees into the Hospital Workers' Union. Because the student physician is part of "the establishment" he is in a unique position to speak out against things that are going wrong. The primary student concern today is with the type of care that they and others around them are delivering to the poor. The important question, which won't be answered for five more years, is what these students will do, as private physicians, to change the posture of American medicine.

B. Action About Health Benefits

A second major area for public concern is in the structure and economics of health care benefits for the poor. There are two areas where the poor need help; the first is in paying for health care on a routine basis, the second in maintaining and caring for the injured and disabled poor. The first step toward making health care a right rather than a privilege for poor people came when Titles XVIII and XIX of the Social Security Act were passed.

Title XVIII, called Medicare, was to automatically cover all citizens over the age of 65, but the physicians' lobby got certain restrictions written into this title which prevent participation by large numbers of poor people. Since we cannot foresee the creation of a lobby of sick septuagenarians, others will have to work for reform of Medicare so that it can serve the very poor. At present, a person must pay the first $40 of each hospital bill he

126

incurs and the first $50 in doctor's visits every year. For a senior citizen on a $65 pension, this is not realistic. Wealthy states generally pay this initial charge for their elderly, but poor states do not. Some accommodation between the need of the physicians' lobby to leave their mark on this "socialized medicine attempt" and the need of the poorest poor to get equal access to medical care must be worked out.

Title XIX, Medicaid, is a program under which the federal government will match state and county grants in order to provide health care to the poor. Much ·leeway is given to the states and much advantage is given to the wealthy states who have funds to match federal monies. In some of the poorer states, Medicaid has not yet been implemented. In rich states like New York and California there already have been cutbacks, and there is very little talk about expanding the benefits anywhere.

A second major health-benefit problem is the disabled. There are two standard categories of disability: temporary and permanent. If a temporarily disabled person is given financial and medical help, he is less likely to become permanently disabled. But few states now grant aid to temporarily disabled persons. In most states, all workers are covered by Workmen's Compensation. If they get hurt or sick on the job, they can draw cash and medical care benefits. Many times, however, employees are threatened with loss of a job if they report an injury (because this will increase the employer's insurance premium). In some states the poorest workers are not covered by Workmen's Compensation. For those unfortunate enough to get hurt on the way home, rather than on the job, there is no standard policy for compensation.

The only national program which theoretically aids the disabled is through Social Security. Congress has said, however, that "disabled" means that the claimant must be unable to do any work at all; it is not enough that he cannot do any work available in his town or county or any work commensurate with his education level. This clause heavily penalizes the poor. Coal miners, for example, are ineligible on the assumption that they could leave Appalachia and secure a clerical job in a metropolitan area. A definition of disabled which is not prejudiced against the poor should be made. In addition, some provision for the medical care of the disabled should be made. The Social Security program does not currently cover this at all.

There should be a single uniform national policy for dealing with people as soon as they become disabled. The need for reform and unification of the present patchwork programs for the disabled is obvious—but the disabled themselves stand little chance of reorganizing HEW to make this happen.

C. Action to Improve Environmental Health

Through their organizations—community action in West Virginia or the farm workers' union in California—workers are saying that even poor people have a right to work under safe conditions. They are beginning to talk about black lung, about unsafe mines, about working in fields where fruits are protected by sprays but where people are not protected from the sprays.

Health indicators have strong political force. A cursory physical examination or a set of hemoglobins to measure anemia can show the toll which poverty takes among poor children. Congressional hearings on hunger are telling Americans that worms are infecting children who don't have sanitary facilities to use, that diarrhea plagues babies who drink water from polluted wells, that malnutrition causes underachievement. Politicians from many camps are talking about hungry and sick children, and hopefully their deliberations will lead them to correct the causes of this hunger and sickness and not lead them only into programs of distributing emergency food supplies. The sick and hungry children are there because health and welfare agencies don't have the political and economic power to change things.

Most public health authorities and medical planners say that the era of epidemic prevention and traditional public health has passed and that the new work is in personal health. This is true for the nation as a whole, but not for the ghettos. The conditions of the Industrial Revolution which prompted the original development of public health forces still exist in poverty pockets in America. Public health forces are not politically aggressive, but they could be made politically responsive if the demand for change is built. There are worms in South Carolina and rats in New York City and spray deaths all over rural California. Like so many other poverty problems, they are waiting to be discovered; then the people with the technical knowledge to change things will miraculously appear. This is where good health for poor people has to start.

FEDERAL STANDARDS AND REGULATIONS
FOR PARTICIPATION

by: Daniel M. Fox

Editor's Note:

Daniel M. Fox is now Principal for the Organization for Social and Technical Assistance, Washington, D.C. He has worked with the Appalachian Volunteers and the Massachusetts Service Corps, both experimental programs in the war on poverty.

Writing from a public administration perspective, he creates a typology of participation which should be compared with Arnstein's and Lazar's.

Some questions:

1. How does the careful statement on civil disorder—rioting has been the most significant tool for citizen impact on participation policy and standards—jibe with arguments in other monographs, such as Piven's?

2. Does the Fox typology of attitudes toward federal intervention— federalist, pluralist, pragmatic skeptic—exhaust the reasonable alternatives, or are there other types implicit in the material?

Dr. Fox has served as a consultant to a number of government agencies and citizens groups. He holds B.A., M.A., and Ph.D. degrees from Harvard.

I. INTRODUCTION

When historians examine the events of the 1960s with the hindsight of another generation, it is possible that they will describe the development of *Federal standards for citizen participation* as the decade's most significant innovation in the practice of public administration. However, neither grass root citizen participation nor federally funded or encouraged participation by the citizen began in the 1960s. One must go back to New England town meetings, Madison's analysis in *The Federalist* and Jefferson's philosophy. But the historical record significant for public officials and citizens today begins in the second decade of the twentieth century. As early as 1912, the Chamber of Commerce of the United States was created to give business and industry a formal advisory role in public decisions. Then came the Farm Bureaus, the TVA and the Resettlement and Farm Security Administration. But it was not until 1954 that the phrase "citizen participation" was introduced to federal practice by the Urban Renewal Administration.

By the 1960s a considerable body of knowledge and experience about citizen participation had accumulated outside the federal government. The federal standards developed and implemented in the 1960s were based upon this outside knowledge and the historic pattern of citizen participation.

II. STANDARDS WHICH AFFECT PROCESS

A set of rules or standards designed to affect *processes* are substantially different, philosophically and administratively, from standards which apply to *products*. It is one thing to prescribe what happens to thieves, or business groups which combine to restrain trade, or contractors who produce or fail to produce component parts of rockets; it is quite another to give a share of a process in which previously excluded citizens (1) can influence public decisions (2) form local coalitions (3) transmute anger or despair into relative happiness in the belief of the possibility of upward mobility.

Even if federal policy-makers reach a consensus about the relevance and utility of a particular set of standards to regulate process, it is almost impossible to evaluate the precise impact of the standards on local affairs. Where social and political change is measurable, for example, it is difficult to sort out the extent to which the change resulted from federal intervention—as opposed to (1) militancy in the community which existed before the application of Federal standards

(2) the personalities and skills of those who organized and provided technical assistance to the citizens (3) the changes in the local or national economic picture (4) the actions of local politicians in search of a constituency.

Moreover, it is difficult to retain or measure impact after grant-in-aid funds have been transferred from federal to local control. For over a generation, federal officials and scholars of public administration have been keenly aware of the difficulties in monitoring and enforcing standards on grant funds designed to produce relatively measurable products—dams, highways, welfare and unemployment insurance payments, school lunches. The transfer of funds, federal, state or local, to bureaucracies over which the federal establishment has ambiguous control compromises any potency in federal standards. Federal power to enforce standards is even more curtailed when grants are intended to have an impact on processes which are not easily defined in quantitative measurements or unambiguous qualitative analysis.

The federal role in enforcing citizen participation standards is usually limited to philosophical debates with grantees or to responding to the complaints of aggrieved citizens.

III. CONCEPTS WHICH AFFECT THE DESIGN OF STANDARDS

The ambiguities in the design and application of federal standards in process and implementation are primarily due to the variety of philosophies and predilections held by those formulating policy. Before one can list the different philosophies or assumptions about citizen participation, one must define the policy-maker's position concerning the role of federal intervention. This position is a result, primarily, of his analysis of how our society works and how it ought to work. For the sake of simplicity, I have divided these assumptions into three categories: federalist, pluralist and pragmatic skeptic. Committed *federalists*, for example, emphasize the complicated interaction among different governmental levels and jurisdictions. According to their view, federal standards should operate to place the maximum power to intervene at the citizen level in government units theoretically closest to citizens—municipalities, counties, states.

Those who view the central dynamic of American society as interaction, confrontation, compromise among various interest groups (labeled as *pluralists*) see the federal role as setting the rules of the game, mediating and arbitrating disputes, and preventing particular groups or coalitions from doing extensive damage to the rights of members of other groups. In the pluralist view, standards are responsive rather than to facilitate change in the distribution of power or wealth.

Neither federalism nor pluralism necessarily implies a commitment for or against public spending, neither does it indicate concern for redress of the grievances of particular groups, nor maintain the extent to which federal power should be used. In fact, it is logically possible for a federalist to advocate either block grants or stringent conditions on grants to local governments, or for a pluralist to be for or against the policy of government as the employer of last resort.

The nature of federal standards, on the other hand, can be deeply effected by a commitment to either federalism or pluralism.

Federalists will devise standards which seek to regulate or stimulate actions by other governmental units. Pluralists will be more inclined to conceive standards regulating or stimulating the behavior of particular constituencies, local or national, organized around narrow or broad issues.

Advocates of the third perspective or philosophy are those whom I term *pragmatic skeptics*. To them the classical definition of the bureaucratic role—constructing and enforcing rules without regard to persons—is abhorrent. Skeptics consider persons more important than rules, and problems more relevant than standards. At the national and regional levels of the federal government, pragmatic skeptics press for a more precise analysis of the complexities in local situations than either federalists or pluralists do. In the continuous process of formulating and reformulating standards, they press for *both* flexibility and the adequate specificity needed to enable federal intervention on behalf of groups for which there is, or may be, a national constituency.

According to this model, neither federalists nor pluralists have adequate insight into our society. Generalizations cannot be made which apply to all state and local governments or to all interest groups. Some local governments' for a variety of reasons, should be stimulated and provided with new tools and assistance; others should be forced to change, or be brought to impotence by federal intervention and the actions— perhaps federally stimulated—of local citizens. The same point applies to interest groups. Federal intervention may be necessary to protect membership from leadership, to reduce the power of some groups and to increase the power of others.

To summarize, from the *federalist* point of view flexible federal standards— vaguely worded statements of minimal or optimal stan-

132

dards—provide the most realistic opportunities for federal leverage. Open end standards, they maintain, allow maximum freedom of decision and action to other levels of government, while preserving accountability to a rational definition of the national interest. *Pluralists* advocate standards as a device which gives competing and coalescing groups maximum freedom to bargain and negotiate in the context of a broadly defined public interest. To *skeptics,* standards provide the framework for strong or weak intervention in local situations, depending on the position of bureaucratic, congressional and/or national constituency power at the particular moment.

In conclusion, the setting of federal standards, by law or by regulations with the force of law, raises the complicated and possibly unanswerable question of the appropriate role for federal intervention in American society.

In addition, federal standards set in our time will reflect the distinctive tensions between federalism and pluralism. However, the tensions emerge less from political theory than from competing constituencies and the individuals involved in the political and/or administrative operation.

The problem of pragmatic skeptics is (1) defining a concept of the public interest which justifies a flexible approach to federal intervention and (2) then developing a potent national constituency which supports that definition.

The terms—federalist, pluralist and pragmatic skeptic—are but typologies of individual predilections which become factors in influencing the determination of federal standards.

IV. STANDARDS AND REGULATIONS

Standards are defined as the minimal rather than the optional, without precise qualifiable elements. Opposite to a standard is a regulation or requirement. But even a regulation can contain the quality of a standard. To illustrate, a minimal or vague standard initially has value by the very fact of its vagueness—the vagueness puts one in the dilemma of interpretation. A self-imposed interpretation, supported by anxiety, tension and/or insecurity, causes reactions. *In the Brown v. Board of Education* case the Court order was vague enough to prompt instant acquiescence, in some cases, resulting in several integrated schools. But as a more lenient view was taken of the decision, the order had to be more tightly defined to reactivate the decision to reinforce

133

the federal position. The decision then contained the element of standard; but by virtue of its specific, defined requirements it became a regulation.

The debate between adherents of standards and regulations is continuously affected by the actions and mood of congressmen and constituencies. For example, it is still not clear whether the conversion of the maximum feasible participation standard of community action into a requirement by Congress that one-third of each board of each CAA represent the poor, or the elaboration of the requirement into a set of standards and procedures by OEO officials, improved or impeded the development of citizens' influence on decisions about their lives. Strong arguments can be raised on both sides of the question. The significant point is not which side of the debate scores more points, but rather the difficulty of assessing the impact on various citizen participation policies—and the elusiveness of the interests of the many publics whom federal policy-makers must consider.

Therefore, the pressure for specific prohibitions is reflected by the rather different views of ways in which federal intervention can effect local processes. The adherents who support specificity, or regulations over standards, do so with the belief that the important aspects of citizen participation can be quantitatively and qualitatively measured. Others maintain that knowledge about what is and is not productive participation is sufficiently codified to warrant efforts to enforce specific federal regulations. Another premise is that specificity protects the rights and clarifies the obligations of citizens and local governments—the emphasis depending on the proponent's political ideology. Some supporters of specificity are optimistic about federal enforcement capacity; others place high value on the strategic utility of the bureaucratic bluff. The argument for specificity can be made from the federalist, pluralist or skeptic position: (1) the importance of improving the wisdom and capacity of local government (2) the need to clarify the interaction of competing interest groups (3) the utility of specific rules which can be applied to a situation when there is a chance of successful enforcement.

The question of importance at this juncture is: have we learned to begin with a standard by evaluating it for its growth or evolution potential for the extensions or additions which will transform the standard into a regulation? Do we recognize the constitutional and political value in the initial vagueness of a standard?

V. ASSUMPTIONS IN RELATIONSHIP TO DETERMINING CITIZEN PARTICIPATION POLICY

Here assumptions simply mean the moral values, or any kinds of committments, which a man has that underlies the action or position he presents as national public policy within the administration.

In recent years, the word "participation," modified by "citizen," "resident," "neighborhood," "maximum feasible" or "widespread," has sparked intense debate among Americans concerned with the politics, policy-making, administration and the success of federal efforts to abolish, comfort or pacify the poor. Adherents of the different definitions of participation see participation as acquiescence, communication, therapy, employment, advising, representation in the coalitions of decision-makers, control over public decisions by those effected—or some combination of these definitions. Opponents of participation in public programs raise cries of patronage grabs, outside agitation, misunderstanding of constitutional arrangements, misuse of public funds and even of Communist infiltration.

Because of the current unavailability of records and the lack of time lapse needed for historic reflection and analysis, only some of the factors entering into the development and implementation of the citizen participation policy in the 1960s will be discussed here. Probably the most important determinant in policy formulation was the influence of widely differing assumptions about the purposes of citizen participation in federal programs. The assumptions, based on an historical foundation, were:

1) *Decentralization.* Throughout American history, citizens, legislators and civil servants have attached particular importance to the virtues of the small constituency and the value of those governmental units which are closest to the people. Moreover, powerful constituencies have long pressed for the transfer of federal powers and funds to local, state and regional authorities. To representatives of these constituencies, citizen participation in federal programs primarily means decentralization of funds and authority to state, local governmental, quasi-governmental or even private agencies which are alleged to be more responsive to citizen needs than distant federal officials are. The act of decentralization, subject to local accountability for federal funds, is assumed to be a sufficient standard to insure adequate citizen participation in decision-making. The Tennessee Valley Authority provides the clearest—and best documented—example of this viewpoint.

135

A variation, used by agricultural, conservation and regional development programs in the past thirty-five years, is for the act of decentralization to include a federal requirement for local citizens' committees—with the composition and primary power structure of the committees delegated to local determination.

2) *Engineered Consent.* Though usually related to arguments favoring decentralization, this cluster of assumptions provides more specificity for citizen participation. The concept of engineered consent does not appear any more malicious than the rationale justifying the mass manipulation of people through advertising—that it plays an important role in sustaining the economy by stimulating and diversifying consumer demand. Applied to public programs, the engineered consent concept assumes that most citizens are less informed than professionals about the causes of and solution to their social and economic problems. Therefore, it seems necessary for public agencies to educate citizens, to provide them with information about proposed programs, to use the skills of advertising and public relations to persuade and to allay fears. The history of citizen participation in urban redevelopment and renewal programs since 1954 provides the best examples of this point of view.

3) *Therapy.* This assumption emerges from the experiences of social workers, community developers, anthropologists and experts on mental health over the past generation. It is assumed that, among certain groups of the population, serious problems of adjustment to the values and attitudes of the larger society (or, negatively put, of alienation from society) are a result of inhibited development of democratic or group skills. Pervasive and diagnosable emotional pathology, or a complex of self- reinforcing and destructive cultural factors, may also prevent participation in the benefits of the most affluent society in history. In this context, the purpose of federal citizen participation policy is to subsidize varieties of group therapy—including group involvement in some form of decision-making—in order to bring the afflicted minority into the larger society. (See Arnstein, below, for similar typology.)

4) *Equal Protection.* It has long been obvious, for those who cared to look, that some citizens have more power than others. Black people, particularly in the South, have been excluded from public decision-making processes for centuries. Indians, Eskimos, Mexican-Americans, Puerto Ricans, poor Appalachian mountaineers, youth and the elderly, have been similarly excluded. The purpose of Federal participation

136

policy is to insure these citizens some voice in decisions which affect their lives.

5) *Employment.* A first principle of public administration recognizes that policy and administration are continuous, and that staff members of public and private agencies make more policy decisions than the formal theory governing board-staff relationships would suggest. This principle strongly suggests that programs which, by design, affect the lives of particular citizens should maximize the employment of people who are most sensitive to and familiar with the life styles, needs and aspirations of the citizens for whom the programs are intended. Overt and covert discriminatory practices by labor unions and personnel officers often prevent members of certain minorities from obtaining employment in federally subsidized programs. Therefore, an object of federal citizen participation policy should be to increase the employment opportunities of citizens affected by particular programs.

6) *Redistribution of Power and Resources.* A significant number of Americans have been denied access to income, decent housing, adequate public services and political participation because of racial or ethnic prejudice. Economic exploitation and the ability of local elites to consolidate and sustain power have further deprived them. Because of its capacity to create and respond to national constituencies, the federal government must intervene with funds and policies to redress the iniquitous distribution of social, economic and political power in particular communities. Citizen participation policy is a tool by which federal officials can (1) include the excluded (2) subsidize the exploited and (3) provide training and technical assistance for those who do not know how power is continually fragmented and rearranged in our society.

7) *Constituency Development.* Related to the distribution of power and the other assumptions is the very important concept (another primary principle of public administration) that a federal agency is only as strong as its national constituency. Decisions about citizen participation policy are determined by the nature, strength and history of an agency's constituency—as well as the nature of its antagonists. For example, policies which focus on the redistribution of power lead to the development of a very different constituency than policies based on the assumptions of decentralization, engineered consent or therapy.

At this point it is of interest to note that, due to the complexity of U.S. public affairs, not one of these assumptions for advocating citizen participation dominated federal policy in determining the scope and

137

dimensions of citizen participation in the 1960s. In the Office of Economic Opportunity, for instance, adherents of decentralization, therapy, equal protection, employment or the redistribution of power fought bitterly. Within the Department of Housing and Urban Development, advocates of decentralization and engineered consent were stronger than in OEO—but proponents of other positions were represented and scored several victories for their views. The Neighborhood Service Program, sponsored by HUD, OEO, the Department of Labor and the Department of Health, Education and Welfare, became a complex, intense battleground—in Washington, regional offices and the cities—for all seven sets of assumptions.

VI. THE IMPACT OF A POLITICAL CONTEXT ON THE DETERMINATION OF STANDARDS

An additional factor in the determination of standards is the political context in which these standards will operate. The primary consideration is in the type and purpose of federal intervention in local affairs. This consideration influences public and private debates about the scope of standards. In addition, the political context affected the philosophies and assumptions adopted by an agency when considering standards at different times in the 1960s.

The most significant actors in the political process which conditions participation policy are rarely the citizens most deeply affected by particular programs. The thesis that federal standards directed at improving the condition of the poor and their immediate environment more truly reflects the "professionalization of reform"—that the constituencies are of technicians rather than representatives of aggrieved people—seems quite accurate. However, the story is more complicated than the thesis suggests. The National Conference of Mayors and League of Cities, as well as individual mayors and governors, had enormous influence on the development and implementation of standards—through Congress, the White House and direct contact with top administrators. Staff assistants to mayors, governors and Congressmen were often able to change the direction of policy standards, as they applied to particular localities, by telephone calls into the middle levels of bureaucracy.

The impact of national and local organizations claiming to speak directly for citizens was less important in determining standards. The fragmentation and continuing debate within major civil rights organiza-

138

tion through most of the years since 1963 made it impossible for them to press effectively for particular standards with any degree of public unity. The Citizens Crusade Against Poverty, an organization established in 1965 to apply pressure on federal agencies on behalf of suffering citizens, was most effective when it called upon its labor and church constituencies or the mass media to reactivate the conscience of the liberal coalition which has been dissolving during the last half of the decade. On occasion, delegations of residents from affected areas lobbied or demonstrated in national and regional offices of federal agencies and Congressmen. However, they were primarily concerned with the funding of particular programs rather than with broader issues of policy.

The most significant citizen impact on the formulation of participation policy, and thus standards, has probably been rioting. Riots dramatized powerlessness, the lack of access to equal opportunity to produce and consume, the negligence—sometimes viciousness—of many agencies of local government. The riots that followed the assassination of Dr. King in 1968, for instance, caused one high ranking federal administrator—an adherent of decentralization and engineered consent assumptions about participation—to speculate that "perhaps conflict at the bargaining table is better than conflict in the streets." Another significant and not entirely cynical argument made throughout the period was that participation standards which transferred considerable power to ghetto residents would create cadres of anti-rioters. However, the total impact of violence on the formulation of policy for standards cannot be fully assessed at this point in history.

From a different perspective, it seems apparent that the policy which determines standards in this area greatly reflects the philosophies and assumptions of the constituencies of a particular Federal agency. In the 1960s, the major citizen participation standards were mounted by new agencies or new clusters of agencies. To create an affirmative political context, officials tried to build new constituencies for their agencies and themselves, while trying to keep natural or traditional constituents unoffended and therefore neutral, or at least not obstructive.

Because standards are developed and implemented in a political context, citizen participation policy focusing on the assumptions of (1) the redistribution of power and resources (2) providing employment and (3) equal protection must mesh with an alienated people who are affected enough by policy to demand consideration and power in the

139

relevant federal and local agencies. Without this meshing—without a formal and informal communication of knowledge about opportunities to citizens—the activities of both federal agencies and citizens groups are useless. The fact is that no matter what model of federal intervention is dominant, or what assumptions about the purposes of participation are written into the standards, the interaction between federal officials and citizens—and not just those citizens in whose primary interest a program is conceived—determines the role and impact of federal power and money.

VII. IMPLEMENTING STANDARDS

The development and implementation of federal standards is a continuous process. Actions produce reactions which lead to new actions. Constituencies, Congressmen, administrators defeated yesterday will be back today seeking new ways to write their interests and ideologies into rules. Regardless of the official citizen participation policy statement in a standard, there is an old and complicated art in participation known as political influence, and it operates outside and around the official position.

There is no guarantee that standards will be implemented even when issued by the head of an agency and supported by instructions prepared by competent staff. No policy designed to effect process rather than product can be unambiguous. Because of the nature of the problems for which standards and regulations are developed, regional officials have wide areas of discretion. Assumptions underlying participation policy are varied, sometimes contradictory, and almost always controversial—a policy standard can be supported or attacked by constituencies, and the agency threatened or supported by the same constituencies. Therefore, the ambiguities permitted in standards are essential for agency survival, credibility and effectiveness.

Regional officials need discretion. No administrator at the national level, unless naive or doctrinaire, could demand that a federal decision-maker in Fort Worth or Austin interpret the ambiguous standards in the same way as his counterparts have in the past in New York or Boston. Officials prefer success to failure, approval to ostracism. They must be sensitive to what behavior will be punished or rewarded. Certain mayors and Congressmen must not be offended. There are political and human limits to the nature and degree of pressure that can be applied to directors of community action and city demonstration agencies.

Federal officials in the field have their own commitments among the assumptions underlying participation standards; and with varying degrees of skill they influence their local contacts to accept or act on particular interpretations of performance standards. There is considerable operational distance from a belief that standards be used to help redistribute local power to the provision for technical assistance to local constituents who lack appropriate strategies and tactics. Similarly, it is difficult for many former social workers or social scientists in federal service to conceive or implement alternatives to the assumption that participation is a form of therapy. Even when the official directive is clear—"you will be rewarded for working to redistribute power in Yokatanawpha County"—implementation of policy standards and regulations may be impossible because the agency cannot supply the appropriate technical skills for the necessary length of time.

Another problem is what has been described as the federal agencies' "refusal to create a range of graduated sanctions to cope with unlawful, improper, and undesirable conduct . . . without having to terminate the grant of funds." In the absence of graduated sanctions, federal officials are limited to persuasion, conspiring with citizens to bring local pressure, withholding special favors from grantees and gambling on their ability to convince their superiors to bring pressure on grantees to enforce standards. These techniques require more bureaucratic and political skill, and often more courage, than most officials have or can be expected to have. It is often easier to overlook violations than to confront them.

A major share of the responsibility for implementing performance standards belongs to the citizens affected by them. There are few instances of ambiguities interpreted and standards implemented in a controversial manner merely because the federal government willed it that way. When controversial interpretations of standards survive in action, it is usually because citizens and their allies mobilize power and devise strategies for escalating conflict in the face of rebuffs. In short citizen participation policies change the content, and occasionally the stakes, but never the substance and style of the American political process.

VIII. CONCLUDING THOUGHTS

The debates over the development and implementation of performance standards for citizen participation will be one of the duller parts of the yet to be written administrative history of the 50s and 60s. But it will be written, for public administrators respond to and help to shape dramatic changes in society. Social historians of the future, for instance, may note that the development of citizen participation policy as a serious task for federal agencies occurred in the same years as the breakup of the Democratic coalition, the emergence of George Wallace as self-proclaimed spokesman for the "unheard million," the revolt of union members against leadership and the transformation of black Americans from caste to ethnic group status. Whether participation standards and regulations can be elaborated enough to confront the problems of powerlessness, restlessness and anger in our society (a feeling and condition not restricted to the poor) remains to be seen.

We may be witnessing the first stages of a new relationship between governments and citizens. During most of this century, public agencies, especially federal agencies, have had relative freedom to be more responsive to one constituency than another at any given time. Until recent years, part of the tacit social contract to which most Americans adhered was that interest groups tended to mind their own business and fought to capture or create public agencies to serve their needs—and once having captured or created an agency, utilized its funds and staff to forward their particular interests. The public interest was fragmented into a series of particular interests. On occasion, interest groups with relatively equal capacity to damage each other came into conflict. The result of the conflict has been a variety of compromises and sometimes the creation of new public machinery.

However, at present, there is evidence that an increasing number of citizens are organizing into new interest groups, and working to change the position of existing ones. The national apathy, leadership by elites and the end of ideology as proclaimed during the 1950s and the early years of this decade seem to be giving way to new militancy, a search for new leadership and the restoration of ideological debate among citizens of all races, ethnic groups and classes. Increasingly, citizens are joining groups and coalitions which, in the name of protecting particular values and interests, are threatening the values, interests, even the security of other citizens. Therefore, new standards and institutions may be necessary to maintain the rights of citizens, the obligations of governments and a coherent definition of the public interest.

Part III

SPECIFIC ISSUES IN
RESIDENT PARTICIPATION

ECONOMIC DEVELOPMENT
THE SWAFCA COOPERATIVE

by: Stanley Zimmerman

Editor's Note

Stanley Zimmerman is a lawyer, a law professor and now president of CONSET, Inc., a consulting firm. He served as a consultant both to OEO and to SWAFCA. His comprehensive reporting of the growth of an indigenous economic organization in one of the most depressed and repressed areas in the United States comes from close observation and participation. His "poker game" description should become a classic example for Dan Fox's study on the public administration of poverty programs.

Some questions:

1. *Would some form of intensive training have helped the organization-building process at SWAFCA? Group process skills for the Board? Alinsky-style organization training? Skills training for staff and boards?*

2. *What weight should be given to the costs and benefits of governmental support to experimental projects? (Compare Bernstein, for example). The Federal government spent hundreds of thousands of dollars in staff time, travel, investigations, evaluations, etc., on this project. How does one evaluate the results, against expenditures for Farmers Home Administration, manpower projects and other federally-funded programs?*

3. *How do Zimmerman's five stages of organizational growth match those in the literature of organizational development? (Compare Gordon Lippitt's* Organization Renewal, *Appleton, 1969). Is SWAFCA an oddity?*

Stanley Zimmerman received a B.A. from Pomona College, an LL.B. from Hastings, and LL.M. from New York University Law School. He was a street worker in San Francisco and worked at OEO both as a lawyer and consultant.

145

SWAFCA is an organization of black farmers in southwest Alabama who came together in the fall of 1966 to find some way to ease their desperate economic situation. The farmers decided to form a new ten-county unit—the Southwest Alabama Farmers Cooperative Association—which would help them grow and market garden crops (cucumbers, okra, southern peas and the like) instead of cotton. They hoped this venture would give them a little economic independence from the southern politicians, land owners, government officials and crop buyers who had made life bad for them and seemed bent on driving them off the land as a response to their civil rights activity.

The story of SWAFCA casts light on the abstract notion of citizen participation and its value in comparison to other ways for improving the well-being of poor people. The participation of the black farmers has been extensive and the development of SWAFCA is largely due to their effort.

Although the activities were sometimes concurrent, the story of SWAFCA has three parts: the organization of the cooperative, its effort to obtain adequate financial assistance from the federal government; and the management of the cooperative. Each involved slightly different tests of the capacity of the poor farmers and, more generally, of their form of citizen participation. The fourth part of this paper draws on the story of SWAFCA to discuss briefly the growth cycle of citizen participation organizations, the roles played by outsiders and the frameworks for evaluating an organization of SWAFCA's type.

I. THE ORGANIZATION OF SWAFCA

Before the cooperative, the economic situation of black farmers in southwest Alabama looked hopeless. For the most part they grew cotton and corn. Some owned their land; most were tenants. Virtually all were tied to whites by their need for credit at the beginning of each year to buy food, seed and fertilizer in return for handing over the crops they produced each fall. The loans were of goods in kind marked up to unreasonably high prices. No cash changed hands. For the few who escaped the credit bind, there was still no open market. The black farmer dealt with the white man in control of his area. He bought or borrowed far above retail and sold wholesale according to the artificial price structure of monopoly markets.

Because of increases in national production and cuts in cotton acreage allotments, by 1960, two-thirds of the farm operators in the ten-county area covered by SWAFCA had a gross income from their

146

farms of $1,500 or less.

The Department of Agriculture seemed to join local whites in working against the black farmer. In 1965 an investigation by the United States Commission on Civil Rights disclosed massive racial discrimination in Department of Agriculture programs. Not only were the few Negro employees segregated, and local boards which passed on applications for assistance entirely white, but the benefits distributed went to the whites in vastly uneven shares. Black farmers often found it impossible to obtain a fair estimate of their acreage for the purposes of the allotment program. Government payments for black tenant farmers were delivered directly to white landlords. Black borrowers from the Farmers Home Administration received substantially less credit than white farmers of identical net worth. Usually the money lent flowed directy to white retailers in checks made out to them instead of the black borrower.

Voter registration drives meanwhile had stirred the whites' long standing fears of black majorities in the Alabama Black Belt. Black tenant farmers began to assert their rights to federal payments under Department of Agriculture programs. Made vulnerable by their declining importance in cotton production and by USDA programs which put a premium on fallow land, black families that had lived and worked in the same place for three generations were told to move on. Entire communities of black sharecroppers and tenants were closed down by white farm owners. In 1964, a study of four counties within the 100-mile wide SWAFCA area located three hundred black families who had been driven off their land within the last year.

Some black farmers had tried to follow white farmers in diversifying agricultural production. Refused admission to the white-dominated marketing associations, they had attempted to form small associations of their own. Each had failed—killed off, so the black farmers thought, by white growers and buyers through economic boycotts and price wars. As late as 1966 several black farmers had to let their tomatoes rot on their land and the few who were able to hire trucks to take their crop to Birmingham to sell for shipment North could find no buyers who would trade with them.

In Dallas County, the rural black people felt that the newly established Office of Economic Opportunity had done nothing to change the situation for the better. In 1965 and 1966 the black farmers of that county had fought several battles to obtain OEO funds in Community

147

Action and Headstart programs, each time losing out to local officials. They believed there was a record of double dealing by OEO leading to programs entirely under the control of the white politicians and serving to continue the racial and economic discrimination of the past. In the summer of 1966 the principal program of the Selma CAP was a public works program employing local Negroes in the repair of roads and the clearing of open drainage ditches, work done previously by prisoners in the local jails. Black farmers branded it as "Mayor Smitherman's nigger in the ditch" program and saw it as illustrative of the OEO effort in Selma.

During the middle years of the 1960's civil rights leaders had hoped that participation in the political process would provide a way out for black people in Southwest Alabama. For the first time since reconstruction days, black men ran for local office in many of the SWAFCA counties where there was a majority of Negro voters. The focus was on the local Alabama elections to be held in the fall of 1966. Through voting frauds and threats of violence and economic retaliation, however, the impact of the black vote had been drastically reduced. Not a single local office in the Black Belt was won by a black man.

In 1966 the story of the black farmer in Alabama was filmed in a moving documentary, "Lay My Burden Down," directed by Jack Willis for National Educational Television. At the end, the commentary summed it up: tragic, unjust and hopeless.

The organization of SWAFCA had its roots in these apparently hopeless circumstances. The farmers involved were led to their bold effort largely because they had exhausted every other possibility.

Residents of each county had carried out the local activities of the civil rights movement over the previous three years, voter registration drives and election campaigns. Local churches and other small community groups had been drawn toward each other, often for the first time.

Even before the local elections some of these groups, particularly those in Dallas and Lowndes County, had begun talking about their economic problems and what could be done about them. In several counties groups had tried to obtain assistance under the federal poverty program. In one county a small credit union had been started successfully. The election results drove home the importance of economic development.

Although most of these efforts had failed to produce results apparent to the outside world, some of the black people involved had changed. They were organized into larger groups. They had learned to

148

speak out for themselves in meetings and before local white land owners and public officials. They were better acquainted with the details of federal programs under which they had been denied assistance. They had developed a sense of what did not work. "Government wasn't going to help," went the talk. "Voter registration wasn't going to help, at least not for another four years. Outsiders with get-rich-quick schemes weren't going to help. There were only two choices. Get out or get with others in the same trouble and do something about it." Some groups talked of credit unions, others of marketing associations and others of cooperative farming. In some counties only a few farmers were involved; in others, meetings drew several hundred.

Only a handful of people involved were known outside their area. Albert Turner had lived all his life in Perry County. After graduating from a black land-grant college he became a professional bricklayer in Marion and a leader in the local black labor union. He was involved in the first voter registration drives of the 1960's in Perry County and in 1965 he joined the staff of the Southern Christian Leadership Conference, becoming the state director in late 1966. Lewis Black was an experienced community organizer from Hale County who had been involved in the civil rights movement in Alabama and later joined the Field Staff of the Alabama Council on Human Relations. Shirley Mesher, a young white woman and SWAFCA's only "outside agitator," was best known in Dallas County where she had come early in 1965 to the Selma demonstration and remained as a field worker. In August, 1965, she was made SCLC Project Director for the county, and later, she left the SCLC staff to continue working with groups in Dallas and nearby counties. These people worked with rural leaders such as Freeman Berry of Dallas County and Percy McSchan of Green County to bring the groups of different counties into contact with each other.

Early in December, 1966, in response to the growing interest in forming a cooperative of some kind, Shirley Mesher contacted the Cooperative League. It suggested that Dr. T.T. Williams from the

Southern University in Baton Rouge be invited to Alabama to talk to the county groups about cooperatives. Dr. Williams had been active in organizing a black cooperative in Louisiana called the Southern Consumers Cooperative, which produced fruitcakes. At about the same time, through a basic education program funded by OEO in Wilcox County, a request was made for an expert in rural programs from OEO to come to the same county meetings. Bruce Kashden, who had worked during the past summer on the development of a farmers cooperative in Fayette County, Tennessee, was sent to Selma.

The two visitors arrived in the middle of the afternoon late in December, 1966, and learned from the small group which met them that the farmers were talking primarily about planting more land with garden crops and starting a marketing cooperative. By combining their baskets of produce into truckloads the farmers hoped to be able to take advantage of more distant markets where the profits were greater. The cooperative would obtain and sell seed, fertilizer and other supplies to the farmers at fair prices during the season and buy their crops at good prices at the end of the season for resale to fresh markets and processing plants at the best possible price. Also, it would assist the farmers in learning the new farming methods required. Williams helped the group work out a schedule of the things which needed to be done and warned them than it was almost too late to begin the effort in the 1967 season.

That night Kashden, Williams, Mesher and a few others traveled to six or eight county meetings attended, in all, by about five hundred farmers. At each meeting the key issues were discussed. Was the group willing to join with the groups in the other counties? How soon could they pick representatives to serve on a central committee which would start the cooperative? To whom could they turn for technical assistance and capital?

The reaction of the farmers was strong. They believed it was impossible to wait another year. Some men had already been threatened with violence and nearly all were afraid that economic sanctions imposed by the whites, would drive them out of the area before the end of another year.

Both Kashden and Williams were impressed by the large turnout and the determination of the farmers. Williams wrote the Cooperative League that it should give the farmers its fullest support, and the League sent $500 to be used in the organization effort. Kashden returned to Washington to urge that at least a small grant be made to the

150

emerging organization.

In Alabama, the county groups went ahead with the organization of the cooperative. It was decided to form a single multi-county cooperative, big enough to stand up to expected white opposition. Each county was to be represented by two board members. In some counties elections were held in meetings of several hundred farmers; in others the small group involved chose representatives informally.

On the night of January 5, 1967, twenty men came to the meeting—two from each of 10 counties—along with Mesher, Black, and Turner and Kashden, who had returned for a second brief visit. The men had notable differences. Four or five of them had been prominent leaders of civil rights activities in their counties and at least one had run for public office. Two men, from Lowndes County, had been associated with the development of the Christian Movement Party. One member was a man of comfortable means, by local black standards, who farmed, ran a funeral home and taught mathematics. At least sixteen were poor. Five or six held jobs in addition to farming and at least one was not primarily a farmer. Most owned their own farms, but some were tenants. Only two had telephones. Two had graduated from college; several had not finished elementary school. But differences which would have left huge gaps between them if they had lived elsewhere in the country were of small importance in Alabama. They were black men. There was a common denominator of poverty and rural isolation.

The most important development of the organizational meeting was the selection of Joe Johnson as President of the cooperative, a surprise to the outsiders. Johnson was a full-time farmer and a very poor man, even among those on the Board. His only income was from a farm which earned less than five hundred dollars a year. He had little formal education. His activity in the civil rights movement had been limited to his own county. But the other men had felt he knew what had to be done and was wholly committed to doing it. Some had also believed it was important that one of the poorest be chosen to show that SWAFCA was really for the small farmer.

Confronted with the schedule that Williams had helped them make, the SWAFCA leaders realized they had to move quickly if they were going to put the cooperative into operation by the 1967 season. The SWAFCA leaders decided to hold an emergency planning session for the representatives of all the government agencies that might provide assistance, at which the cooperative could present its plan and ask what the government could do to help. Fearful that government officials would

151

pass the responsibility for replying to levels of their agencies not represented at the session, the SWAFCA leaders sent invitations to both the local and Washington offices of each agency.

On January 14, 1967, representatives from about twenty government offices and a number of private organizations came to the meeting. After the Board members and farmers made a presentation of the problems they faced and their plan for a cooperative, the government officials were asked to meet privately to discuss the possibilities for federal assistance.

The representative of the Farmers Cooperative Service, who had been selected to make the initial statement for the group, indicated that no definite commitments could be made. Some of the government representatives voiced general approval of the idea of a cooperative but questioned whether it should cover a ten county area and advised that the cooperative should wait another year.

The Board met following the meeting and concluded that the heart of the matter was that nobody, including OEO, was prepared to offer anything, at least in time for the 1967 season. The members of the Board felt that all the government people either didn't believe they could establish the cooperative or, worse, didn't really want them to try. Many of the members were bitter, anguished and discouraged. Some of the members proposed a more modest effort, starting with only a few counties in 1967; other members argued that this would fatally weaken the cooperative. Finally, the members decided to go ahead in the full ten-county area in the 1967 season, recruiting membership, urging farmers to shift to garden crops, using the few dollars which could be raised to buy truck loads of fertilizer and bags of seed and, at the same time, somehow finding enough money to keep going.

Over the next few months Johnson and the other supporters of SWAFCA went from meeting to meeting, and from farmer to farmer, signing up members of the new cooperative. The choice of Johnson as President proved to be inspired. He was a poor man who risked everything on the cooperative. Other poor men listened to him and decided to join.

By the beginning of the season, over eight hundred farmers throughout the ten county area had joined SWAFCA. Together, they were by far the largest number of black men to join in a single economic venture in the history of the state. Most believed they were taking a step which permitted no turning back to traditional farming

152

and marketing arrangements with the whites; if the cooperative failed, they would be forced to leave their farms.

Johnson preached strongly what the members came to call the "Spirit of SWAFCA," a dream of justice and an end to the separation between rich and poor. They see it as an organization which symbolizes their pride, their love of the land and their capacity to do someting worthwhile for themselves.

This beginning gave the citizen participation in SWAFCA three distinctive features:

1. A boldness that bypassed the white controlled economic and political institutions but which saw that they could begin realistically with the existing skills and resources available to them—land, time and large families.

2. A commitment that required great personal courage—the farmer had to refuse to deal with whites who traditionally supplied him and thus faced ostracism and the possibility of physical violence.

3. An insistence on control—the skeptical SWAFCA farmers believed that government agencies and politicians would try and take over the cooperative and kill it.

II. FEDERAL FINANCIAL ASSISTANCE

SWAFCA could be started without outside help, but it could not be fully developed without financial assistance. As Calvin Orsborn put it, those in power in Alabama fought to maintain the status quo and to kill the idea "of low-income farmers working for themselves. . . to handle their own finances and organization."

In early February, 1967, work started on a proposal for OEO funding in both Selma and Washington. The original idea from the farmers concerned a shift to garden crops and the marketing cooperative. The OEO staff pressed for the exploration of non-farm enterprises. The SWAFCA leaders—skeptical about non-farm enterprises as an initial step for their farmer membership—finally decided to include such an effort in their proposal to be undertaken after the cooperative was underway.

Late in February, 1967, Joe Johnson, William Harrison and Shirley Mesher were invited to Washington by OEO. They arrived at Gerson Green's office in the evening and were faced by representatives of the many units of OEO involved in review of the proposal.

To many of the OEO people it was a fairly routine meeting but to the SWAFCA leaders, it was a grueling and demoralizing experience.

153

"What is this project supposed to demonstrate? We have ample evidence that the small farm does not represent a viable alternative for the rural poor."

"I see no sign that you've been in contact with the Department of Agriculture. Why aren't you seeking assistance under their programs for cooperatives?

"We have two established Community Action programs in your area. Have you cleared with them"

"Why aren't there any white farmers in your organization? Is this part of the black separatist movement?"

At the end of the evening, the session left them believing they had no chance to obtain assistance. Only after the larger meeting broke up and a few stayed behind to begin reworking the proposal did they begin to think they might still have a chance.

On one point, the SWAFCA leaders and OEO staff disagreed sharply. Interested in improving the political prospects for funding and also concerned about the lack of experience of the SWAFCA leaders, OEO staff pressed SWAFCA to permit the grant to be made through one of the nearby colleges, which would also provide technical assistance. SWAFCA leaders were adamant in their refusal to take shelter under this arrangement. As an alternative the OEO staff proposed that the cooperative make a comprehensive management contract with an experienced firm which would run the cooperative for the Board. A representative of the firm went to Selma to explore this possibility with SWAFCA. He was coolly received and quickly dispatched. Finally OEO shifted to a third approach and agreed to the hiring of a large technical staff as orginally proposed by SWAFCA. This was accepted by the Board.

About a month after the Washington meeting word of the pending proposal became public knowledge in southwest Alabama. Led by the Mayor of Selma, a meeting was called of representatives from eight of the ten counties covered by the cooperative, most of them elected officials. At the meeting the group declared its opposition to the proposed OEO grant.

SWAFCA leaders and OEO staff supporters had anticipated a major political battle for the funding of the cooperative but had thought it would come later, after the grant had been announced by OEO and Governor Wallace exercised her expected veto. Caught off guard, they worked frantically from both Selma and Washington to line up support.

In Selma, SWAFCA leaders turned to the more prosperous black residents of the city. A meeting at the Negro Elks Club obtained the

154

support of the thirty who attended, demonstrating that SWAFCA had supporters other than farmers: men who were black, but plainly not black separatists. The meeting was led by Calvin Orsborn, a prominent black businessman in Selma. He owned a cotton gin and other equipment and facilities used for sorting, packing and shipping crops—the only such facility owned by a black man in southwest Alabama. He was respected as a successful, capable member of the community. During the Selma march of 1965 he had led the black middle-class of the city in supporting the march, throwing open the doors of his house to shelter and feed the marchers. At the Elks Club meeting, Orsborn announced that he had agreed to become the general manager of the new cooperative. He received solid support from those present and a petition supporting the funding of the cooperative was sent to Washington.

The SWAFCA opponents and the SWAFCA leaders both obtained audiences with the Deputy Director of OEO concerning the proposed grant. The two delegations arrived a week apart, on April 5 and 12, 1967. The opponents of SWAFCA seemed to have a good case. They claimed that local officials, including the Director of the Selma Community Action Program, had been bypassed; that a duplication of the effort of existing marketing cooperatives and education services offered by the Department of Agriculture was involved; and that the Board Members and staff of the cooperative lacked necessary business experience and refused to accept advice from local officials. Moreover, the local officials were able to bring along to the audience every member of the Alabama Congressional delegation. On the other hand, the impact of telling points was reduced by groundless statements about Black Power and Communist involvement in the cooperative. Members of the delegation hammered at the point that they represented the true view of the people of Alabama, although their group did not include a single Negro.

The SWAFCA leaders improved their position considerably in their meeting with the Deputy Director. They arrived without activists Turner, Black and Mesher, who had become the subject of controversy as an outside agitator, in order to demonstrate their independence and determination to speak for themselves. The Board members sought to dispel any notions that SWAFCA would oppose the participation of white farmers and claimed that a few poor white farmers had, in fact, joined the cooperative already. But it was the statements of Calvin Orsborn, the newly hired general manager, which had the most impact. Orsborn's practical and intelligent statements about the plans of the cooperative did much to dispel any doubt that the farmers could manage such an undertaking.

At the end of the meeting top OEO officials were clearly sympathetic to funding SWAFCA, but the final decision still hung in the political balance. In addition to expected support from Walter Reuther, civil rights organizations and members of the National Council of Churches, SWAFCA gained the support of important groups with expertise on rural life such as the Cooperative League of the USA, the Southern Regional Council, the National Sharecroppers Fund and the National Caltholic Rural Life Conference.

OEO announced the grant a month after the meeting with the SWAFCA delegation, on May 12, 1967. That week the Opelika *Daily News* editorialized bitterly:

> What it all boils down to is that SNCC, militant civil rights groups and their sympathizers have more influence and power with OEO and its operations than do all the elected officials of the counties and the state involved in the grant.

In the following months, Governor Wallace vetoed the grant and her action was vigorously supported by SWAFCA's local opponents. OEO was prepared to exercise its power to override the veto, which it did. Although it came too late to help in the first season, the Board had obtained the money to hire technical staff and field representatives to organize and manage the cooperative on a full scale.

The second campaign for financial assistance took place under quite different circumstances. By October, 1967, when SWAFCA made application for a loan from Farmers Home Administration (FHA), it had been in operation for a full season and it was a veteran of the political battles which had led to the OEO grant. During that conflict, the Department of Agriculture had indicated its cautious support of the cooperative and expressed its willingness to assist in a variety of ways, including a special effort to provide economic opportunity loans and farm operating loans to cooperative members through the FHA. Further, the Department had suggested, "FHA will be willing to consider a cooperative type loan to the marketing group." SWAFCA leaders nonetheless felt they were tackling one of their giant opponents which had stood against the black man in Alabama for decades.

This time the political battle went on in muted tones while the cooperative struggled with the massive and hostile bureaucracy of the Department and with high level officials who seemed out of touch with the SWAFCA realities.

The first battle concerned the size of the loan. In January, 1968, SWAFCA provided FHA with a feasibility study in support of a loan of $850,000. The study strongly endorsed a substantial revolving fund for cooperative purchases and the construction of distribution and receiving facilities in each of the ten counties as essential to reaching the full potential membership of the cooperative. FHA replied that a loan of $450,000 was sufficient and proposed full service to only five counties. Also, FHA wanted to retain control of the funds until the Farmers Cooperative Service approved the specific location, design and acquisition of each county facility.

On January 16, 1968, representatives from OEO, FCA and FHA held a joint meeting with the SWAFCA Board of Directors in Selma to resolve the matter.

It was, as William Harrison described it later, a kind of poker game. SWAFCA needed the funds. FHA was under pressure to make the loan, probably to avoid a highly publicized failure to deal successfully with black farmers and possibly to shift primary government control over the cooperative from OEO to the Department of Agriculture.

Everyone had his say and then, suddenly, only FHA and SWAFCA were left in the game. FHA's principal representative, dropped $450,000 on the table. . .

(The excerpts are from the minutes)

"The Principal Representative: This is what FHA is offering, $450,000; this does not mean to imply that the cooperative cannot be eligible for another loan somewhere in the future, but this is all that FHA has to offer at this time . . . he (FHA) wished that the board of directors would make a decision now, today, in order that they could quickly process the application and SWAFCA could get the money that it so badly needs for this phase of its development.

"Mr. Harrison pointed out that the board could not possibly make a decision intelligently on the spur of the moment like this. They needed time to discuss this, to deliberate on the matter.

"Mr._____, proposed supervisor for SWAFCA from FHA, arose and admonished SWAFCA and the board of directors to take the money now since it may be gone tomorrow. Someone else may have the money if we wait and not make a decision on the matter now.

157

"Mr. Harrison let Mr.＿＿＿＿＿＿＿＿ and those present know that we (the board) do not think this is true. Washington (FHA) cannot expect to come down here and discuss something as mammoth as this and expect the board to act immediately when so much hangs on this."

FHA agreed reluctantly to a one day delay and the Board met privately all the following morning. That afternoon, Harrison delivered SWAFCA's message to FHA. He explained it would be the ruin of the cooperative to mortgage all its assets for only half the money needed to do the job. SWAFCA would go elsewhere for a loan.

FHA checked its cards—and folded. It agreed to make the larger loan.

A second and more basic conflict was developing over the degree to which FHA would control the action of the cooperative during the 30-year loan period. By April, 1968, FHA had tentatively approved the loan cf $852,000, but on terms which the SWAFCA leaders believed would place the cooperative entirely under FHA control. Extensive powers were to be exercised at the local level by an FHA Assistant County Supervisor under the supervision of the FHA Alabama State Director who so strongly opposed SWAFCA that he had threatened to resign if a loan were made to the cooperative.

The SWAFCA Board objected to these controls, arguing that they went far beyond what was necessary for the Government to protect its financial interest.

In local meetings with SWAFCA, FHA representatives made it clear that the agency was not merely concerned with protecting the financial interest of the Government. The powers were to be used to provide management assistance to the cooperative so that it would develop along the lines of proven past success. SWAFCA would not be permitted to pay more than FHA appraised value for land, although black people frequently were required to pay a premium for land in Alabama because of the reluctance of whites to sell to them. It would not be permitted to make loans of over 30 days to members under any circumstances, although the economic well-being of the cooperative was tied to that of its members and many of them had not been able to obtain credit from other sources, including FHA. It would be required to follow the advice of the Farmers Cooperative Service on the location and construction of all sub-stations, although SWAFCA had its own technical staff which had been in basic disagreement with the FCS on

158

the size of the initial loan and the timing of the expansion program. It would be required to deal exclusively with the bonded construction contractors, although many competent and trustworthy black contractors were unable to obtain bonding services in Alabama.

FHA, on the other hand, agreed to nothing, not even to make the full loan to SWAFCA. In the confusing morass of documents required for the loan—some fifteen in number—there was not one place for an FHA signature and not one line which recognized the powers of the Board or rights of the members of SWAFCA. FHA officials even refused to provide the Board with copies of the FHA Instructions which, through reference in the loan documents, were binding on its activities, explaining that they were internal to the agency.

During March, April, and May, SWAFCA leaders went from Selma to Washington and back to Selma again in an effort to open negotiations on a more satisfactory arrangement.

The delegation returned to Selma and obtained a final meeting with these officials during the first week of May. At the end of five hours FHA had refused to make a single alteration in the forty pages of documents involved, even in one instance when an error in the typing was acknowledged.

Finally one Board member who had been silent during the entire meeting ended the technical discussion with the comment which brought the session to a close.

"I've listened all night and all I hear is FHA. . . I won't vote for that and the people in my county won't vote for it either."

A few weeks later, FHA made another "final" offer to SWAFCA. It offered several minor changes of policy and warned that unless SWAFCA agreed to the loan promptly it would be postponed for another year.

Over the following weeks SWAFCA leaders worked nearly full time laying the groundwork for a second major political battle. A white paper was prepared outlining the issues of control, and circulated to organizations which has supported SWAFCA in the previous year.

Meanwhile, a development took place, through the United States Commission on Civil Rights, that was to have great impact on the outcome of the SWAFCA negotiations with USDA. The Commission held hearings in Alabama and, partly through the efforts of SWAFCA leaders, the FHA State Director became the subject of much of the controversy. Pressed to explain at a hearing why black farmers received smaller loans than white farmers with farms of the same size, he insisted

159

the only difference was that, "In many cases our nigger population has small acreage." Pressed further on the issue of racial discrimination, he referred to his own personal philosophy: "In the animal kingdom the strong take from the weak and the smart take it away from the strong. It's the same in the human kingdom."

In Washington the Secretary of Agriculture agreed to a meeting on June 12, 1968. This meeting, and the negotiations that took place on the following day, were the zenith of SWAFCA's effort to obtain the financial assistance. The amount of the loan was substantial, but more than that was involved. In many parts of Alabama, the Office of Economic Opportunity was regarded as a temporary agency, controlled by northern liberals who were part-and-parcel with the troublemakers of the Civil Rights Division of the Department of Justice. But the Department of Agriculture was a permanent and important part of southern economics. If SWAFCA obtained a substantial loan from USDA, it meant that the cooperative was endorsed, no matter how unwillingly, by one of the most powerful of southern institutions.

Gradually the meeting worked around to the question of the FHA State Director in Alabama. As SWAFCA leaders told the story of his opposition to the cooperative, William Taylor, the Staff Director of the United States Commission on Civil Rights, passed a note to them asking if many of SWAFCA's problems would be solved if their loan were supervised directly from Washington. When they replied it would be a useful beginning, Taylor made the proposal. The Secretary appeared to be prepared in advance and quickly accepted this change as a basis for a full review of the loan terms, to begin the next day under Assistant Secretary Baker's supervision. The next day, after a few introductory remarks, Secretary Baker left the meeting. It became apparent that the remaining USDA officials were not authorized to agree to any changes. The SWAFCA delegation promptly broke off the negotiations and left with a promise to return when officials could be present who were authorized to act. Secretary Baker quickly returned and the meeting resumed.

Secretary Baker, an attorney, discovered that the FHA staff was using legal documents and forms developed for other FHA programs, some of them years out of date and not remotely applicable to the cooperative loan. After several hours, during which he demanded explanations of conflicting and ambiguous provisions from other officials, he and the other attorneys present began to draft a new set of documents and forms. The negotiations finally ended some twenty-two

160

hours after they had started.

Under the arrangements negotiated and drafted at the session, SWAFCA became FHA's first demonstration project. It deals directly with Washington and is not bound by existing or future FHA regulations applicable to other borrowers. The loan agreement expressly recognizes the right of SWAFCA to manage the cooperative. SWAFCA administers a working fund of $400,000 which is not subject to prior FHA review of expenditures. On the other hand there are provisions which hold SWAFCA strictly to a fixed repayment schedule and require it to develop annual plans for the use of FHA loan funds. If SWAFCA should default on its loan payments, FHA has extensive powers of foreclosure.

The FHA loan, along with a second OEO grant made routinely in 1968, brought to a close SWAFCA's efforts to obtain the financial assistance needed for it to be permanently established. Beyond these, it had hopes to get funds from OEO to continue the special technical assistance staff for several more years and funds from the Economic Development Administration to explore the possibility of starting non-farm enterprises.

In less than eighteen months Johnson, Orsborn, Harrison, and other SWAFCA leaders had passed from the first demoralizing encounter with Washington officials at OEO to negotiating and drafting the loan instrument which would govern SWAFCA's unique relationship with the Department of Agriculture.

Finally, and most important, the cooperative had obtained adequate financial assistance without relinquishing its independence to those who supplied its funds. SWAFCA still stood for a group of poor farmers, "field-hand financiers," who proposed to manage their own cooperative.

What remained to be demonstrated, as they had said to the Secretary of Agriculture, was that they could do it.

III. THE MANAGEMENT OF THE COOPERATIVE

As SWAFCA developed, the management of the cooperative became the farmers' most critical test. Failures could erode support for the ideal of self-management, which was at the heart of the cooperative's success in organizing the black farmers in obtaining financial assistance from OEO and FHA.

The SWAFCA concept of self-management meant that all expert and professional personnel would be under the close control of the farmer-managers and largely restricted to technical roles. At the beginning, the argument that the farmers could not run the cooperative successfully could be met with the argument that they had never been given the chance to try, whereas the professionals and experts in the Department of Agriculture had demonstrated their unwillingness or inability to provide assistance to the black farmer.

As the operation of the cooperative became a major SWAFCA activity, however, the primary issue changed. Was the cooperative being managed successfully by the SWAFCA leaders, almost all of whom were farmers? If not, members and potential members could become highly critical of SWAFCA management and turn away from participation in the cooperative; SWAFCA leaders could lose confidence in their abilities and give up responsibilities to outside experts and professionals. Government officials could conclude they could not defend their continued support of the self-management approach for SWAFCA against the powerful opponents of the cooperative.

The opponents of self-management were placed in a much stronger position. In effect, it became necessary to show only (1) that some particular management failure had occurred and (2) that some outside expert or professional would have handled the management problem differently. SWAFCA supporters were left with the more speculative arguments about whether the recommendations of the outside experts and professionals would actually work.

The management of the cooperative involved four basic business objectives:

— Contact potential members, persuade them to join the cooperative and to shift substantial amounts of land and family effort to the production of garden crops, and provide them with needed technical advice.

— Arrange for capital and heavy equipment needed by the farmers for efficient farming.

— Set up and operate systems to purchase seed, fertilizer and other agricultural supplies and to sell them to the farmers at a reasonable price and at the time needed.

— Set up and operate facilities for collecting, grading, purchasing and reselling crops to fresh market wholesalers, frozen food producers and canners at a price which will permit the cooperative to pay the farmers a good price for their crops.

162

The risk of failure was so great, even with the best possible management, that probably no competent management team with a profit motive would have undertaken the venture without some form of absolute guarantee from the government. In agricultural production, circumstances beyond human control could create risk and restrict management options—weather conditions, for example. Also, there are fixed times within relatively narrow ranges for preparing the land, for planting, for laying down supplementary fertilizer and providing other care, for harvesting the crops and for shipping them to market. Opportunities must be taken on schedule or missed entirely; failure in the production process tends to be cumulative, whereas success does not.

The venture had to meet unusually fierce competition. SWAFCA intended to develop a substantial business enterprise which, if successful, would cut deeply into the profits of established business with monopoly markets. From the outset SWAFCA would be required not only to compete with these businesses in the usual sense but to fight off their combined attempts to kill the cooperative at almost any short range cost. Suppliers of fertilizer and lime boycotted the cooperative and its members. Produce buyers within the state also boycotted SWAFCA and undertook price wars by purchasing substandard produce at top prices for short periods of time in order to divert farmers from selling to SWAFCA. A story circulated that one farmer carried 500 pounds of pickles to a SWAFCA station where he received $4.80 for the pickles that SWAFCA accepted; then he took the culls (or rejects) to the pickle company's station and sold them for $5.50.

Local white officials were bitterly opposed to the cooperative. The Post Office often lost SWAFCA mail; the telephone company sought to charge $700 for the installation of four telephones; local Extension Service employees spread rumors about the poor management of the cooperative and urged farmers to stay with established produce buyers; local police stopped SWAFCA trucks on the way to market for extended safety checks; local judges granted the Mayor of Selma a temporary order restraining the operation of the cooperative which had

to be enjoined by a Federal District Court; the Alabama delegation to Congress was able to get the General Accounting Office to make a full investigation of SWAFCA activities only three months into the first season after SWAFCA received federal funds.

The cooperative's membership had other problems stemming from backgrounds of poverty and racial discrimination. Many of the farmers could not read; they lacked knowledge of new farming methods or lacked the confidence to try them. They lacked the necessary capital and credit opportunity to begin on any substantial scale and thus would be wholly dependent on success each year with no capital reserves to pull them through a bad season. Many did not have even the conventional small farm equipment, much less the heavier equipment which could make their farming more profitable. Most did not own a motor vehicle, and they were spread over an area which measured in excess of one hundred miles length and breadth at its most distant points.

The financing arrangements for the SWAFCA venture were entirely inadequate at the outset and, at best, promised to involve the cooperative in a shaky and troublesome arrangement with the federal government. It could be expected that a major effort would be required to maintain a good relationship between SWAFCA and its sources of capital. Both OEO and FHA agencies were subject to continuing pressure from opponents of the cooperative; and they placed a high premium on the forms of orderly internal management: written organization plans, job descriptions, audit systems for cost control and financial accountability and other such measures. The cooperative was subject to a steady stream of report requirements, poverty-watchers, consultants, advisors, evaluators, investigators, inspectors and auditors. An inadequate response to any of these could place continuing financial support in jeopardy.

A combination of these factors created several major management problems for SWAFCA during the first two years. SWAFCA found it almost impossible to hire and retain competent professional talent during the first two years, largely because the financial support for the cooperative looked so uncertain and because local whites and SWAFCA competitors put a great deal of pressure on such persons not to work for SWAFCA.

A second problem was that the combination of factors often made management policy decisions extremely difficult because they pulled in different directions. It became clear that, in the short run at least, the interests of the cooperative members and the cooperative were not always identical. One early instance of conflict involved the failure of SWAFCA to collect promptly on loans made to members during the 1967 season. The members were hard pressed; some would have found it impossible to repay the money without great sacrifice, if at all. SWAFCA, on the other hand, needed the money and needed to

164

demonstrate it could manage loan-making to members according to usual business standards of responsibility.

By far the most important problem resulting from the combination of these factors was the tremendous pressure they created on SWAFCA managers. Major crises, each of which would have warranted the full and studied attention of SWAFCA managers, sometimes arose at a rate which made this kind of consideration absolutely impossible. For example, in one extremely difficult 30-day period during June and July, 1968, SWAFCA conducted a full scale campaign to obtain a loan from the Department of Agriculture, dealt with the effect of a serious drought on its marketing commitments, underwent a close review of its internal operations by a team of GAO investigators; collected, graded, sorted and shipped more truckloads of cucumbers than it had ever handled before; and resolved long standing differences between the Board and the General Manager by accepting his resignation.

In all, not more than thirty people were substantially involved in the management of the cooperative during this period. By conventional standards most of them appeared unsuited by background and experience to run the kind of enterprise they sought to establish. The first year, Board members played a dominant role in both the management and execution of the venture. There were no clear lines between the functions of the Board and of the SWAFCA staff, headed by Calvin Orsborn, because substantially the same people were involved. Without compensation, the Board members and Black and Turner acted as the Field Representatives of the cooperative and as working foremen. They recruited members, estimated the acreage and yield of produce crops to be expected, advised the farmers on new methods of farming, distributed seed, fertilizer and other supplies; and graded, sorted and shipped the crops which were produced. Many members of the cooperative who were not on the Board performed similar functions. A farmer would arrive in Selma to pick up his fertilizer and stay to work all night unloading the railroad car full of fertilizer which had just arrived.

The Board met frequently, at least every two weeks, and considered matters in great detail. It approved each arrangement for purchasing goods and equipment, each marketing contract and the hiring of each employee. Subcommittees of the Board also met frequently and considered matters of similar detail. A later observer of SWAFCA reported that during the first year the organization was more like that of a Greek city of classical times than a modern business venture. There

165

were no set procedures and everyone involved was able to consider all of the problems with about an equal voice in what the cooperative should do.

As the first season reached its climax, mistakes, omissions and weakness in the operation became apparent and it appeared likely that SWAFCA would be unable to make marketing arrangements for many of the crops produced. But Ben Fink, the newly hired marketing advisor, was able to make the marketing arrangements. The cooperative, while losing some money itself, was able to return about $40,000 to its members which they would not otherwise have earned. In addition, by forcing local companies into a more competitive situation, SWAFCA brought the local price of fertilizer down from $50 a ton to $36 a ton and raised the price paid for cucumbers and southern peas from 2-4 cents per pound to the cooperative's price of 6½ cents a pound.

The key management issue that emerged at the end of the first year was the allocation of responsibility between the Board and Calvin Orsborn. As General Manager, Orsborn felt more of the administrative matters should be left to him or, at least, to him and Johnson, as President of the cooperative. He objected to the delay caused by the interference of the Board and felt justified in acting without its approval. Also, he felt the Board did not realize the difficulty of some of the things it asked him to do or the amount of time required. On the other hand, at least some members of the Board felt not only that Orsborn and Johnson were acting independently on matters which should have been submitted to the Board, but that Orsborn often refused to follow the Board's orders on important administrative matters. They felt that Orsborn was giving too much time to his other businesses, which he continued to maintain, and not enough time to the cooperative.

Dissatisfaction with this situation and the management of the cooperative led to a change in Board composition and leadership in February, 1968. Most of the old Board members were reelected by their counties, but four or five were replaced by new men some of whom had been active in helping the cooperative during the first year. At its first meeting the new Board elected William Harrison president. During the first year, he had been one of the Board members most concerned, and most articulate, about the management problems.

One of the first actions of the newly constituted Board was to confront Orsborn with its dissatisfaction. The results were far from satisfactory, but neither would break off the relationship. They were tied together by a common concern for the impact of an open break on SWAFCA's chances for the FHA loan and the cooperative's need to use Orsborn's cotton gin facilities as its main distributing and shipping point.

In the second year, the first season after the OEO grant, the activities of the Board members in managing the cooperative remained largely the same. There were some permanent additions to the headquarters staff, but the most important addition took place in the field where some men with degrees in agricultual science were hired as Field Representatives. It was expected they would take over much of the work done by the Board members in the first year; but it became apparent that many were not effective with the farmers, who placed a high premium on practical farm experience and were suspicious of advice from nonfarmers who were also outsiders. The Board members continued to play a major role and local farmers with reputations for farming success were hired in place of some of the original Field Representatives.

Taken collectively, the increased associations of the federal government with the cooperative provided an important supplement to SWAFCA management. The consultant firm hired to monitor SWAFCA's development and members of the OEO staff in Washington made many suggestions to SWAFCA Board members and staff.

Despite the management problems which arose, SWAFCA finished the second season with a success similar to that of the first year.

Although the cooperative lost money again, it marketed 1.4 million pounds of produce and returned almost $60,000 to its member farmers. It forced prices in the area to still more competitive levels and worked out arrangements by which FHA lent about $273,000 to 338 SWAFCA farmers, most of whom had not been able to obtain assistance from FHA in the past. But even more acutely than the first year, when the operation had necessarily been smaller because of the lack of financial assistance, omissions and mistakes in management caused problems for SWAFCA. Failure to deliver fertilizer, seed and other farming supplies to the farmers on time, a similar delay in purchasing trucks and equipment needed by the cooperative staff, and inadequate training and supervision of the Field Representatives were some of the management deficiencies which constituted major problems.

The key issue of the second year was the need for a basic change in the structure of the cooperative which would make it more like a conventional business organization. OEO urged SWAFCA to adopt a

167

written organization plan which contemplated the restriction of the Board to matters of general policy and left the day-by-day management of the cooperative to the General Manager and the staff. OEO consultants, GAO investigators and the CPA firm hired by SWAFCA urged closer adherence to systems for financial control. A discovery that Orsborn had placed $85,000 in a bank account not known to the Board and without proper authority dramatized the inadequacy of these controls—although there was no showing that the funds had been shifted with any wrongful intent, and all but a disputed $10,000 was returned shortly after the discovery. SWAFCA Field Representatives, Board members working in the field and SWAFCA farmers complained about lack of support for field activities and wanted more orderly arrangements made. Some experts and professionals associated with SWAFCA coplained they could not work with the cooperative because the farmer-managers "would not follow instructions" and Shirley Mesher and the other advisors often opposed their advice on technical matters.

Resistance to the changes arose for several reasons. Initially, many of the Board opposed the changes because they would have given Orsborn more authority and they doubted his ability or willingness to manage the cooperative in accordance with their wishes. But more generally many of the Board members and the three advisors were concerned that the changes might cause the real management of the cooperative to be taken away from the farmers by the experts and professionals who were employees of SWAFCA. Judging from the nature of the criticism, there was real cause for alarm. While Board members would agree when pressed by OEO that the advisors often caused problems in the management of the cooperative by their opposition to the plans of the technical staff, they were well aware that the advisors were important SWAFCA allies: they were willing to stand up to the government and attack excessive influence of outside experts and professionals on the growth of the cooperative.

The experience of two seasons with the cooperative was the best possible preparation of the Board members for the changes that were finally made. Because they were closely involved both as managers and staff, they were able to see first hand some of the disadvantages to the more communal approach to management which they had taken initially.

The resignation of Calvin Orsborn as General Manager in July, 1968, removed a major impediment to the adoption of a more conventional

168

structure with greater decision-making power vested in the full-time staff. During the fall and winter many of the changes were made. They were matched by a significant shift in the positions of members of the Board. Harrison, who had been acting informally as the General Manager of the cooperative since July, resigned his position as President to become SWAFCA's General Manager. Another Board member who had been working informally as Field Representative resigned his position on the Board to join the staff on a permanent basis.

Thus, at the beginning of the third year, SWAFCA entered into a new phase of development. It had been reorganized along more conventional lines. An organization plan had been adopted. Systems for cost control and financial accountability have been established. Many of the original Board members have stayed with the cooperative through the transition and some occupy key positions on the cooperative staff.

It is too early to say that the SWAFCA farmers have met the test of developing the cooperative successfully. Under any circumstances a venture of the size and complexity of SWAFCA takes more than two years to establish, and SWAFCA has operated only one year with even the minimal amount of capital needed to put the cooperative into full operation. Many problems continue.Pressure to respond to new government requirements may sap continued control by the membership.

But the cooperative, even at this point, has come further than any similar effort in the south to help the black farmer. Many of the external factors which created problems for SWAFCA may be under better control. For the first time the cooperative begins a season without the need to search for additional funds. Over the winter it was able to hire many of the persons needed to fill its technical staff. The local white community has grown less openly hostile, perhaps in part because SWAFCA has started paying with checks which make the local merchants aware of its economic impact on the area. Much of the local opposition of the Department of Agriculture employees has been neutralized by support from the Washington level of the Department, even in the face of a report of the General Accounting Office which was critical of SWAFCA.

IV. ORGANIZATIONS DEVELOPED THROUGH CITIZEN PARTICIPATION

The story of SWAFCA is meaningful as an account of successful action by poor people to affect the circumstances that kept them in poverty. It is also important because it sheds light on the concept of

169

citizen participation organizations and the worth that such organizations may have as instruments to end poverty. Based on the SWAFCA experience, this section draws together some of the important principles likely to be present in the growth of citizen participation organizations and the roles played by persons outside such organizations to aid in their growth. Then, it suggests three frameworks for evaluating citizen participation organizations such as SWAFCA and the likely conclusions with respect to that organization.

A. The Growth of the Organization and the Roles Played by Outsiders

It is to be expected that the growth of citizen participation organizations will fall into several distinct, although overlapping, phases that are brought about by their efforts to meet new problems. The struggle involved is likely to be inevitable, painful and essential to the full development of a strong organization. Although SWAFCA has not completed this evolution, its development suggests that the growth of citizen participation organizations should be viewed in at least five phases: organization, validation, management, decentralization and proliferation. The culmination of this growth is the spawning of new citizen participation organizations that are likely to go through the same phases of growth.

Organization. In the organization phase it appears that individuals and smaller groups come together, settle on a common aim, select leaders and decide to work toward their objective as an organization. Somehow, they must choose wisely and begin to move forward as a cohesive group.

SWAFCA's story suggests that it is vital for a citizen participation organization to be freed from the paralysis of waiting for help to come from outside the organization. Often, it seems that members of the organization start by thinking what others might be willing to do for them. They accept the idea of outside help eagerly and are prepared to follow those who assure them it can be obtained. Only when they are convinced by personal experience that assistance from others will not bring an end to their problems are the members prepared to form an organization that in aims and leadership will respond to what the members are determined to do for themselves. From this position, judging from the SWAFCA experience, the members are likely to work out perceptive and realistic decisions about aims and leaders for the organization. They know what is important to them, what they can do

170

about it and whom they are prepared to follow.

The greatest danger for the organization in its first phase seems to be that it will move too quickly to formal organization, structure and association with particular goals. All of these things inhibit the development of a strong active membership convinced it can play a part in what is to come and prevent it from making a full exploration of ideas and the capabilities of potential leaders. Standing committees and officers elected for a fixed term impose a hierarchy on the rest of the membership and encourage them to play only a passive role, leaving it to others to carry the organization forward. Formal organization is a public act which not only contemplates much of this structure but, because of its public nature, tends to associate the group with certain aims and leaders at the expense of others. Moreover, the act of formal organization often initiates a new level of accountability for the organization. It can no longer move with the same ease through a process of trial, error and new trial on an experimental basis.

Validation. This is a useful term to encompass all the ways in which other institutions come to acknowledge and support the new organization as a factor in their own plans and activities. As formal organization is the achievement of a new status for persons who form the group, so validation is an achievement of a new status by the organization.

For example, SWAFCA was validated by the wholesale marketing concerns and the frozen food packers who valued its products, by national civil rights organizations and church groups who valued its impact on racial discrimination in Alabama; and by government organizations, such as OEO initially and FHA at a later time, who saw it as a means of furthering the objectives of their programs and, perhaps, of enhancing their own credibility as institutions of a certain kind.

The organization must obtain validations from institutions that will establish its status and permit it to have the influence and resources necessary to accomplish the aims chosen by the membership.

The SWAFCA story suggests that during this phase a large share of control over the growth of the organization shifts to a relatively small group which acts as a task force in the conduct of the organization's activities. Timing, flexibility and speed of reaction are critical factors in obtaining the desired validations. Only on

171

occasion can the membership of the organization participate directly in the process. Even on these occasions, as when a mass demonstration takes place, the role of the membership is a fairly passive one in which they follow the directions of their leaders largely on trust.

Judging from the SWAFCA experience, it is critical in this phase for the task force group to recognize that, apparently, a price is always required for validation, although it is not always made explicit. The group must be able to estimate precisely, in terms of its own aims, the value of what is offered and what is sought by the validating institution. Usually the price is some degree of influence or control.

The trade-off between the organization and its validating institutions must leave the organization in a position to meet its commitments to both the membership and the validating institutions. The danger is that the two sets of commitments will conflict.

Management. During this phase the organization must operate its selected activities in a way that passes on expected benefits to its members and maintains its status with essential validating institutions. The dynamic core becomes the officers and staff who are working with the operation on a daily basis. Even regular and frequent meetings by the Board may not serve to keep its members centrally involved.

It seems important, if the organization is to be successful in this phase, that increasing specialization among the management group take place gradually. Those who are the designated leaders of the organization must resist pressure to assign special authority to individual members of the group on a permanent basis until they understand fully what they are being asked to relinquish and what the individual must be expected to do in return. If they do not understand some aspect of the operation, as they will not at first, the answer is not for them to assign it to an employee or some other specialist but to retain absolute control over it until that employee or specialist has taught them what is involved and they understand it fully. The guiding principle is that the designated leaders of the organization should delegate only those tasks they know how to do well themselves.

Over a period of time the group must develop systematic procedures for handling the business of the organization. The most

172

important purpose of these procedures is to route matters quickly to those who have the authority and responsibility for making the necessary decisions and taking the action that must follow. The most important classification is that which, from the perspective of the leaders of the organization, separates matters which are routine from those which are not. When a matter becomes routine for the leaders it should be delegated to someone else with instructions as to how it should be handled. The principle to be grasped here is closely related to the guiding principle for making delegations: Nothing is intrinsically routine. The same matter will not be routine for all leaders in all organizations. The criterion for deciding what is routine from the perspective of the leaders is whether the possibilities for handling the matter are fully understood by them and they are clear on how they want the matter handled in the future.

In general, there is a good chance that the management group will understand fairly quickly the importance of anticipating the demands arising from those aspects of the operation of direct and immediate importance to its membership. They are much less likely to understand initially that attention must also be given to those of direct and immediate importance to validating institutions providing support to the organization.

In theory, many of the requirements arising from dealings with validating institutions should make the organization better able to perform the activities of importance to its membership. In practice, the requirements usually make competing demands on the time of the management group. Some requirements will stem from the validating institution's notion of what systems, structure and practices are best for the organization in the conduct of its affairs. Since these requirements are usually based on general experience rather than detailed experience with the particular organization, there is no assurance that they will be best at the particular time they are sought to be imposed.

In the case of SWAFCA, OEO pressed strenuously for the officers and Board to pass a resolution defining the responsibilities of staff employees and delegating authority to them to act in their areas of responsibility. Later (as OEO no doubt correctly anticipated), the cooperative was criticized by the General Accounting Office for failing to take this step. But, although the proposed organization plan may have been reasonable, the Board probably

173

was justified in refusing to act. While the adoption of the plan would have satisfied OEO, it may have required the release of control over aspects of the operation that the leaders did not fully understand. Moreover, at the particular time OEO was pressing most vigorously for the adoption of the organization plan, there were fundamental differences between the Board of SWAFCA and its General Manager on the proper scope of his responsibilities and his ability to perform to the satisfaction of the Board. Despite the obvious need to establish a formal structure for the staff, the Board was probably reluctant to take this step because, indirectly, it would increase the authority of the General Manager. At the same time, the Board was not ready to ask the General Manager to resign or accept his resignation. It was in the midst of a campaign to obtain funds from the Department of Agriculture on favorable terms and feared that the public loss of the General Manager would weaken its position.

As problems are anticipated, resources are made available to meet them, and more and more activities become routine, the organization faces a new problem. The success of the organization brings a larger membership and the needs of the more experienced members change. Even if the organization performs its work well, it begins to lose its sensitivity and responsiveness to at least a substantial portion of the membership.

The response of the membership is to increase pressure for a more important role in the guidance of the organization. This pressure brings the organization to the beginning of a new phase.

Decentralization. In this phase the growth objective of the organization is to shift control of its operations to smaller units where there is increased opportunity for it to respond to the guidance of the membership. The dynamic core of activity in the organization shifts from the single management group to management groups of local units.

Because SWAFCA appears to be just entering this phase, the principles and problems to be drawn from its experience can only be inferred in most general terms. But certainly, a major problem faced by organizations in this phase will be to overcome the resistance of the central management group to the loss of its power. Their resistance will be supported by validating institutions, for whom it is easier to deal with a highly centralized organization.

Decentralization could take place for SWAFCA through the

174

strengthening of the county organizations that already exist. At this level, community boards could begin to make many of the decisions affecting their area. This development might be stimulated by the planned construction of receiving and distribution stations in each of the SWAFCA county areas. Some staff members of the central organization are already assigned to work in particular counties and, as the work increases in each area, additional staff members are likely to be added on this basis. The next step may be for some of these staff members to move their base of operations out of the central headquarters to the receiving and distribution stations in the county where they work. Local boards, perhaps stirred by their presence, should begin to take a special interest in their activities. Reports to the local board will become more important to the staff than reports to the central headquarters, and formal control over their activities may be shifted to the local board. The board and the staff in each county will form the management team in their area.

The end result of decentralization for the organization can be renewal of close ties between the membership and the leadership of the organization. At the same time, as local management groups become increasingly important the pressure may grow in some areas for changes and additions which are not desired by the entire organization. This pressure, particularly if it is supported by a far-sighted central management group, can bring the organization to its final phase.

Proliferation. The growth objective of this phase is to assist in establishing other organizations to be developed through citizen participation. These organizations may adopt aims similar to those of the older organization or they may adopt aims which are possible because they relate to the success of the older organization. Thus, for example, if truck farming becomes a successful operation for a large number of families in the area served by SWAFCA, another group may be able to form an organization to build the wooden packing boxes needed to ship the produce.

The role for the older organization in this phase is to act as a validating institution for the new organization and to help it receive validation from other institutions. In the case of the box factory discussed above, SWAFCA would become one of the principal purchasers of the new organization's product. It could also offer technical assistance to the new organization during the early portion of its management phase.

175

The full development of the old organization is achieved in this phase where, in this way, it is in a position to help create new organizations to be developed through citizen participation.

In the development of organization through citizen participation it is basic that the primary role must be played by the membership and the leaders under their control, but many persons outside the organization are also involved.

The fundamental requirement for those who mean to help is a commitment to citizen participation as a primary means of developing the organization. Many who accept this principle in theory do not follow it in practice. They intervene in the effort of the organization to conduct its own affairs and take on the role of a leader. Professionals and technicians fear that poor people will not do a good job in conducting the affairs of their organization and want to protect the citizen group from harmful mistakes. They intervene to help the organization cover a particular crisis and then withdraw. As a result of the successful handling of the situation the organization moves to a more complex level of activity; existing leadership is sustained. Another crisis arises and those permanently involved are even further out on the limb of their own ignorance and inexperience. They are even more likely to make mistakes and the mistakes are likely to do even greater harm to the organization.

Another reason causing professionals and technicians to intervene is that they are distressed at the unjust way that poor people are treated by an important institution—OEO or FHA, for example—and they intervene to lead in an attack on the institution. But even if the organization obtains just treatment in the particular case, the institution is not made wiser or more concerned about just treatment of the poor; it is encouraged in the notion that just action need only be a consideration when it deals with an organization led by a professional or technician.

Still another reason given for intervention is that poor people suffer great injury because they are required to do without the assistance to which they are entitled, and intervention can often win benefits for the poor that they would not otherwise obtain. This intervention tends to add another condition to obtaining assistance from such institutions— the presence of a layer of professionals and technicians as leaders or "advocates"—which most poor people will not be able to meet in organizations developed through their effort because they cannot attract needed professionals and technicans from the short supply.

Many professionals and technicians are subject to racial and class bias, particularly when the poor people involved are black. They believe that success for the organization can only come through their intervention or, at least, through a leadership that follows their guidance faithfully.

The fact is that professionals and technicians may be wrong in what they propose. A notable example concerns the decision of the SWAFCA Board to start the cooperative on a ten-county basis. Almost all those professionals and technicians involved, including many who were sincerely interested in helping the organization, would probably have started the cooperative in a smaller area during that year, if at all. Yet, with hindsight, some of those involved have wondered with good reason if the decision to start on the full ten county basis was not critical to generating support for the cooperative and in obtaining funds from both OEO and FHA because its size made it more difficult for a single local unit of government to assert an exclusive right to dealing with the organization. The area involved was well in excess of any possible jurisdiction of the Selma Community Action Agency or, indeed, any single local unit of city, county, state or federal government.

Failure is not the greatest danger for citizen participation organizations. Most of the poor people involved will not be defeated by failure. What does often defeat them is believing they can't bring success to the organization through their own action. For many, the steps leading to success for the organization appear to be part of a mysterious process dominated by near-magical forces. The most important task of professionals and technicians is to dispel this false magic and to convey to the people involved the awareness that they can cause the organization to succeed.

Three important roles involving outsiders in direct contact with the organization are those of the community organizer, the promoter and the staff member in an institution which may fund the organization.

The community organizer. He is the key contributor to the organization during all phases of its development. In the broadest sense, the objective of the organizer is to help the membership of the organization find a sense of its own potency and of the need for it to take matters into its own hands instead of waiting for help to come from others. The danger for the organizer is that he will lose sight of the need for a basic orientation toward the membership and become involved in management of the organization as an assistant to its leaders. In the later phases of its development, when the leadership becomes separated from

177

bership, the organizer must continue to serve the membership, helping it to build ties with its leaders and to form new groups.

The promoter. He may play a significant role in assisting the organization during the second phase of its development when it is seeking validation and support from other organizations or institutions. Essentially, he is a broker who seeks to make arrangements satisfactory to both the new organization and the validating institutions. He capitalizes on his ability to communicate with two vastly different groups of people and on his knowledge of both the new organization and the validating institutions.

The danger for the promoter in working with the organization is that he will push it into an arrangement which does not serve it well. One possibility is that the arrangement will give too much control over the organization to the validating institution. Another is that the responsibilities of the citizen participation organization under the arrangement will be more than it can manage in the next phase of its growth. He should insist that the organization tell him the kind of validation and support it desires. The promoter should become involved only when the need for him is well defined. He should do his work and leave.

The project officer. The project officer of a funding institution makes his most important contribution during the validation and management phases of the organization's development. In both phases his key function is to interpret correctly and communicate to the organization the requirements and objectives of his institution. When the organization seeks validation and support from the institution the project officer can help it present its proposal in the terms most favorably related to the interests and programs of the institution. He can also press the merits of the organization in these terms to officials of higher levels of the institution during their consideration of the proposal from the organization. When the organization is in the management phase, he can act as a reliable control point for imposing and ordering the requirements imposed on the organization by his institution and aid in turning unreasonable or unduly burdensome requirements away from the organization.

He is often under pressure to produce a number of proposals attractive to the institution in terms of its requirements and objectives and, in the absence of others who perform these roles, this may drive him to act as a community organizer and promoter for the organization as well. The danger of undertaking these activities is that they conflict with the project officer's position within his own institution. When he

178

is driven to retreat into the task of representing the institution he is likely to find his credibility destroyed within both the organization and the institution. To the organization he is one who offered a different kind of assistance and then failed to provide it. To the institution he is one who becomes so closely allied with the organization that his judgment about the best interest of the institution may no longer be reliable.

B. Judging citizen participation organizations

Intuitive reactions in favor or opposition to citizen participation organizations are not adequate to resolve the conflict which exists about their value. A set of rational standards, commonly accepted, can help guide those who wish to encourage the development of citizen participation organizations. Equally important, the adoption of rational standards for judging these organizations can help protect them against attacks based on other standards, often unstated, which would not be commonly accepted if plainly acknowledged as the basis for the attack.

The report of GAO on SWAFCA illustrates this kind of attack. The report recommends that OEO reevaluate the cooperative to determine whether continued federal funding is warranted and that, "if the Government continues with its support of SWAFCA, it should provide technical assistance to SWAFCA and ensure that such assistance is fully utilized."

In less euphemistic language, the burden of the report is that GAO doubts that OEO should give any additional funds to the cooperative and, in any event, urges FHA to establish traditional controls over SWAFCA that would effectively end the citizen participation. The report is highly critical of SWAFCA because the cooperative failed to establish or follow adequate procedures for management and financial control and this failure resulted in harm to the operation and possible losses of federal funds. Although almost everyone would agree that deviations from adequate management and financial controls are fitting subjects for concern, the basis for the leap from the identification of such deviations to the concluding recommendations is a step which requires careful explanation. Yet the report is absolutely silent on this point. The assumption which seems to be implicit is that these deviations are the exclusive standard against which the performance of citizen participation organizations should be judged.

179

The following are three suggested frames of reference which might be useful in judging a citizen participation organization of SWAFCA's type.

(1) *SWAFCA as a mechanism for delivery of benefits.* From one perspective, SWAFCA is part of a system to distribute needed benefits to poor people in rural areas under federal programs. The Department of Agriculture has been charged with this responsibility, among others, for many years. Despite the different approaches used and the different relationships with the Department which exist, organizations such as SWAFCA can be compared with local FHA units and county level offices of the Extension Service, and some judgement then formed about their relative value in accomplishing the Department's general objectives.

The Department of Agriculture, at least since World War II, has been unable to reach poor blacks in Alabama with any significant amount of the assistance to which they are entitled under the law. The reasons for this are complex and not all attributable to a desire in the Department to discriminate against black people, but the fact is plain.

Compared with the use of local FHA or Extension Service units, SWAFCA represents a tremendous advance in reaching black people under Department programs. Support given to SWAFCA is passed on by that organization to over 1500 poor families, almost all of whom are black and have needed assistance to which they were lawfully entitled for many years.

One common denominator for judging more precisely the capability of the three kinds of units with respect to the target population of rural black people in this area is the increase in the income earned by these people as a result of their farming activities which can be attributed to the effort of each kind of unit. No very sophisticated consideration is required to indicate that SWAFCA's impact measured in these terms has been vastly greater than that of the other kinds of local units.

The absolute cost of local FHA and ES unit operations may be almost as high as the cost to the government of the SWAFCA operations; yet, the return in dollars of income earned by poor black people in the area as the result of SWAFCA's activities is likely to be far higher than the returns attributable to the activities of each of the other units. In future years there is a good chance that an increasing amount of SWAFCA's cost of operation attributable to servicing persons eligible for Department assistance will be met through revenues to the cooperative from its marketing system. The cost to the government will be reduced accordingly. There is, of course, no possibility that the local FHA or Extension Service unit will become self-sustaining in any degree.

180

It might also be important to consider the indirect impact of each unit on the full amount of Department assistance provided to the poor black people in the area. A distressing problem for the Department of Agriculture has been the tendency for local units to direct their assistance toward those who are least in need and even toward those who are so little in need as to raise questions about their eligibility for assistance. Thus, Extension Service employees appear to focus on advising the owners of the larger and more successful farms in the area, and FHA county supervisors follow a similar practice in making loans. To the extent that the local FHA or ES unit departs from the most efficient distribution of its effort among levels of the target population in terms of program objectives, there is a hidden extra cost to the government.

Initially SWAFCA undertook to make loans to individual farmers on the grounds that they were not being serviced by FHA local offices. FHA responded by significantly increasing the number of loans to them with the assistance of SWAFCA in identifying those who needed assistance and making collections for FHA. This improvement in Department assistance should be attributed to SWAFCA and should also be considered in judging the cooperative as a local unit for the distribution of federal benefits.

(2) *SWAFCA as an economic enterprise.* A second way to view SWAFCA is as a business which is part of the economic activity of the area. In this context the cooperative might be judged in terms of how it improved the economic opportunity for poor people in southwest Alabama and how this improvement compared with the other opportunities available to them either in that area or elsewhere.

No force, either government or private, appeared able and willing to provide an improved economic opportunity. SWAFCA was able to attract government subsidies—a loan and grants—which probably could not have been obtained through any other kind of effort. The sale of farm supplies, fertilizer, and seed and the purchase of the crops produced created higher incomes for those who dealt with the cooperative; many additional farmers also benefited indirectly through the fairer prices offered by other concerns as a result of SWAFCA's competition. Investigation would probably also disclose that SWAFCA through its business activity as an export industry added appreciably to the wealth of the area—with at least some "trickle-down" benefit to poor people not engaged in independent farming operations.

Nevertheless, it is reasonable to consider whether there are economic justifications for the continued development of the organization through citizen participation. The argument might be made that the best decision in economic terms for the poor people of the area is to now put the business in the hands of professionals and technicians.

SWAFCA was started through citizen participation, and it has resulted in a substantial increase in economic opportunity for the poor. Ordinarily a change in management approach is not dictated by a previous record of success. Moreover, the most important external factor in achieving this success was the government subsidies won by the citizen participation organization. If professionals and technicians were to take over control of SWAFCA, one very likely result is that the organization will lose, through the withdrawal of its citizen leaders, almost all the power which made possible these subsidies. It is even possible that the loss or reduction of this power would leave the organization unable to protect itself against the political pressure to withdraw present government assistance to the cooperative. At best, it appears likely that the organization would become a captive of the government agencies involved through the impositions of technical government management requirements. This would weaken the organization in every way, including its ability to make profits for the poor people served by the cooperative.

The impact of such a change in management on the prospects for other economic opportunities for poor people in the area appears to be still more unfavorable. Given the natural cycle of organization in citizen participation, it is likely that SWAFCA will pass through phases of decentralization and proliferation. The result could well be the creation of a number of citizen participation organizations which would vastly improve the economic opportunity for poor people in the area. Such an evolution is much less likely to take place if professionals and technicians take control of SWAFCA during the management phase. If citizen participation is ended in SWAFCA, organizations may still be developed through citizen participation, but a potential training ground for new entrepreneurs would be closed off, and, perhaps, outside resources would be discouraged from pursuing the citizen participation route.

(3) *SWAFCA as a vehicle for social and political development.* A third point of reference for judging SWAFCA and other citizen participation organizations is as a means for aiding in the social and political development of poor people.

One of the most illuminating aspects of the SWAFCA experience is how fundamentally such an organization is concerned with the social and political development not only of its membership, but of all poor people in Alabama. The choice of economic activity by the members was not a rejection of other forms of social and political action but a means of enhancing that action. At least in the Alabama situation the decision to seek economic improvement cut at the heart of the political and social domination that made voter drives less effective and frustrated individual efforts by the poor, and particularly the black poor, to rise in the social and political structure of southwest Alabama.

Participation in SWAFCA has been a continuing experience in social and political development through group action. The explicit focus of the organizational phase is on the formation of groups and the discovery of the strength that arises through group action. During the validation phase the task force supported by the membership was required to undertake major political battles to obtain funding from OEO and FHA. In later phases the membership has undertaken new efforts through group action to control its leadership; and it may move on to establish new organizations developed through citizen participation.

Although the experience is most intense for those directly involved in each instance, the opportunity for involvement passes from group to group during the full cycle of the organization's growth. It is not limited to a single group of leaders who occupy the center of the stage during each phase. Moreover, new members are drawn into the organization and may become involved in the experience of social and political development through group action.

The impact of success achieved in Alabama by a group of poor black people is likely to be of even greater importance as an example. To others who are poor and black it suggests that they, too, may be able to improve thier situation; to those who are wealthier and white the message is that those who are poor and black are not inherently unable or unwilling to achieve social and political advances for themselves.

This discussion suggests that citizen participation organizations such as SWAFCA may be judged with creditable results in more than one framework. In any particular situation the value of the organization is cumulative. As a mechanism for delivery of benefits, as an economic enterprise and as a vehicle for social and political development an organization of SWAFCA's type has a many sided value for poor people and society generally. Its benefits are not likely to be equalled by any other single kind of institution.

PARTICIPATION ON THE BLOCK

by: David Borden

Editor's Note:

David Borden came to intimate involvement in the East Harlem community from similar involvement in Puerto Rico, where he was a Peace Corps trainer.

Peace Corps community development experience and ideas make up much of the structure of his story—and much of his emotional thrust against big government and big organizations generally. His monograph does give one of the clearest pictures of the "trees," while so many of the others concentrate on the "forest."

Some questions:

1) Is the block communities experience a New York phenomenon, tied to the essence of East Harlem, or does it have broader applicability?

2) What are some of the ideological strands which makes Borden's attack on OEO so different from the criticism in Piven's, Bernstein's and Fox's monographs?

3) How does Borden's training emphasis on attitudinal change among the poor contrast with the focus on systemic change in many of the other articles? Is this training what Arnstein would call "therapy"?

Borden is now President of Victoria International Corporation, New York City. The Corporation is engaged in training and community development work.

I. INTRODUCTION

"I think the one that needs the program should administer the program. And if this is done the people that need it would get it. But if you associate the program with those that don't need it, they will be getting the bulk of the funds that is needed for the people that need the program."

Thus spoke a resident of East Harlem in 1966, in a taped interview conducted by one of his neighbors who was a trainee at Block Communities, Inc. This is a brief story of that program's efforts on some fifty blocks in New York and a commentary on the efforts of the anti-poverty program as it affected those same neighborhoods. I separate the two because, unlike most offspring of the battle against poverty, Block Communities, Inc., is a very specialized drive to develop community participation and control on given blocks around all facets of the residents' lives. Its entire product is community participation.

II. THE ORIGINS OF BLOCK COMMUNITIES, INC.

Block Communities and its predecessor organization, Block Development Project, have performed with a spirit of idealism not unlike that which gave birth to OEO. Block Development suffered from naivete, but its idealism was also what attracted its friends and staff. It was founded on the following principles:

(1) Citizen participation and ultimately citizen control cannot occur without a direct, day-by-day contact with the resident citizens. The first step toward community control is to help people learn the slow painful process of assuming civic responsibility. Only as this process takes place should specific projects be initiated.

(2) Communities of poor people, like poor individuals, can grow in spite of tremendous odds. Poverty produces attitudes of despair and helplessness, but these attitudes can be replaced with a sense of confidence in an individual as he confronts community and individual problems.

(3) Participation and control do not necessarily mean mass demonstrations. Communities must learn more sophisticated, and ultimately, more effective techniques of getting things done. Most important, they must learn never to confront unless there is a prospect of success.

(4) The only type of person to effect change on a block is at once

185

highly skilled and tough. The best person potentially is someone residing on the block.

(5) Change must start at the block level with a small number of families and one person should work not more than one block.

(6) People without experience in doing so have to be trained to manage their own affairs. Otherwise they will continuously be dependent on the efforts (good or bad) of others.

This concept was a brainchild of many people. For me, it came from a year's work with the Peace Corps in rural Puerto Rico where my assignment was to expose new volunteers to the concept of community development. Perhaps I learned more than the volunteers. Most important, I learned that communities could learn to initiate the solutions to their own problems, and I came to appreciate the absolute necessity for a highly skilled person to assist in that process.

Two years in a settlement house in East Harlem illustrated to me that the same basic techniques could be applied in an urban community. By the end of that experience we had organized the first credit unions known anywhere in public housing and, in addition, we developed a thriving block organization. (This organization was responsible for four of its young people attending college in the fall of 1965 where none had before.)

Initially, the block organization was a very tight social group, as most people (including myself) considered the "real" problems too awesome to tackle. We organized dances, beach trips and spent long hours talking. Then the beach trips began to take on a new dimension. By the end of the summer, the kids were renting four buses on a weekend and charging their families $3 a seat to go to the beach. Collecting several hundred dollars in dues, they set up a storefront club and began to deal with some of the real problems. Returning from vacation, I discovered that the community had moved without me. Movies were being shown in vacant lots and plans were underway to establish day care centers which eventually were, in part, responsible for the East Harlem Block Schools. One of the families had even purchased a building on the block.

Buoyed by this block movement, several of us wrote a proposal in 1964 for an anti-poverty program to affect East Harlem. The initial stage was to involve local people, training them in community organizing and assigning them work on one block in the area. They were to be the catalyst in the long slow process of bringing people together around common issues. Nothing else should happen for at least one year.

The second stage was to create a "community chest" with an elected board from all the blocks involved. The function of the community chest would be to provide technical assistance and capital for self-help projects. It was anticipated (correctly) that most of the generated block activities would not require money, and therefore, funds would be distributed on an investment basis rather than as charity. The community chest would put funds only in projects which would make a maximum, permanent impact—special attention being given to projects not requiring annual refunding, but which generated their own income.

Finally, the proposal stated that great effort would be expended to build a broad operation of effective services from the existing maze of social service agencies. This would be accomplished by creating teams of service personnel, such as health aides, nurses aides, teachers, case workers and Bureau of Child Guidance officials. It was not anticipated that this effort would be expensive, but would only be a matter of bringing public servants together and retraining them so they would have a greater impact.

Tremendous emphasis was placed on finding the best talent in the community, regardless of the talent's origin. In addition, an attempt was made to avoid defining the issues around which the community might organize, feeling that each block must set its own priorities.   l

In summary, the task was defined essentially as one of training individuals and communities to develop their own capabilities in dealing with problems. Once this capability was developed there would be little need for a continued federal subsidy. We considered OEO's support as a five-to ten-year effort at the most.

To say that our proposal efforts were blocked by other groups would be a gross understatement; "strangled" might be more accurate. The program was blocked primarily by social workers and "do-gooders." But in fairness, it was also hampered by our own inability to conduct political in-fighting. We were all young. We all lived in the community. But we had not acquired an understanding of the use of power for survival. Sadly enough, we were not blocked on the merits of our program.

In 1964, East Harlem spawned two separate poverty efforts, both of which continue, to this day, to battle each other. Both have had their detractors and allies in the Wagner and Lindsay administrations. Both administrations were, and are, afraid to lay down adequate laws of operation to these groups. The result has been a great deal of cynicism on the part of community residents who seem primarily divided between those who want to profit from the pork barrel and those who ignore it all and lead complacent lives. It would be difficult to measure or define how the community has been tangibly or permanently improved by the efforts of these organizations. Certainly, the community would have benefited far more had they cooperated.

Failing to influence this conflict, we went "underground" and focused on the blocks. We found ourselves dealing with a totally invisible community which was being completely ignored by the poverty program.

In late 1964, we established our first program, the Block Development Project, as a private, nonprofit corporation, and it made almost every possible mistake for an organization of this type. Most of the mistakes were due to the simple fact that a person coming from a ghetto environment is not initially the most able to effect the change in a ghetto. The reasons are many, but the most important is that the ghetto and the society which systematically sucks its blood destroy the ghetto citizen's faith in himself. The ghetto resident, labeled inferior by the world around him, too often reflects that evaluation. Also in 1964, those young people most confident and aggressive on any given block wanted to get as far away from that block as possible.

In addition, the prospect of effecting change by acting alone on your own block is an absolutely terrifying proposition. Even the most confident person walking into the average East Harlem block is soon swallowed up by the apathy or is eaten alive by the illegal forces working the block. Of the first five workers for the Block Development Project, only one lasted the length of the project. Among those who resigned were some of the original visionaries of the project. Their frustrations were brought out in their reports:

> "One man told me today that it was dangerous to make friends, and so he avoided the practice. What the hell is going on here? How can one person affect this attitude in two to three thousand people?"
> "Waited until 9:30 for everyone to show up for the meeting. No one came."
> "It really gets to a person when he gets all sorts of suspicious, evil scorning, untrusting looks."
> "In order to function in East Harlem, you have to be either very tough or very wise. I am neither."
> "It's the people. You can't do nothing without the people. They're

188

the ones who make the change."

"When everybody knows everybody else, it's easier to live in a place."

"I was invited today to my first cup of coffee in the block."

Finally, we relied too much on instinct and good will and too little on technique and knowledge.

In the Spring of 1966, the Block Development Project ran afoul of its own board. The board, composed entirely of community residents systematically hired by one of East Harlem's two warring anti-poverty groups, threatened to have us become a tool of that group. The staff made a painful decision not to permit this, turned down more than $1 million dollars in OEO funds and resigned from the project to form Block Communities, Inc. The city awarded the money to neither Block Development nor Block Communities, nor anyone else, leaving East Harlem no federal funds for another year.

III. THE BCI TRAINING PROGRAM— THE HEART OF THE EFFORT

Block Communities survived and grew because we had learned to train ourselves for our job. First, we hired a psychiatrist, Dr. Efren Ramirez (who later became commissioner of the city's new Addiction Services Agency). He was a good instructor in community organization. He met once a month with staff, helping to determine goals and evaluate the means by which to pursue them. He instructed the staff in specific skills, especially how to deal with apathy, hostility and fear. Toward the end of that summer, he brought in Victor Biondo, a giant of a man, both compassionate and tough, a most highly skilled trainer.

We made heavy use of Biondo's good sense and experience. Gradually we evolved the training program used at BCI today. The overall purpose of the training programs is to help a person develop the confidence, skill and commitment needed to be effective in changing the adverse factors in his own community. The principles this training followed can also be read as a list of things we learned over the last four years:

1. Permanent change takes place in a community only when people grow to take responsibility for changing that which is affecting their lives. The best person to help people grow is one who has grown himself and understands the process on a personal basis.

2. To work in a community as an agent for change requires an

incredible amount of skill. This skill can be taught to people who are willing to learn through (a) experience (b) group discussions and (c) exposure to what other people are doing.

3. Confidence is essential to the agent trying to foment change. Confidence is built primarily on the development of ability, not by short-term ego-building such as the approval of one's peers, superior or constituency.

4. A social revolution can only be fought by people who are self-disciplined and proud. The gentle process of classic social work has tended to emasculate people. To become both confident and self-disciplined is a process which cannot be sugar-coated by Freudian psychiatry. In this light, it is better to help a person decide whether he wants to continue following a certain course of action than to inquire as to why he followed it in the past. If the decision is made to place some of the burden for change on the people who are the victims of the system, then some demands must be made which will help them take an effective role in the revolution. This cannot be done by offering excuses or tolerating unproductive behavior. Freudian psychiatry seems to me to be a way of helping a person understand that there are a variety of valid reasons to justify silly behavior. When applied to a black youth this becomes one more act of emasculation for him by cutting off his anger and excusing his behavior. Groups like the Panthers and the Muslims recognize this and therefore place a tremendous stress on positive, disciplined behavior.

Our block workers encountered youngsters who had been "social workers" and had learned all the sociological excuses for their actions. One block worker, a particularly tough individual, said that one member in a group of kids with whom he was working had informed him that he couldn't be expected to do all his homework because he came from a "matriarchal society." The block worker asked the individual if he would like to have his mother join the group. If not, he did not wish to hear any more about the matter.

We thus evolved a philosophy of action which could well be called "existential charity." The purpose of our work was to help people move to a crossroads situation. Once there, they had to make a choice. Are you going to do something about the garbage the superintendent is allowing to pile up in the hallway? Are you going to cope with the fact that the police never seem to answer your calls? Are you going to fight for a better education for your kids? Are you going to challenge the myriad of other problems about which you complain?

190

Intrinsic to this philosophy is the reaffirmation of potential in every individual to control the situation around him. What we learned to say to the block resident is that, in spite of the matriarchal society, in spite of a rotten political system, in spite of the exploitation perpetrated against you for centuries, you are not helpless. And in the final analysis, no one is going to do anything for you—you must do it for yourself.

Therefore, the final purpose in the training program was to help the block worker apply this approach to his own life and then in turn to relate this learning to promote action on his block.

The Techniques Used

The primary form for the block worker's training was group discussion. In this context information can be more easily and effectively imparted, especially if effective questions are asked by the trainer. Not only can an experienced trainer define and help develop an intellectual understanding of the problem and its solution; but he can also lead people to make the connections, to exercise logic.

In addition, the group is an extremely effective way of helping individuals to respond to personal attitudes as they relate to the job.

Attitudinal training was an important part of BCI training. It asks:
1. "What do you want to do?"
2. "How do you think you are going to get there?"
3. "What problems are in the way?"
4. "What do you think you can do about them?"
5. "What are you going to do this week?"

What happens essentially is that the average young ghetto male, when confronted with this dialogue, undergoes an incredible strengthening process. For perhaps the first time, someone is caring enough about him as an individual to confront him on his behavior, to assume at the outset that the revolution begins with him and his actions.

The process of becoming a block worker at BCI is based on levels of attainment with clear-cut goals at each level. Initially, a person attends training sessions in his neighborhood one night a week to learn the workings of a community organization and how it would fit his block.

Often these sessions prove a jolt to the prospective worker. Someone is throwing the ball in his court, without promising him anything, least of all a job (there are as many as thirty candidates for a single job—a fact we tell the trainees). The training at this stage focuses on the problems of the trainee's block, what can be done about them and what

191

is he going to do this week to rectify them (as a volunteer!). The results are regularly amazing. If a person attends three meetings, he attends ten. Often the impetus during training causes him to find a steady job which will pay more than we can, but he continues as a volunteer.

By the time a man is hired, BCI knows him well and he knows BCI. Once hired, the trainee is put through two months of intensive training on the specifics of community organization. He learns:

1. How to explain his presence on the block.
2. How to bring groups of people together around common interest.
3. How to deal with hostility, indifference, apathy, fear.
4. How the city, state and federal governments operate.
5. How the Mafia functions.
6. What other community organizations are doing.

At the same time the trainee is apprenticed to a functioning block association. Here the association and the block worker can teach him the trade.

Now the block worker moves onto his own block. His first tasks are (1) to get to know every family on the block (2) to explain why he is there and (3) to attempt to enlist their support. The usual response is one of polite uninterest and skepticism. But during this survey period, he begins to accumulate allies who, if not overtly helpful, are at least cheering from the sidelines.

Once the survey is finished, the block worker begins the long arduous task of changing people's attitudes to the point where they begin to believe that something can be done.

IV. THE RESULTS

The kids on both George's and Carlos' blocks had formed baseball teams and were seeking competition. On July 12th, at one of the playing fields in Central Park, the 102nd Street Royal Tigers met the Little Elks of 123rd. In our eyes, the important thing here wasn't the game itself, but the fact that these kids had formed their own teams, chosen their own captains and were in the process of forming their own league. At any rate, it was the first game of a new era and the score was 24 to 2.

The next day the Royal Tigers met to analyze their defeat. I was at this meeting and I am going to describe it in some detail, as well as the events that followed. On that afternoon those kids accomplished a wonderful thing. I feel that what they did symbolizes what any tenement neighborhood can do if it is just given the time and the belief and the ultimate responsibility.

When I arrived there were already about fifteen kids gathered around. Their epic defeat the day before had seemed to invest them with a sort of optimistic humiliation—as if they felt that whatever happened from now on, at least they couldn't do much worse. After everybody was accounted for, Carlos asked them why they had wanted to have a meeting.

"To find out why we took gas, man, 24 to 2!"

And all at once there was an explosion of voices, an eloquent onslaught of swear words and complaints and accusations. At last they refined the reasons for their loss down to two things: Hector, their best player, had played one-man team and ought to be kicked off the club; and Papo, their captain, had failed utterly, and ought to be replaced at once. After they had arrived at this decision, Carlos asked them, "Okay, so you want a new captain. Who do you want?"

There was no immediate reply.

"Well, who do you think will be a better captain than Papo?"

After a long silence, somebody grudgingly admitted, "Nobody."

Papo shrugged his shoulders and tried to display nonchalance. Carlos asked, "You think Papo is the best guy for captain? Then why do you want to kick him out?"

"He's stupid, man!" said a kid named Tito.

"You dope, Tito! If he's stupid, we're more stupid!"

There was a loud outburst, and then Raphael, a quiet, modest, quixotic sort of kid, stood up and shouted for silence. "I got somethin' to say!" he cried, and slowly the noise subsided. "I got somethin' to say," he repeated.

"Well why don't you open your mouth, man, and speak it!"

"How can he open his mouth when you keep screaming?"

"Forget it," said Raphael, and started to sit down.

"Come on," urged Carlos. "If Raphael has something to say why don't you let him say it."

There was an expectant hush. Raphael stood up again and cleared his throat. "Well, we lose yesterday, 24 to 2. And maybe we been blamin' Papo so we don't have to blame ourselves."

For a moment when I heard Raphael utter these words I wanted to embrace him. In fact I almost fell off my chair. It was almost as though he had stumbled across one of the secrets of the universe, and through my mind ran all the excuses for mankind's failure and for individual

193

failure (including my own) that had probably ever been offered. What irony that a 16-year-old kid could see this, and tell his friends to toss aside these excuses, to cease condemning others and to look inside themselves.

"Yeah," said a fat kid named Amos, with a titantic finger mit. "Yesterday we was always fighting with each other!"

"It's Hector's fault," said someone. "The way he play every base and run into you, man!"

"Hector gave me a bump on the head and he make me drop the ball! He don't stay put in his position!"

A couple of more remarks like this were made and, for the moment, the blame was passed to Hector. He was a rough kid, 13 and hard, like someone small and durable patched together with cement—the block's best athlete and it's biggest troublemaker. About a month before, he had thrown a garbage can at Carlos' wife. Now Carlos asked him whether he thought the others were justified in blaming him.

Hector shrugged. He had a sullen old felt hat pulled down over his forehead so that his eyes could look out from darkness; he could see without being seen. "I don't know," he mumbled. "Anyway, they already kick me off."

Carlos turned to the others. "Was it because of Hector you lost the game?"

Nobody answered right away. Then Hector said, "They play terrible!"

"Yeah, when we tell you to cut out hoggin', the next time you just stand there and let the ball go through your legs!"

"This is just like in the game!" said Papo. "We always fighting with ourselves!"

"Anyway, we already kick Hector off!" said Tito.

"Maybe we kick him off but we still fighting with ourselves!"

Amos, the rotund rightfielder with the big mitt, cried, "What good it gonna do to kick Hector off, and he can play good ball!"

"Give him another chance," a voice muttered, and there was an undercurrent of assent.

"You want another chance, Hector?" asked Carlos.

Hector shrugged. His eyes did not look up.

"We give him another chance," said Papo, "But he better stay at third base where he belong!"

"How about it?" Carlos repeated. "Hector, you want another chance?"

194

For at least half a minute Hector didn't move. Outside, a truck roared by. It's shadow briefly cut off the glint of sunlight in the hall.

"Come on, man, you wanta play or not?" cried Papo.

Hector shrugged again, and then imperceptibly nodded his head. There was a general release of tension, and a feeling of complacency seemed to occupy the room. Carlos killed this at once. "Okay, so Hector's gonna play," he said. "Does that mean that necessarily you're gonna win your next game?"

The kids grumbled in a downcast way. They had unscapegoated both Papo and Hector, and consequently were now confronted with the inadequacy of the game they had actually played. A prolonged and solemn discussion followed. At length it was decided that they required, above all, two things: more practice and a place to practice in. With respect to the latter, somebody suggested the empty lot on the block.

"What? You wanta play in all that stinkin' trash?"

"Man, the city oughta clean that place up and make it a playground!"

Papo suggested, "Why don't we write it to the Mayor?"

"What do you want the Mayor to do," Carlos asked, "Show up here with a shovel?"

"Well, what you want us to do, man, clean that lousy place ourself?"

Carlos smiled. "Who else is gonna do it?"

"Sure, maybe we clean it up, but all those people gonna throw their garbage there again!"

"Yeah, who's gonna stop those people from dumpin' their junk inside the yard?"

"I don't know," said Carlos. "You're the only guys I know who even want to stop them."

Raphael got to his feet again. "We could make signs," he said, "and write a letter for our folks to read."

This was all agreed upon and the Royal Tigers formed a club. Then Carlos asked them when they thought they'd clean the empty lot.

"How about Thursday, man?"

"I won't be here Thursday," said Carlos.

"Why do you need you?" said Papo. "We know how to clean that junk!"

A few minutes later the meeting broke up and the kids drifted out into the street. Carlos and I stayed behind for a while talking, and then we went outside too. Carlos' house is down near the corner of 102nd

195

and Park, and we strolled slowly up the street discussing something about the project's training program. Then we drew abreast of the empty lot and were stopped short, dumbfounded. The staggering panorama! The theoretical breakthrough into commitment! The Royal Tiger technique of instant community action! Somehow those kids had acquired a couple of shovels and rakes, and now they were piling up garbage with a wild speed that resembled the rapid movements of comedians in old silent movies. Nor was there anybody urging them on, no hero shouting messages of encouragement to them. Carlos and I, in fact, simply leaned against a car fender and watched. This was slum self-help in the grand sense of the word.

Papo, who had the biggest shovel, was clearing a path through the litter to the back fence. All along the way, kids were piling up old bed frames and boards, yanking them from the earth where they'd been abandoned long ago. Then, out of a basement marched three kids lugging immense barrels, trashburners. And from the other side of the lot another kid materialized with, of all things, a wheelbarrow.

Meanwhile, up above the scene of this activity, one by one in the windows of the tenements lining the yard, spectators—women, mothers, grandmothers—appeared. Here and there was the face of a young girl. On each face was registered not surprise so much, or even shock, as out-and-out disbelief.

Finally one of the mothers could bear it no longer. She leaned out beyond the window ledge and yelled, "Willie! Willie, is that you?"

"What you want?" said Willie looking up. He was a thin kid, a 15-year-old not much wider than the rake handle he was wielding.

"What you doin' there?" his mother cried.

"What does it look like?" said Willie. "We gotta have a place to practice ball." He bent over to resume raking, and then looked up again. "Don't you throw no junk down here! Give you fifty dollar fine!"

The best way to change attitudes is through action. As we begin to take some action with our lives, we develop confidence and are more ready to cope with the next step. (Perhaps the crowning achievement of OEO was to create large numbers of people who came to distrust charity even more and therefore relied on their own efforts.)

On any given block, the legacy of a block worker is visible in many ways. There is a block association with a hard core of active members. There are several young people going to college where before there were none. There are rent strikes. And, often, there are summer programs funded by OEO but entirely managed by the block association.

But the greatest result is intangible—for the time at least. This is a sense of optimism on the part of many people who were once callous and cynical. There is the awareness that things will never be the same.

V. THE FAILURE OF OEO

There are those who cite OEO's stress on "maximum feasible partici-pation of the poor" as the cause of its imminent demise. All the shouting and screaming initiated by OEO programs and activities, they say, caused a backlash which produced, among other things, the Green Amendment making OEO a toothless tiger.

But it seems more realistic to contend that, if anything, OEO did not emphasize citizen participation enough. Little money was allocated for self-help efforts at the local level, and even less attempt was made to organize programs of self-help. It is my contention that OEO has never expected very much of the poor. If it has, it has never made these expectations explicit.

OEO's failings are many:

1. From its inception, OEO remained a patchwork of ideas and projects which have failed to evolve into a program. It has been devoid of goals to which a constituency could relate and respond. It is little wonder that the so-called constituency focused *only* on acquiring the ability to get services from OEO, rather than developing the means of providing those same services in an effort at self support.

2. OEO failed to organize effectively at the grass-roots level. For two weeks in July, 1966, Block Communities conducted interviews of over 500 poor people covering every block in East Harlem. Mothers were interviewed, junkies, teenagers, old men, civic leaders, welfare recipients, priests. These interviews were conducted by three local residents in training to become block workers. All interviews were taped. Out of 500 residents, only 72 were participating in some way in the program. Of this 72, 64 were either kids or counselors involved in summer youth projects. This leaves 8 people out of 500 participating in the program on a year-around basis. Extending these figures to all of East Harlem, it means that out of a community of 180,000 people, less than 3000 (1½%) were directly connected with the program.

3. OEO failed to develop a technology which would allow for indi-vidual and community growth. This technology would require an

intensive training program affecting all levels, within all agencies, which concurrently developed the ability of personnel to make effective demands on community groups.

4. OEO never fully realized that it was not a retreaded WPA. Thus, many people were hired, not because of ability, but because they needed a job. Had OEO been a $20 billion project, jobs could and should have been provided, without regard to ability. But under a limited budget too many jobs were handed out without regard to talent. There are talented people in a ghetto but they have to be sought out and trained. This generally has not happened. OEO jobs were scarce. Scarcity bred power and power bred corruption. In no small way, OEO at the local level helped to supplement the already corrupt *modus operandi* of the community power vendors.

5. The concept of community participation, by far the most unique of all OEO's concepts, was not only too narrowly conceived but its practitioners were too ready to accept form rather than substance. Community participation is not an end but a means to control over those institutions which surround us. Participation, and ultimately control over the forces which affect us, are absolutely vital for happy and productive lives. But participation, being construed so narrowly by OEO, involved only a tiny number of people. It tended to ask them to participate in programs which had little or no long-term relevance to the very institutions which they, for so long, sought to control—such as the school and the police.

OEO failed, not because of its commitment to participation, but because it did not place enough of its initial emphasis on participation and control; the latter would develop a genuine constituency before acting to meet the demands of its predetermined constituency.

VI. CONCLUSION

What does this indicate for the future? It means there must be a renewed commitment to citizen participation defined as self-help. OEO should divest itself of all service functions and instead become a Department of Community Development with the focus on teaching self-help in the hollow, on the block or barrio level. A highly trained national service corps tapping VISTA and the Teacher's Corps would provide only one-half the manpower for this effort. The rest would be well-trained, talented people from those neighborhoods to be affected.

Once the impact of this effort is felt, two things will happen: First, communities will initially look to their own resources rather than seeking charity from the outside. Second, the communities will make a much more effective use of resources available from the outside. They will take charity as an investment, not a dole, and will bargain better with those who want to help (sometimes to the discomfort of the do-gooders).

On my way to the office this morning, I saw Mr. Lugo and two teenagers out on the sidewalk sawing up boards from the burned-out building. "What are you doing?" I asked, trying not to look too amazed.

"We're making benches for the summer program. We've been here since 7:30.

We have had few spectacular successes on our blocks. But hundreds of people like Mr. Lugo know that something can be done about their lives—they are acting on their behalf and on behalf of their community. They have learned how to translate concern to movement and the result is a kind of tough optimism.

And BCI continues. Its headquarters is a rambling loft where block workers are being trained, where techniques are being refined under the patient tutelage of Tom Watkins. But the action continues to be on the street. In Brownsville, East and Central Harlem, the Bronx, South Jamaica, block workers (all of whom are now from the blocks where they work) continue to push and challenge people to confront issues and do something about the problems around them.

What BCI is doing could, with refinements, apply to any community, rich or poor, urban or rural, white or black in this country. The process of community development can be practiced by housewives serving as volunteers in their own community, by clergy, by teachers, by basketball coaches—anyone can learn the basic techniques of helping others to help themselves. It is a basic antidote for crime and deteriorated housing and terrible schools. But it is also an antidote for alienation, for boredom, for race hatred and for individual helplessness in an impersonal society.

199

COMMUNITY REPRESENTATION IN 20 CITIES

The Brandeis University Study

Editor's Note:

In June, 1966 the U. S. Office of Economic Opportunity granted funds to the Florence Heller Graduate School for Advanced Studies in Social Welfare of Brandeis University to make a comparative study of resident representation in community action programs in twenty cities.

The study was designed to provide (a) a description of the patterns and processes of representation of target area residents in CAA structures (b) a description of other forms of resident participation in CAA programs (c) insights into factors which make for differences in the extent and quality of participation (d) beginning information on the effects of difference in the extent and quality of participation (d) beginning information on the effects of differences in participation on the policies and programs of the CAA.

The actual time framework of the study was January, 1967–June, 1968. Following is a synopsis of the selection process, issues, findings and conclusions.

The selection of a sample of CAAs for intensive study was the first task for the research staff. The potential study population was reduced to 79 cities through application of the following restrictions: (1) the core urban community in which the CAA was based should have at least 50,000 population (2) the CAA should have received a grant for one program component other than Headstart by June 30, 1965 (3) the exclusion of New York City and Los Angeles because of size and complexity in relation to the research resources available. Of the 79 cities, Chicago, Detroit, Philadelphia and eight other cities were then excluded because they were already included in other major studies or because of their extreme distance from the study center.

Next the 68 cities were grouped by geographic region. Most of the cities fell within three general regions: Northeast-North Central, Southeast and Southwest. Nine cities fell outside these general regional clusters. This left a total of 59 cities stratified by region. A proportional sample was drawn using random numbers. It contained twelve in the Northeast-North Central area, four from the Border South and four from the Southwest-West Coast. For analysis purposes the Northeast and North Central regions were treated separately. The study cities were as follows:

Northeast
Hartford, Conn.
Waterbury, Conn.
Providence, R.I.
Scranton, Pa.
Wilkes-Barre, Pa.

Southeast
Charlotte, N.C.
Durham, N.C.
Huntington, W. Va.
Chattanooga, Tenn.

North Central
Cleveland, Ohio
Cincinnati, Ohio
Lorain, Ohio
Akron, Ohio
Flint, Mich.
St. Paul, Minn.
Milwaukee, Wis.

Southwest
Laredo, Texas
San Antonio, Texas
Phoenix, Ariz.
San Jose, Calif.

"Grass-roots," "asphalt-level," "citizen" or "community" participation in the planning and administration of community service programs has been a public issue since the beginning of large scale, federally financed service programs in local communities. It has been a central concern in the TVA, the county agricultural programs of the Department of Agriculture, urban renewal and the community action programs of the Office of Economic Opportunity. Recently it has become a critical issue in Model Cities planning and in the administration of public welfare and public education.

There is no single phrase which accurately summarizes the concept. "Community participation" and "citizen participation" are too general and inclusive to describe the particular emphasis of community action programs. "Participation of the poor" is not actually accurate since the involvement of individuals in decision-making within the CAA network has been more frequently tied to residence within particular geographic areas than to actual individual or family income.

The term "target area" has been used widely within the OEO to describe those geographic community areas which receive the most intensive service through the CAA. This term is part of the military campaign image implied in the phrase "War on Poverty"; but there is no other term which is as widely used and which has as consistent a meaning for persons involved with OEO programs at all levels.

Target area participation involves both community political issues and an organizational management issue. These issues overlap and have often become confused with each other. But they are different.

The issue at the community political level is direct representation in the formal control of service programs, governmental and non-governmental, of those community interests excluded from such positions. The power to control the operations of a community service organization normally rests with a group of individuals drawn from traditional community leadership groups. This power is exercised through the consensus decisions of the total membership or of a consistent majority on the policy board. The addition of target area representation on the policy board in sufficient strength to exercise a veto or block action by the majority dilutes the power of non-target area individuals and the interests they represent.

If this occurs in a series of organizations throughout the community, a share of the community authority which has been solely in the hands of those groups economically and politically dominant will shift to groups which have not yet achieved any significant economic or political power. This authority can be used by emerging groups to advance their own interests. Such a shift of authority will be resisted by those community groups which have traditionally held control. This creates a political issue in the broad sense of the word "political."

The issue at the organizational level is the strong, direct representation in the control and management of a service organization for the users or consumers of the services provided by that organization. The bureaucratic or corporate model of a formal organization includes a hierarchy of status and of authority. Policy-makers and management personnel are at the top of such a hierarchy. Persons receiving the services of the organization are considered to be at the bottom of the hierarchy or not actually part of the organization. Differences in status positions within the organization are generally, though not always, similar to status differences between the same individuals in the community outside.

Placing representatives of a consumer population that has low community status in positions of authority within the organization may disrupt traditional assumptions about status positions within the organization. Persons responsible for directing the operation of formal or bureaucratic organizations normally try to avoid such disruptions.

The inclusion of representatives of consumer groups in positions of authority also may result in demands upon the management of the organization which conflict with the recommendations of staff, or with the demands of other interests such as taxpayer groups or governmental funding sources. These demands add to the complexity of organizational management and may become an important organizational management issue.

At both the community political level and at the organizational management level, target area participation in strength will mean some change in the authority and power of other groups and interests and some increase in the level of difficulty and complexity involved in carrying out an organizational program.

Disagreements, controversy and conflict over the implementation of target area participation can be expected regardless of the nature of the program or the nature of the community setting. The actual form of the conflicts will differ between those that involve essentially organizational management issues and those that involve broader community political issues. In some situations both types of issues may be involved.

203

Many of the discussions and judgments about the role of participation reflect the assumption that, because there are federal legislation and federal guidelines, there is a common pattern of participation in CAAs and community action programs at the local level. Actually, a number of factors have led to a high degree of ambiguity in the relationship between the federal intent in participation and the actual development of target area participation in local communities.

There has been a variety of interpretations of the primary purpose of the CAA. There have also been various interpretations of the meaning of "participation." The lack of federal clarity, the fact that local CAA organizations were being established before the OEO administrative structure was completed, the urgency of beginning local programs as soon as possible in 1964-65, and local interpretations of participation made by civil rights and welfare rights organizations—all contributed to the possibility of having a variety of patterns of participation in individual communities.

The analysis of the data from the Community Representation Study indicates that there are, in fact, several patterns of target area participation which have developed in local communities under the same basic federal requirements. There are variations in the extensiveness of target area participation, in the degree of emphasis on the organizational or the political dimension of participation and in the extent to which target area board members and neighborhood associations have organized an adversary coalition within either the CAA or in the larger community.

These patterns of target area participation have a systematic relationship to characteristics of the community in which they are located.

A general model can be described which includes characteristics of cities, characteristics of the CAA, the pattern of target area participation, and relationships among these key elements. While this model does not account for all of the variations found among the CAAs and while the experience of any one community may vary on certain details from the overall model, the patterns described in the model are generally prevalent throughout the group of 20 cities.

The following are the key elements of the model:

1. The cities fit into four categories on the basis of a combination of demographic characteristics and form of government. These characteristics are (a) size—50,000 to 150,000, and over 150,000 (b) proportion

of black population in 1965 — 0-9%, and 10% and over (c) form of government—council-manager/commission or mayor-council. The four categories are:

- Small cities, those of 150,000 population and under.
- Large cities with a low proportion of black population, under 10%.
- Large cities with a high proportion of black population and council-manager governments.
- Large cities with a high proportion of black population and a mayor-council form of government.

2. In mayor-council cities a staff person from the city government participated with staff from non-governmental social welfare and education in the initial drafting of the plan of the CAA organizational structure. In council-manager cities the staff for this initial planning came from the non-governmental community welfare planning council and/or board of education; the city manager's office was not directly involved.

3. The basic structure of the CAA as established in all four categories of cities, in 1964 and early 1965, closely resembles a non-profit, non-governmental social welfare agency.

4. Two different patterns of initial CAA structure appear within the· framework of this basic organization form. The first pattern has a relatively large board (20 members or more) and a relatively small staff of persons employed directly by the CAA (under 20 employees). This can be described as a "representative" model, emphasizing broad representation of local organizations and interest groups, with the responsibilities of the CAA limited to planning, coordination, fiscal control and research. In this pattern direct service program operations are delegated to existing organizations. The second pattern, which can be described as a "management" pattern, involves a small board (under 20 members) and a relatively large CAA staff (over 20 employees). A smaller number of organizations, primarily those with direct operational responsibilities in the inner city or representing major power interests in the community, are on the board while the CAA responsibilities include the direct operation of some programs, and therefore the employment of operational staff. These two patterns of board-staff sizes do not have a direct relationship either to the categories of cities or to the patterns of target area participation.

5. A basic structure for target area participation in nearly all cities by mid-1967. It has these features:

a. The organization of voluntary associations almost exclusively on a neighborhood or locality basis.

b. Staff assistance to these associations from CAA staff employed in neighborhood service centers.

c. Target area representatives are one-third of the total membership of the CAA board, and have an attendance record which is equal to or higher than that of other board members in the same city.

d. Neighborhood associations have budgets of less than $100 a year for operating expenses and have few other organizational resources.

e. Sixty percent of all of the important issues acted on by neighborhood associations concern improvements to a single neighborhood.

f. Basic structures for target area participation emphasize participation of target area representatives as single members of the CAA board and action by neighborhood associations on concerns of individual neighborhoods; it is focused on organizational advisory participation, which does not include control of program or personnel. The structure does not encourage joint action by target area groups or individuals on common issues.

6. Around the general characteristics of participation there are four different patterns of participation structure and participation activities. These are systematically related to the four categories of cities:

Small Cities

Neighborhood-related units not begun until 1966-67.
Small proportion of black participants.
No inter-association council.
Neighborhood organizing is minor emphasis.
Pattern of target area participation activities at neighborhood level and within the CAA board is identified as *Limited Participation*.

Large City with Small Black Population

Neighborhood-based units begun in 1965.
Small proportion of black participants.
No inter-association council.
Neighborhood organizing is in support of service provision but is major emphasis within CAA.
Pattern of target area participation activities including neighborhood

associations and target area board members is identified as *Active Advisory Participation.*

Large City with Large Black Population, Mayor-Council Government

Neighborhood-based units begun in 1965.

High proportion of black participants.

External council formed by neighborhood association leaders to take joint action on issues within the CAA.

Neighborhood organizing under CAA is for support of service provision but is major emphasis.

Pattern of participation activities including participation of target area board members and of neighborhood associations is identified as *Internal Adversary Participation.*

Large City with Large Black Population, Council-Manager Government

Neighborhood-based units begun in 1965.

High proportion of black participants.

External council organized by neighborhood association leaders, and internal council organized by CAA.

Neighborhood organizing is separate from service programs and is major emphasis.

Total pattern of participation activities including activities of target area board members and of neighborhood associations is identified as *External Adversary Participation.*

Joint action among associations on community-wide issues outside the CAA primarily around issues of common interest to black citizens.

7. Attitudes of some groups of participants within the CAA structure show differences among the patterns of participation on key issues.

    a. Target area individuals, including association presidents, target area board members and non-professional staff, support protest activities and political activity by neighborhood associations in CAAs which fit the *External Adversary Participation* pattern.

    b. Target area individuals in all other types of CAAs disapprove such activities.

    c. Private board members in large cities identify social conditions as the cause of poverty and recommend action on such conditions as the solution to poverty; private board members in small cities do not support such an interpretation of the causes and solutions for poverty.

8. CAAs with either pattern of adversary participation have in common (a) an external council among associations and (b) neighborhood associations and target area board members who are almost entirely from a single minority ethnic group. In external adversary CAAs there were demands from groups acting for ethnic minority citizens and low-income citizens for representation on the initial CAA board, and such representation was provided. In internal adversary participation CAAs there were no such demands at the beginning of the CAA, or such demands were refused. There was pressure from ethnic groups both within and outside of the CAA for increased representation after the CAA board was established; this continued to be an issue even after one-third of the CAA board was made up of target area representatives.

When the actual distribution of data from the 20 cities and CAAs is compared with the dimensions used to describe the general model, there is a close fit. The location of a city in one of the four city categories leads to a correct prediction that 14 of the 20 cities fall into the four categories of target area participation patterns. Two of the special cases involve small cities where key staff members concerned with neighborhood organizing came from outside the local community and brought to the community a strong emphasis on organizing for action on community issues. In two large cities with large black population and council-manager form of government, which do not fit the pattern, a broad and firm community leadership consensus is dominant and has permitted little development of systematic neighborhood organizing from within target areas.

Conclusions

1. The requirement for "maximum feasible participation" has had an impact on the CAA in every city. It has created an opportunity for citizens from low-income neighborhoods to have a part in decision-making in an important community service program. It has encouraged groups of such citizens to organize to bring about changes in community conditions that perpetuate poverty. Such opportunities have not existed in past community service programs, and no other organization now extends such opportunities as widely as the CAA.

2. New opportunities for participation have been created primarily through two types of action by the federal government: (a) enforce-

ment of the requirements that one-third of the membership of policy-making bodies of the CAA must consist of target area residents, democratically selected and (b) financial support for neighborhood organizing as a program activity of the CAA.

3. The federal government has also been the source of major limitations on the opportunities for effective participation within the CAA: (a) through the restriction on the use of program funds and a reduction in local initiative funds and (b) by increasing the complexity of federal administrative rules and supervision, which reduces the ability of the CAA board and executive director to plan a local program appropriate to local conditions.

4. The use that is made of these *opportunities for participation* in a particular community has been largely determined by local conditions and local forces. Federal support for the concept of participation is a *necessary* condition, but it is not a *sufficient* condition to ensure that any specific pattern of participation does, in fact, take place.

5. A variety of participation patterns have emerged in local communities. These patterns are systematically associated with the characteristics of the city in which the CAA is located. The actual content of participation in a particular CAA is more directly affected by local conditions than by OEO requirements. The range of patterns extends from CAAs with no significant participation to cities in which participation has meant the organizing of action groups exclusively within black neighborhoods for a broad attack on community conditions harmful to black citizens. Both extremes fall outside the formal federal interpretation of participation.

6. The most important city characteristic associated with the level of participation activity is the population size of the city. Large cities in general have a more active pattern of target area participation within the CAA board and through the activities of neighborhood associations than small cities.

7. Within this study about one-third of the CAAs have a pattern of target area participation which results in no significant impact on decisions within the CAA or on other community service organizations; in about one-third of the CAAs target area participation does influence some decisions within the CAA, primarily through an advisory relationship between target area associations and spokesmen and the CAA, but there is little impact on other organizations; in the remaining one-third of the CAAs there is a regular and continuing influence on decisions within the CAA, including decisions on which representatives of target

area interests are opposed by other interests within the CAA, and there have been changes in the policies and programs of other community service organizations as a result of target area pressure.

8. In the one-third of the CAAs in which participation has had a continuing impact on critical decisions or has resulted in changes in other organizations, there is an action coalition among target area associations and target area members of the CAA board. Part of the structure of such a coalition is the establishment of a council of associations. Where such a coalition exists, one-third membership on the CAA board is sufficient for target area interests to win positive board action on controversial issues.

9. The most important city characteristic associated with the development of a coalition is the size of the black population within the city. Cities with an action coalition among CAA neighborhood associations are cities which have a large black population and in which most of the neighborhood associations are predominantly black.

Focus on Factors Limiting Participation

In the course of this study it has become evident that there are a number of factors in the operation of CAAs which generally restrict the scope and impact of target area participation, though their significance may vary from community to community. Some of the most important of these are described below.

The significance of target area participation through membership on the CAA board is reduced by restrictions on the ability of the entire CAA board to make important decisions. Federal earmarking of funds for particular programs and reductions in local initiative funds have reduced the range of program choices with which the board can deal. Moreover, these choices must be made during an intensive budget planning process which is concentrated in a few weeks out of the year. Fiscal complexities in program funding, funding delays, detailed fiscal and program accounting procedures and the practice of OEO regional staff in dealing directly with the CAA director rather than through the board on these details leaves the CAA board in the position of ratifying staff recommendations on complex packages of programs and budgets without information as to possible alternatives.

The significance of participation is also limited by a restricted definition by the CAA board of its responsibilities. The prevalent view at the local level is that the board is basically responsible for planning and overseeing the management of a particular group of program operations, funded by OEO and operated by or under the supervision of the CAA. This view excludes action on broader community issues, particularly if they are controversial, or action directed at the operation of other community service organizations whose services affect the program of the CAA. This narrow conception of the responsibilities of the CAA board prevents the CAA as a total organization from fulfilling its role as "advocate of the poor on matters of public policy which affect their status promoting institutional improvement and desirable changes in social policy." (CAP MEMO 80, February, 1968)

The potential impact of target area participation is also restricted by inherent limitations in the pattern of organizational associations on the basis of residential neighborhoods. Organizing around neighborhoods emphasizes the unique problems and interests of separate geographic areas rather than the interests of low-income persons throughout the city. The selection of target area board members by individual neighborhoods also serves to make them spokesmen within the board for a single area. The potential strength of associations and of neighborhood representatives on the CAA board is fragmented. Issues chosen by associations for action emphasize improvements in a single neighborhood. The membership of CAA neighborhood associations, as is true of most neighborhood associations, is predominately composed of women, and the issues chosen by the association reflect the interests of women as homemakers and mothers. Problems of out-of-school young adults and unemployed and underpaid men seldom receive much attention. Few of the issues on which action is taken at the neighborhood level deal directly with the problem of poverty. Most of them reflect the general inadequacy of public services and city housekeeping resources, which exists in all cities and affects most neighborhoods.

A pattern of program organization that makes neighborhood organizing and the support of neighborhood associations part of the program of individual neighborhood service centers, together with provision of a variety of specialized services, leads to an emphasis on the association as a program advisory group—a group which will provide community support for the center—rather than on its role as an independent action group. The potential for the development of the association as an action group is further restricted if service center staff carry responsibility for both service out-reach and providing assistance to an association. The ability of the association to operate independently is also restricted by the assumption that, with the resources of the service center available, there is no need for organizational resources, including operating

211

funds that are directly controlled by the association itself.

Another significant limitation on the effectiveness of participation is the confusion and ambiguity which exists in the relation of the CAA executive to target area groups and representatives. The CAA executive's role can be defined by various persons as: (1) local representative of a nation-wide federally administered program (2) staff assistant to the CAA board with responsibility to carry out its decisions (3) administrator of a large community program operating within broad policies set by the board (4) coordinator of diverse programs administered by a variety of independent agencies that deal with problems of poverty, the inner city and racial discrimination (5) the senior staff leader of a diverse staff of professionals and non professionals carrying out a difficult program which is frequently under community attack and requires constant defending (6) spokesman for the larger community in its relations with citizens in low-income neighborhoods (7) spokesman and advocate for those citizens who are the victims of discrimination and poverty. There is no agreement on which of these roles is more correct; no single executive can be all of them. Because there is no certainty as to what the role should be, it is not possible to agree on a formal channel called "participation" which involves the executive. Yet the widest range of decisions within most CAAs is made by the executive director.

Focus on Factors Supporting Participation

Other factors appear to be consistently associated with an active pattern of participation having a broad impact on the CAA and the community.

The significance of target area membership on the CAA board is increased if the CAA board itself controls a wide range of substantive decision-making. This may mean resisting efforts by OEO staff, by the CAA executive, by delegate agencies and even by individual service center boards or councils to remove areas of decision-making from the board. The active involvement of the CAA board in substantive decision-making not only means exposing such decisions to the possible impact of target area opinion, but also increasing the knowledge of board members about issues involved.

Effective organizing of citizens in low-income areas into associations that can take action on conditions which create and perpetuate poverty requires some basis of a sense of common identity other than being

212

poor. The traditional approach within the CAA, as in other social welfare approaches, is to assume that living together in a particular neighborhood provides that sense of common identity. But ethnic identity, age, common work situation or involvement with a single organization (public housing tenants, welfare rights) are often more powerful factors than neighborhood residence in creating this sense of common identity.

The impact of neighborhood organizing as a program activity of the CAA is increased when it is identified as a specialized program separate from the administration of service centers, organized on a community-wide basis and headed by an experienced administrator who is directly responsible to the CAA executive. While this removes some of the camouflage which has sometimes been used in introducing neighborhood organizing as a program activity, it makes it possible to carry out programs of training for staff and neighborhood leadership directly focused on methods of effective organizing. It can contribute directly to the development of patterns of joint action among various groups within target areas. This also makes it possible to bring into the CAA staff persons with experience in the development of organizing programs, and with a clear commitment to citizens associations as a method of action on critical community problems.

CHAMBERS OF COMMERCE
PARTICIPATION AND THE ESTABLISHMENT

by: Ivan C. Elmer

Editor's Note:

Ivan Elmer himself points to the peculiarity of including in this volume a monograph on the Chamber, the NAACP of the white middle class. The organizational techniques he cites are most appropriate to participatory efforts, however. His helpful hints—on organizing effectively, attracting people to an organization, using them productively, and using professional and volunteer leaders—have important overlaps into participation of the poor and minority groups.

There is also a poignancy to the historical development of the Chamber which may be satisfying to those who are already pessimistic about the future of the citizen participation forms of the 1960's.

Some questions:

1) How do Elmer's organizational principles contrast with those in the Zimmerman and Borden articles?

2) Are these analogies to the historic changes in participation in Chamber affairs in the history of the Urban League, the Urban Coalition and other bodies to which top business leaders give their names?

3) Beyond the examples cited, are there Chambers of Commerce which operate by the principles and policies set forth in the monograph? Or do others move in other directions?

Mr. Elmer has B.A. and B.J. degrees from the University of Texas and was active in intergroup relations work when he served as manager of Chambers in three Texas cities. He is Director of the Urban Action Clearing House and Committee Executive to the Urban and Regional Affairs Committee of the U.S. Chamber of Commerce. In 1969, he served on the President's Task Force on Voluntary Action Programs.

I. INTRODUCTION

It may appear absurd that those who would involve the poor more effectively in influencing their own futures would turn for guidance to that stereotype of Establishment Status Quo, the Chamber of Commerce movement, for examples of citizen participation.

Yet, when the cliches are brushed aside there appear countless examples of organized, voluntary community-wide action under the guidance or sponsorship of local chambers of commerce.

Strong supporting trends in the chamber of commerce field reinforce the desire for "maximum feasible participation." The history of chambers of commerce holds important cautions, however, on what may be feasible and on the methods by which participation can be maximized.

Chambers of commerce were not originated to provide a vehicle for citizen participation. They began, as the name implies, as assemblies of men with commercial interests seeking to promote, to protect or to change, as their interests required. They are voluntary, independent and—with rare exceptions—financed entirely by dues payments of their members.

But being business oriented, chambers of commerce tend to be pragmatic about what can get a job done, rather than holding to theory as a primary guide to action. Experience over more than 200 years told an evolving but increasingly clear story: economic benefits can only be realized in a reasonably stable, prosperous community; and broad participation is an essential part of success in community improvement activity.

Today total involvement is "the word" in chamber of commerce circles. This does not mean that chambers try to become an organization to do all things for all people; it is a businessman's organization and will continue to be. But chambers are now expending great energy encouraging their constituents to recognize the need for involvement of all community elements in the community decision making process. They are devoting an increasing effort to forming the kinds of local mechanisms that can give other groups as well as the businessman an effective voice in determining the community's future course.

II. HISTORY OF THE CHAMBER OF COMMERCE MOVEMENT

The first chamber of commerce in America—and the first completely independent commercial organization ever formed—was the New York Chamber of Commerce, founded April 5, 1768. Its Latin motto, "Non

Nobis Nati Solum" meant "Not Born for Ourselves Alone."

The Houston Chamber of Commerce, formed in 1840, was the first known to be created with a primary motive of serving the community. The capitol of the Republic of Texas had just been moved from Houston, currency was devalued, loans were cut off and yellow fever was nearing epidemic rate. Businessmen formed the chamber in part to combat growing sentiment to abandon the city. Almost immediately the chamber organized programs to improve health conditions— including a rat control program that worked.

As late as 1900 there were fewer than 100 local chambers of commerce. Their objectives were commercial; their activities were regulatory, promotional and developmental. Late in the period they began articulating the relationship between primary aims and broader needs— the inescapable facts that business could not be better than the environment in which it operated.

Early decades of the 20th Century brought more and more chambers of commerce, and many of them included in their statements of purpose the words ". . . cultural and civic improvement" along with business development.

This was a period of flamboyant growth and expansion in America. Business possibilities became more closely tied to developing new cities and new areas. Boosterism was at its giddy peak, with extravagant descriptions, noisy trade promotion tours, community picnics and county fairs—the type of activity that came to characterize the chamber of commerce movement.

Yet chambers of commerce also led actions to secure paved streets, sidewalks, city parks, better schools, city planning and good government, street cars and touring opera.

The Chamber of Commerce of the United States was chartered by Congress in 1912 to assist in bringing the views of the business community to Congress and to be a co-ordinating force in focusing the energies of voluntary organizations on progress of America's communities.

Chambers of commerce were changing internally in several important ways at this time the most important being the extensive broadening of the base of support and participation that accompanied an expanding range of activities. A series of cause-and-effect relationships can explain the change.

First, the effects of a broader effort were widely felt in the community. (In other words, benefits of the chamber fell upon more people than the top business leadership). Performing the expanded programs cost money, time and effort. The small top group was unwilling to pay all this cost, since the benefits were widespread.

In this way came a pressure to gain financial support from a broader base of citizens, albeit still primarily a business base. This brought the second cause-and-effect link: just as the larger supporters were unwilling to finance all of an effort from which they did not gain all the benefits, so the individuals and smaller businessmen were unwilling to share in financing the effort unless they also shared in the decisions as to what would be done.

By the end of World War Two, chambers of commerce were thorough-going community organizations, willing to speak for (or about) their communities to all who would listen. Their numbers had grown from less than 100 at the turn of the century to more than 5,000. They were frequently the best-financed and most fully staffed of any organization in their city. They tended to be community-problem solvers on a wholesale level.

Reducing unemployment, raising family incomes, cleaning up slums, providing adequate services to all areas of our cities, setting up adequate building and housing codes, replacing sub-standard homes—these "social" goals were listed in the objectives of practically every chamber of commerce in the land.

But the local chamber of commerce leadership abhorred "do gooder" projects initiated by bleeding hearts or social workers. To the chamber, it was "a matter of dollars and *sense*". So the chamber of commerce went its way, interpreting all its actions in economic terms for the benefit of its business constituency. And what could not be couched in money terms was frequently excluded from discussion with a curt, "That is not our concern; that is a job for Welfare or the United Fund or the Church".

Few chamber leaders attempted to deny at this point the social or moral implications in economic decisions. Nor did they deny economic effects from social decisions. But, by and large, chambers staked out for their own goals those actions that produced direct economic improvement or directly influenced economic gain. The trap was that no one could predict when or how much a social problem might escalate into a major economic problem.

Every device within reason was used to involve chamber members in setting the goals and program of work of the chamber. The phrase, "Let them write it and they will underwrite it," became an axiom for assur-

217

ing continued financial support. This involvement of chamber members, however, did not mean rapid changes in direction.

Key business leaders awakened sooner than most professional chamber of commerce leaders. And the mass awakening for chambers began when many of them recognized they were losing the active participation of these top leaders in the local chambers. The chief executives were becoming "too busy" and began suggesting second or third echelon officers to represent the company on the Chamber board of committees.

To attribute all such change to this or any other single cause would be over-simplification. But in case after case chambers had defined their scope of operation more narrowly than the top business leader believed could be effective in representing the company. The chamber had defined itself out of its traditional place of high influence with business itself at a time when financial support mounted to record levels.

The nation had changed. Laws had changed. The business system had come through 25 years of shock from depression, war and armed stalemate to find that it could survive and prosper under conditions previously considered to be fatal. Many of the nation's historic economic goals had been met, and continued yammering about them was no longer productive.

The chamber movement, sensing danger, asked itself with more feeling than ever before, "What are we? What is our place in the world?"

III. POINTING THE WAY

Chambers of commerce, uncertain about their role in society, faced a dilemma on their dual loyalties to business and to the community. While disagreement was widespread within the movement as to what should be done, there was little doubt that the way chambers of commerce approached community improvement needed improving.

There was something badly wrong in our cities, and it was not confined to the chamber movement. City government, other institutions and an increasingly restless citizenship were equally frustrated at the course of events, the conditions of our cities and their ineffectiveness in dealing with problems.

A way must be found, said leaders of many groups, in which we can more harmoniously work together to meet urban needs. The National Chamber had launched a series of businessmen's conferences on urban development in 1947, continuing at intervals until 1958. A special ad-

218

visory committee to the Construction and Civic Development Department of the National Chamber was formed in 1955 with representatives of community organizations, government and national organizations concerned with community affairs. The advisory groups prepared an Urban Development Guidebook, intended for municipal and business leaders. In this Guidebook appeared far-reaching suggestions for involving the citizenship more effectively in community affairs. A section of the Guidebook contained the following recommendations:

Citizen Participation Must Be Organized

An astonishing amount of help for urban development activities can be obtained by inviting, receiving and considering suggestions for such a community improvement program. However, this form of citizen participation is not automatic. It must be organized.

In sizeable communities the organization of citizen participation must be set up as a full-time job. This is a job which should not be done by the local government. A municipal administration which is active in urban renewal programs is under pressure to justify its every action. There would be a temptation to use the machinery of citizen participation for this purpose. Therefore, it is a protection to the public and also to the public officials to have the organization of citizen participation established beyond any possibility of official municipal control.

In many cities the chamber of commerce may be the appropriate place for the organization of citizen participation activities. The chamber is concerned with all the activities of urban development and usually has accepted the responsibility for building community support for urban development programs.

Flexibility of Participation Program Needed

One more reason for having adequate organizational facilities behind citizen participation programs is the need for an occasional change of focus. At one time the whole community will have to be aroused to support community-wide activities such as the enactment of a housing code. At other times the citizen participation must be spotlighted on a specific neighborhood or project area such as would be done in the relocation of displaced persons. The obvious change of attention from area to area requires a system of communications which will function under all conditions.

219

Merits of this approach, compared to generally used approaches, seemed apparent to many leaders at both local and national levels. But the concept was not filled out with enough specific action steps so that it could be truly helpful.

In 1959 the National Chamber agreed to underwrite the production of guidance materials that could be adapted to local conditions across the nation. Another representative advisory council was created to prepare these materials.

Their work produced the Balanced Community Development program. It turned attention back to two basics: people and existing organizations. The preface to pamphlets in the Community Development series, published in 1960, contained this explanation:

The techniques and procedures suggested in these pamphlets for coping with community development problems are based on four assumptions:

1. That no single organization in any community—including the local government and the chamber of commerce—has within itself all of the resources required to accomplish balanced community development.

2. That the methods and procedures now being used by communities have not proved to be wholly adequate for solving many of the complicated and controversial community development problems.

3. That some procedure to ensure broader and more effective citizen participation will be required for dealing with many of these problems.

4. That existing community organizations and institutions, with coordinated leadership and widespread citizen understanding and support, can find ways to develop acceptable local solutions to even the most difficult problems.

It is notable that while citizenship participation was the central theme of the 1960 series, the actions called for from the citizenship process were directed at the physical problems of the cities.

The chamber movement had not yet been able to bring itself into the arena of individual "people" problems. But that was to come.

A series of case reports were compiled in 1963 and published to show how 18 of the early pioneers of this approach had organized themselves. By 1965 the Balanced Community Development concept had been tried in many cities of a wide range of sizes. For the most part it had seemed to work best in smaller cities. In 1965 the concept was

meet social needs as well as physical
concept of crosssection leadership
ine and set priorities for meeting

ons, incorporating the refinements,
"Forward Thrust—A Process for
ces."

ed about more community matters
day are joining groups that involve
Ironically, however, there has been
portunity for involvement that is
es, there is no common forum for
ms together. There is no common
eeded to explore problems objec-
cedure to develop consensus and
of great public concern. There are
le and groups to pull together.
odern America—fragmentation in
d federal activities, fragmentation
racial and religious backgrounds;
themselves; fragmentation among
or and civic organizations.
nication gaps among groups, to
cooperation, to mistrust and sus-

eloped from the most successful
indispensable role of true citizen

gether people and groups in a
objectives, (2) name problems
ojectives; (3) examine available
ems, (4) establish priorities, and

nent of success for FORWARD
majority of citizens feel they
futures because of FORWARD
angible successes give little com-
they do not "belong," that they
are unimpressed by "progress,"
, for they know the progress is

not of their doing, not for their benefit. If the answer is "Yes", the community has taken a towering forward step regardless of immediate physical results, the climate is being created in which future problems can be forestalled or solved. The essence is people—people working together, involved, participating in discussions, finding a personal meaning in the community in which they live and work.

Numbers of chambers of commerce have taken aggressive steps to build opportunities for citizen participation in vital community decisions, following generally the concepts of FORWARD THRUST.

Two basic approaches seek this goal from differing angles. In one of them the community leadership structure solicits a frank and continuing dialogue with leaders of citizens and civil rights groups. The dialogue does not broaden to include the average citizen. Citizen group leaders are encouraged to strengthen their groups and involve them in defining and working at solutions to problems.

Hartford, Conn., and Schenectady, N. Y. illustrate this approach by chambers of commerce.

The Greater Hartford Chamber of Commerce had directed many of its efforts toward improving conditions of its minorities and poor for a dozen years. Its leaders estimate that 80% of its total effort now goes to meeting socio-economic problems. In 1964, as the business leadership watched the growing fragmentation of the metropolitan community, they organized a modern-day counterpart to the old New England town meeting, called "Town Meeting for Tomorrow." Its purpose was to bring together all possible community group leaders and to let them talk with each other and with experts gathered for the series of meetings to suggest new approaches to stubborn problems. Hundreds of people participated, but all were leaders in some degree. Top business leaders challenged citizen group leaders to take information from the meeting to their constituents and to bring back information from their people to future meetings. Discussions in "Town Meeting" have been reconvened periodically up to the present.

In Schenectady, the chamber called leaders together in 1965 to respond to a community crisis. The community needed to clarify its thinking on what its future should be and how it would go about achieving that future. From this start came a regular informal, frank exchange among leaders of the chamber, local government, and citizen groups, especially civil rights organizations. These leaders talk priorities, methods and resources to meet community needs. Job training and low-cost housing on a large scale have been two of the community actions that have resulted.

The second basic approach to build opportunities for more citizen participation is to organize a formal public effort to solicit the views and action of all possible citizens. The Dayton, Ohio, chamber illustrates this approach.

In Dayton, citizen participation has probably been carried farther in direct influence over chamber of commerce policy than in most other localities. In late 1965 the chamber set up a 25-member community development committee to communicate with all the major interest groups of the Dayton area. The chamber proposed that the committee review all public capital improvement needs and suggest priority schedules. Within a short while the committee could be seen falling short of being an adequate communication or study group because there was too large a task and too few participants. In 1967 the Dayton leadership created an Area Response Council composed of a representative of every neighborhood or civic organization in the area. Membership soon passed 250 persons, who became the core of a large grass roots information apparatus. Monthly discussions air current key issues and serve as a basis for a formal balloting by the member organizations on the most crucial community needs.

The Council depends on organization response, and local government units rely heavily on this response in making decisions about public questions. The Dayton Area Chamber of Commerce Board of Directors has agreed not to endorse any public proposal without prior approval by the Area Response Council.

These four chambers of commerce illustrate actions by hundreds of such organizations—perhaps a majority of them. They point to one direction the chamber movement can pursue. And they show how greater citizen participation can result through this and other existing institutions.

These changes must be placed in perspective. Yearning for effective involvement by more people did not begin with passage of the Economic Opportunity Act in 1964, any more than it began with the chamber of commerce movement 200 years earlier. Throughout history, the search for greater voice and influence has spurred individuals and classes and societies to improve old institutions and create new ones. The changes in the chamber movement offer substantial reason to hope that more nearly perfect (or "maximum feasible") participation can be achieved by improving, rather than discarding, the institutions we now know.

PARTICIPATION IN THE URBAN SCHOOL SYSTEM
A WASHINGTON CASE

by: Gail Saliterman

Editor's Note:

In the aftermath of Ocean Hill-Brownsville and IS 201, it may seem peculiar to read a case study of so genteel a school confrontation as this Washington case.

Gail Saliterman had a most unusual vantage point, however. Now an adjunct lecturer at Herbert H. Lehman College of the City University of New York, she served from late 1964 to 1966 as Assistant Director of the Model School Division of the D.C. school system. She was executive assistant to the chairman of the Advisory Committee and directed an experimental in-service training program.

Her "insider's" thesis is helpful: she shows the present rigidity in institutionalized educational bureaucracy; describes the great skill and sophistication used to bypass citizen participation; and makes clear the parameters of successful efforts by citizen groups to restructure public school systems. Some questions:

1) Compare the D. C. Model School case to the events in Ocean Hill. Does it hold, for example, that "the wider the scope of the conflict, the more the advantage accrues to the weaker groups?" Where does a strong teachers' union fit into the power scheme laid out in the study? Can the games run on the D. C. group be run in 1969, with the Black Power experience of the past two years? Isn't D. C. a special case in any event, with its plantation traditions and lack of representative government? Or, are public school systems similarly insulated in other cities?

2) Are alternative systems of education—peoples' schools, street academies—the answer to the effectiveness of current school bureaucratic structures?

3) Is there inevitably a confrontation between school bureaucracies and citizen groups wanting change? Are cooperation models extinct?

Miss Saliterman received her B.A. from the University of Michigan and M.A. in Political Science from Yale. She attended the London School of Economics and is completing a Ph.D. at American University. She has worked in Latin America and for the Education Division of Xerox Corporation and has been a consultant for several government agencies.

Introduction

The heightened intervention of the Federal government in education through its review of civil rights compliance activities, support of curriculum development projects, and special efforts to aid the disadvantaged has forced school issues into the national political arena, forcibly dispelling the 70-year myth of a non-political education system.

The ideology that a public institution, maintained by allocations of public funds, could be non-political if it so chose, served the efforts of educators to professionalize their occupation without jeopardizing their reliance on governmental financial support. The writings of the late 19th century muckrakers, exposing instances of obvious manipulation of school jobs and budgets by local political machines, gave weight to the demands of educators for more autonomy. As a result, the public school sytems were able to sever their explicit ties with the two-party system. Separate, ostensibly non-partisan, Board of Education elections, separate taxing capacities, and separate budgets—all contributed to an ideology that greatly enhanced the ability of each school system to isolate itself from the normal public review of public institutions. It required the failure of schools to educate the deprived and segregated, a new awareness of the poverty cycle, and the growth of black militancy to initiate demands for a change.

The demands for change have been of two basic types. One is the demand for new programs, special courses, team teaching, non-graded schools, and so on, all designed to help students, particularly ghetto students, learn more.[1] The organizational resistances to these innovations, to be expected in any large organization, particularly a service organization that operates without the sweep of the profit motive, triggered the second demand for citizen participation. In its most radical form, this demand is for community control of educational decision making. More mild forms of involvement may include using local parents as aides or activating parent-teacher-association-type organizations.

Advocates of citizen participation believe that once the citizens are involved, the school system will become more responsive to their

[1] By far the vast majority of . . . educational innovations thus far developed do not demonstrate any special knowledge of lower-class patterns and therefore they are not uniquely beneficial to lower-class students. If anything, those that work probably work even better for middle-class students, widening, rather than narrowing, the gap between the two classes.

interests and this, hopefully, will result in more effective education, particularly in the disadvantaged areas. They derive their arguments in support of this concept from the two most often opposing traditions in American political thought of classical democracy and modern pluralism. [2] The contemporary theory of citizen participation is like the democratic theory of Rousseau, James Mill, and John Stuart Mill in that both believe participation in political affairs is vital first, for an individual's self-improvement, second, as the primary means of protecting his self-interest, and third, as a way of building a sense of community. Yet, while the classical democrats believed that through universal participation a general will of all the people would emerge, today's supporters of citizen participation reject the notion of a single general will as utopian. Instead, they accept the basic theoretical assumption of the pluralists that politics is the process of resolving inevitable conflicts among various interests, but see no basis for concluding, as do the pluralists, that the presence of multiple centers of power means the American system of government is basically equitable.

Quite the contrary, citizen participation is viewed as a way of organizing those individuals who are presently excluded from policy decision-making arenas in order to ensure that their interests are taken into account. Thus, having observed that there is no single general will, but many heterogenous wills, the advocates of citizen participation simply want to rectify the fact that the will of the poor, because they are least articulate, have the fewest resources, and most apathy, is ignored. The absence of the poor from political decision-making processes must end because it has permitted the institutionalization of biases that, in and of themselves, perpetrate a state of poverty. In other words, citizen participation is no longer considered a device for arriving at some ideal general consensus; nor is it merely a way of helping individuals to improve themselves. Instead, it is an organizational method for altering the existing social order.

Yet, given this ideology of citizen participation, in combination with the recent demands for changes in the educational systems, local school districts still seem able to continue with almost universal success to inhibit any citizen participation that strives to alter the existing policy bias in favor of its middle-class clients. In New York City, efforts to

[2] For a discussion of classical democracy and contemporary pluralism, see Charles A. McCoy and John Playford, editors, *Apolitical Politics, A Critique of Behavioralism,* New York (Thomas Y. Crowell Co.,) 1967. Also see Cahn & Cahn article, above.

increase community control through school decentralization not only caused the entire school system to be closed down for three months, but to the extent that a tentative resolution has been possible, it is founded on the intervention of the state government, further inhibiting the possibility of local citizen participation. Similarly, a recent article on the Philadelphia school system pessimistically reported that "the North Philadelphia Model School District is dead, and the experiment in community participation at the proposed Pichett School in Germantown is mired in a confused confrontation among administrators, community groups and the board."[3]

If institutions like the school system are particularly successful in resisting citizen participation, is it necessary to conclude that the concept should be forgotten? It is the purpose here to discuss one attempt to use a citizen's group to change an urban school system and to derive, from this analysis, a strategy to be used to undermine the generally effective resistance with which efforts at citizen participation are usually confronted. Only if a strategy for change is employed will citizen participation fulfill its promise as a device for bringing about basic social change.

Specifically, the case study documents the unwillingness and inability of a large urban school system to relinquish any management control or decision-making power. It is a particularly interesting instance of citizen participation because the individuals involved were not the poor, but were prominent, articulate members of the middle-class community; their failure, therefore, reflects the difficulties all outside groups have in trying to confront and to alter any ongoing organization, independent of the usual problems associated with organizing the poor. Understanding the ways in which contemporary American bureaucracies resist outside interference may help advocates of citizen participation develop a strategy for effectively limiting this tendency.

The Schools and the Disadvantaged

A school system's superior access to the poor—it touches every child—may make it the institution best able to coordinate new efforts to eliminate poverty. School personnel are confronted every day with evidence of the effect of a child's background on his ability to learn.

[3] John P. Carr, "School Reform Died in an Angry Turmoil," Philadelphia *Inquirer*, December 29, 1968.

228

Although other institutions may be created to meet the external needs of the child and his family, the school could hire personnel to ensure unity and access to the array of services being made available to the community—legal assistance, medical care, welfare benefits, and job retraining. At the same time, representatives of other institutions, such as police and probation officers, by working more closely with school staff, may more effectively carry out their primary task of preventing more serious problems from arising.

School systems will have to alter radically their own philosophy and structure if they are to cope with these new tasks. There is growing realization that the rules which govern the existing school system are such that the disadvantaged child may enter with handicaps so great the probability of his succeeding is extremely small. These rules are being changed. Schools have tried to compensate the educationally disadvantaged with longer school days and with remedial programs. Either those in need do not participate or their participation makes little difference. Educators are realizing that supplementary services are necessary for some children, but they alone are not a sufficient answer to the problem of teaching disadvantaged children.

The institutional structure of the school needs to be redesigned to permit and encourage activities which will affect the motivation and success of the disadvantaged children who participate. The ability to succeed in school and thereby be further motivated to learn is particularly important for children in ghetto areas because not to learn in school is a more disabling phenomenon for them than it is for more fortunate children. While the advantaged child is exposed to a number of educational experiences, all of which can compensate him if he is not able to utilize his formal educational experience to its fullest extent, school may be the slum child's only hope.

New sources of funds for education have recently generated a large number of demonstration projects in schools. Few of these efforts have been rigorously analyzed.[4] But even if the data from the programs had been more carefully collected, it would have provided little information about the impact that changes in the structure or organization and meaningful citizen participation can have on learning. Most of these programs have been limited in scope and superficial in their institu-

[4] See for example two excellent descriptive but unquantified reports: *Progress Report*, Higher Horizons, Board of Education of the City of New York, January 1963, and *The Annual Report*, 1963-64, The Phoenix Project in Pupil Motivation, Phoenix, Arizona.

tional changes and almost none have permitted local members of the community affected by the school system to be involved in the educational decision-making process. Thus far, most school systems receiving new funds designated for helping the educationally disadvantaged have sought to do so through "additions to school programs, staff, curricular programs and related services."[5] For example, most of the monies that school systems have received from the Elementary-Secondary Education Act of 1965 have been used for remedial specialists and counselor-social worker teams. Although such projects "may *add* something to the educational scene in each respective community . . . (they will *not*) necessarily change anything about the educational structure, or process or goals of the community."[6]

The disadvantaged have not demanded the services they need from the school bureaucracy for three reasons. First, this clientele lacks the political, verbal and motivational muscle to demand better education for themselves and their children. Second, and because of the first factor, funds for education have been distributed along a gradient of influence, with those most in need receiving the least.[7] And third, the school bureaucracies, isolated from community pressure, have become ingrown and rigid in their responses.

Such rigidity reduces conflict and uncertainty, at the expense of innovation.[8] Thus innovation is inhibited at the very time that the schools need most to be devising new methods of meeting new, as well as old needs.

For the middle-class parent the school offers driver training, social dancing, shop work and college placement. The disadvantaged child does not always even encounter a curriculum which insures that he will pass the minimum tests to be an apprentice in a union. He rarely finds courses scheduled to meet his needs to work as he studies. Outside groups, aware of such facts, need to link the total services of the community—city government, welfare service, legal aid, labor unions and so on —to the schools. School systems will then be better able to meet the needs of this presently less-helped community. Given new ties, demands for greater services would be made on the schools to which

[5] Robert Dentler, *Strategies for Innovation in Education: A View from the Top*, Public Policy Institute, Oct. 15-16, 1964, pp. 2-3.

[6] *Ibid.*, p. 16.

[7] *Ibid.*, p. 22.

[8] Victor A. Thompson, "Bureaucracy and Innovation," *Administration Science Quarterly* June 1965, p. 4.

they will be able to respond. For example, once discussions between labor unions and school officials begin, it should be possible for the unions to help develop curricula which would permit rapid assimilation of graduates into apprenticeships. In response to this and other new pressures the school system would hopefully begin to make appropriate changes.

Recognition of the special needs of the disadvantaged is not new, but efforts to organize members of the community as a way of bringing new solutions to bear upon them is new. The creation of the Model School Division and its Advisory Committees is one such recent effort.

The Model School Division

On June 17, 1964, the District of Columbia Board of Education approved the creation of the Model School Division as an organizational means of providing a new educational experience for disadvantaged students. The Division, located in a low-income area, included a vocational school, a high school and the three junior high and fourteen elementary schools which fed into it. Five pre-school centers opened in local churches on October 1, 1964. The funding for the Division, above and beyond the normal school budget, was to come from the local action agency, slated to receive funds under the then new Office of Economic Opportunity (OEO).

The concept of a Model School Division was first proposed by a panel on education sponsored by the U. S. President's Science Advisory Committee. The panel outlined a number of substantive ideas for improving education in ghetto schools in a report, *Innovation and Experiment in Education.*[9] The panel members concluded, however, that the simultaneous implementation of more than one or two of these innovations required more administrative flexibility than is usually present in large urban school systems.

To counter this tendency towards inflexibility, the panel recommended that any school system attempting to implement a number of new ideas should create a "model sub-system" within the existing

[9]*Innovation and Experiment in Education*, The Panel on Educational Research and Development, Washington, D. C., (Government Printing Office) March 1964, pp. 34-36. These ideas included innovations such as curriculum development, teacher education, extra hours, new housing, flexible zoning, use of inspired amateurs, nongraded schools, team teaching, teacher resource rooms, preschool centers, work study programs, music and art center, and student book allowances.

school district. The sub-system would perform all the services necessary for running schools, but also it would "be an experimental system, with freedom to experiment across the board—curriculum, recruitment of teachers, utilization of teachers, the management of the system itself."[10]

To insure the continual infusion of new ideas and to create additional pressure for lessening the reluctance of any complex organization to depart from existing procedures, the panel members argued that "the model sub-system would have its own lay advisory council or 'board,' including members of the school staff, members of academic faculties of universities and artists, musicians, writers, lawyers, and other interested people from the community."[11] In other words, citizen participation from a wide rage of groups in the community was viewed as a device for bringing about organizational change. The inclusion of these outsiders in the "cooperative direction of a comprehensive experiment" offered a way to check the propensity of the Superintendent and other school officials to treat both programs—the regular and the experimental—alike.[12]

In addition, the panel members believed the existence of an Advisory Committee would benefit the sub-system both by providing a broader perspective within the experiment and by helping to involve new community resources. With new sources of funds, new ideas, new community contacts, and administrative freedom to experiment across the board, the sub-system would have an opportunity to make a major breakthrough in the current efforts to educate the disadvantaged.[13]

[10]*Ibid.*, p. 36. Generally, school officials from the central office have functional responsibilities, such as purchasing, research, pupil appraisal, personnel, and maintenance, that comprehend all schools in the district. In theory, at least, an independent, self-contained unit would not be responsible to these officials; instead, arrangements would have to be made within the sub-system itself for the carrying out of these functions. To the extent that such independence were not granted, the freedom of the sub-system to experiment would be reduced. It may, however, be unrealistic to expect a complex organization to free completely any sub-unit without intense internal struggle.

[11]*Ibid.*, p. 37.

[12]*Ibid.*, p. 38.

[13]Other educational reformers have, subsequently, had similar insights regarding the linkage between the organizational structure of school systems and their ability to implement new programs, and they have advocated some form of independent district or gradual decentralization as a way of ensuring administration freedom. See for example, Marilyn Gittel, *Participants and Participa-*

Shortly after the Board of Education approved the recommendation to establish a Model School Division, the Superintendent appointed an Assistant Superintendent to be in charge of it. Together, the Superintendent, the Assistant Superintendent of the Division, and the Director of the Community Action Agency funding the Division appointed thirteen individuals to a citizen's Advisory Committee. The staff member of the Office of Science and Technology who had drafted much of the panel's report, although not officially a part of the appointment process, was also involved in selecting the Advisory Committee members. As a result, the members selected represented a wide range of interests and backgrounds.

One of the thirteen appointed was the Chief Judge of the District Court of Appeals. He was elected Chairman of the Committee. Two of the thirteen were members of the Board of Education. Their views as to the role of the Advisory Committee were, however, by no means identical. The fourth member was an officer of the national parent-teacher association and the fifth was the head of the local Urban League. One member was a noted philanthropist and two members taught at Howard University. Only two of the thirteen members could purport to "represent" the community directly affected by the Model School Division. One was a resident of the community and the other was a minister with a congregation in the area. Finally, the other three members were practicing professionals in various fields.

It is perhaps testimony to the progress of the ideology of community participation that, in 1964, when the Superintendent and the Board of Education first agreed to implement the sub-system, the federal commitment to the idea that the citizens most involved with the institutions and policies under experimentation should participate in their decision-making processes was quite new.[14] Thus, although adherence to the phrase "maximum feasible participation of the poor" had been employed, at least nominally, in the selection of the board of the Community Action Agency, no one, not even OEO or the local Community Action Agency, viewed the Advisory Committee as the forum in which the views of the Advisory Committee would be represented. In fact, quite to the contrary, the supporters of a committee to

tion, *The New York City School System*, New York, (Praeger Publishers) 1967; *The Report on New York School Decentralization* (The Bundy Report); David Rogers, *110 Livingston Street*, New York (Random House) 1968.

[14]Adam Walinsky, a review of Daniel P. Moynihan, *Maximum Feasible Misunderstanding*, The New York *Times Book Review*. February 2, 1969, p. 1.

permit citizen participation in school decision making viewed the problem as one that required a blue-ribbon committee; it was sufficient that the board of the Community Action Agency, with its representatives of the poor, approved the recommendations for membership.

The selection of members for the Advisory Committee raises an important question regarding the "representativeness" of any citizen's committee, rich or poor. In the case of the Model School Division Committee, it was assumed that the invitation to be a member, along with the search for diversity, would enhance the effectiveness of the Committee. Yet, in actual operation, the apathy of some members, enabled others within the Committee to have far more power than the original balance intended, and the diversity would have probably caused internal dissension, had the Committee ever been able to function according to the panel report outline. Furthermore, the invitational selection process meant that the Committee was not the product of a specific position to be taken vis-a-vis the school system. Its members were neither motivated partisans nor full-time professionals.

In contrast, if citizen participation is organized around the support of a compelling issue, both apathy and crippling dissent may be avoided or minimized. Such a strategy also eliminates the question of representativeness by focusing on the issues that generate the maximum interest rather than on the individuals who purport to speak for the most people.

The Citizens' Advisory Committee

Once the Board of Education recommended that a model sub-system and an advisory committee be established, at least three alternative courses of action were open to the Superintendent of Schools and the Executive Director of the local Community Action Agency. One was to appoint the Advisory Committee and charge it with the task of creating an operational sub-system, developing programs, and assisting their initiation, in the manner implied by the Science Advisory Panel. This, needless to say, would have been a departure from the usual school system procedure.

A second alternative was to give the Assistant Superintendent of the Model School Division and his staff, who were already involved in developing the specific projects to be implemented in the designated schools, the authority to develop the administrative structure and pro-

234

cedures needed to implement an innovative program.[15] This may or may not have involved the use of the citizens who were at this time in the process of being appointed members of the Advisory Committee, but it would have been a step in the direction of real decentralization of power.

Instead, the school system followed a third alternative. It illustrates the techniques and methods available to a large bureaucracy for suppressing any attempt to involve outsiders who threaten the status quo or to redistribute resources within the system. Under the guise of supporting change, the activities of the school system involved the use of five different barriers to citizen participation to which any complex organization has access. These barriers included 1) delaying the first Advisory Committee meeting; 2) diluting the potential power of the Committee by appointing other committees; 3) limiting the information available to the Committee; 4) limiting its funds; and 5) appealing to legitimate legal restrictions that limit the possibilities of change. Each of these barriers will be discussed below.

The Model School Division staff was asked to continue to concentrate on developing specific projects, unconcerned with administrative arrangements. At the same time, a team of outside consultants, selected by the Superintendent, was asked to develop "the broad administrative organization and scope of the plan for the 'model school subsystem.'"[16] Meanwhile, the newly appointed Advisory Committee members were informed that the school system did not want to convene the Committee or take any other action, pending the report of the

[15] The planners, according to the Superintendent were to concentrate on 1) adult education, 2) curriculum and instruction, 3) enrichment of living and instruction, 4) extended education program, 5) in-service training for teachers and principals, 6) physical plant and education, 7) preschool education, 8) remedial and compensatory education, 9) supportive services for children and teachers, 10) work-study and work experience, and 11) research and experimentation, although the proposals submitted to the community action agency for funding did not include all these areas. *Letter to the Board of Education* from the Superintendent, September 23, 1964.

[16] *Letter to the Chairman of the Advisory Committee*, from the Acting Superintendent of Schools, August 10, 1964. The consultants were J. Bernard Everett, Assistant Superintendent of Schools, Newton, Massachusetts; Roderick F. McPhel, Assistant Professor, Graduate School of Education, Harvard University; Donald P. Mitchell, Executive Secretary, New England School Development Council; David V. Tiedman, Professor of Education, School of Education, Harvard University; Dean K. Whitla, Director of the Office of Tests, Harvard University.

consultants. Thus, the school system, observing the very first beginnings of citizen involvement, responded by delaying the advent of the Advisory Committee and diluting the impact of any one group by establishing others, such as the Superintendent's consultants.[17]

Furthermore, the school system limited the recommendations that the consultants could make by confining them to a series of guidelines that specified that the Model School Division remain "an integral part of the regular school system."[18] Thus, for example, the consultants cited the administration of the District of Columbia Teacher's College as precedent for giving the Assistant Superintendent of the Model School Division autonomy; but as long as they remained within the confines of this guideline, they could not develop an independent administrative structure for the Division. As a result, the consultants reaffirmed the wishes of the Superintendent and other school officials by suggesting that all regular programs should continue under the school authorities ordinarily responsible for them and that only the special programs should have "wide freedom of application . . . . What is needed is the usual school budget and allocations procedures operating through regular channels *plus* special programs and funding mechanisms which recognize the *extra-school* dimensions of the required effort."[19]

The consultants' failure to recommend changes in regular procedures negated the entire concept of a sub-system. In addition, acceptance of the guideline requiring that the Model School Division remain an integral part of the total system ignored the fact that, almost by definition, any program that fulfilled its goal and had an impact on the learning of the educationally deprived would have to affect the regular system. Failure to establish an administrative structure that could develop

[17] Other commentators have discussed the use of delay and dilution as two standard techniques used by school systems to avoid change. See, for example, David Rogers, *110 Livingston Street*; Peter Schrag, *Village School Downtown*, Boston (Beacon Press), 1967. Not only was the impact of the Advisory Committee reduced by the appointment of the consultants, but this same technique—dilution—was used to blunt the possible effect any one Model School Division project could have. By planning so many projects, the school system could claim to be trying out new things without ever permitting the new ideas to be of sufficient magnitude to make a significant difference in the operation of the system.

[18] Donald P. Mitchell, et al., Preliminary Report: *Model School System*, September 15, 1964, p. 16.

[19] *Ibid.*, p. 19.

responses to problems automatically limited the kinds of new programs, curriculum, and supportive services which could be implemented.

More relevant for this case study, the consultants were particularly vague with regard to the role of the Advisory Committee, merely recommending that it be used "to assure that the Model System will in fact be an integral part of the system while still having the flexibility to initiate different programs."[20] Moreover, the suggestion that the Superintendent, the Executive Director of the local Community Action Agency, the District Commissioner for Welfare Services, the President's Advisor for National Capitol Affairs, and the Assistant Superintendent of the Model School Division be *ex officio* members of the committee and act as an Operations Group to screen all projects before they were submitted to the Advisory Committee would have obviously reduced the responsibility of the appointed committee members.[21]

Throughout this period of delay, several members of the Advisory Committee, particularly those recommended by the staff member of the President's Science Advisory Committee, were demanding that the Advisory Committee be convened so that its role might be defined and its power vis-a-vis the Model School Division and the rest of the system understood. The Committee's only clout, however, was the earlier acceptance of the vaguely defined idea of a sub-system with citizen participation.

A second source of power for the Committee derived from the prominence of its members, but in reality the prominence hardly meant more than the ability to attract attention in the press. The school system was sufficiently concerned to react to these threats and try to avoid a confrontation; ultimately, however, the mere existence of the Advisory Committee was not enough to force the school system to permit much citizen participation in the implementation of the Model School Division.

In fact, the Superintendent received the report of the consultants and used it to further restrict the role of the Advisory Committee. In a report to the Board of Education, which it adopted immediately, he ignored the question of the autonomy of the Model School Division to focus entirely on the Advisory Committee, defining it as a public interest group:

1) To evaluate proposals submitted to it by the Assistant Superin-

20*Ibid.*, pp. 19-20.
21*Ibid.*, p. 22.

237

tendent in charge of the Model School Division;

2) To evaluate proposals submitted to it by the Board of Education;

3) To propose programs for consideration by the Board of Education as they may be developed out of the experience of and from the public interest point of view represented by the membership of the Committee, (the Committee is not a research organization but it may properly suggest proposals for analysis by the Research and Development Section of the Model School Division);

4) The Board of Education makes a final determination as to each proposed project; and

5) To assist in securing funds for approved projects.[22]

The recommendations left the Committee without any useful function:

(The Advisory Committee's role lies) in distilling relevant experiences in other parts of the country and bringing new ideas to the Board of Education and to the School Administration . . . It is well to remember that money to support the Model School program is expected to come from sources other than the regular school budget, and that the impetus behind the Model School Sub-System lay with the educational panel of the President's Science Advisory Committee. Had the . . . Committee been formed by the Superintendent to study schools in the Cardozo area, it might have seemed appropriate for it simply to react to the Administration's proposals and to communicate ideas to the Administration for such consideration as the latter chose to give them. But this was not the derivation of our Committee. The broad base of the Committee reflected the need to bring new ideas and a different focus to planning for schools in the Cardozo area with its complex problems of cultural deprivation, poverty and substandard living . . . *In conclusion, if the Committee is not to exercise independent judgment in planning for the Model School Sub-system, I would question whether it has any useful function to serve or whether it would merely be window dressing aimed at obtaining additional funds for District of Columbia Schools.*[23]

[22]Superintendent of the District of Columbia Public Schools, *Review of Consultant's Proposals for the Model School Division*, submitted to the Board of Education of the District of Columbia, November 18, 1964, pp. 5-6.

[23]*Letter to President of District of Columbia Board of Education*, Novem-

Despite the school system's unwillingness to define a useful role for the Advisory Committee, members of the Committee and other advocates of the idea agreed that the Committee should attempt to function as though it had a charter to carry out the panel's original idea. In so doing, the Committee encountered the third and fourth barriers used to thwart outsiders attempting to become involved in decision-making processes: providing the Committee with little or no information regarding the planned or operating projects in the sub-system and giving the Committee no access to funds for consultants, staff or other operating expenses.

At the first meeting, for example, the Committee members requested their chairman to consult with appropriate staff in the school administration and the community action agency to obtain information on the current status of all proposals relating to the Model School Division. After repeated requests, the Committee was informed that there were no written documents describing the ideas and developments of the last eighteen months as they related to the Model School Division, but that when the proposals were ready for Board of Education approval, the Advisory Committee would "receive a package of proposals for review."[24] When the package arrived, the Assistant Superintendent of the Model School Division stated that he was submitting *"for the information* of the Advisory Committee a copy of the proposals for the Model School System *which have been* submitted to the Office of Economic Opportunity for review and funding."[25]

He suggested that time had prevented him from involving the Committee to a greater extent. "Due to the need to develop proposals for submission rapidly and the delay in convening your Committee, we have had to proceed at top speed. This in no way indicates any attempt to by-pass the advice and assistance of your Committee. We desire and welcome the high level assistance you and your Committee will offer."[26]

ber 20, 1964, (emphasis added) from The Chairman of the Advisory Committee.

[24] *Letter to the Chairman of the Advisory Committee*, from the Assistant Superintendent of the Model School Division, November 5, 1964.

[25] *Letter to the Chairman of the Advisory Committee*, from the Assistant Superintendent of the Model School Division, November 19, 1964 (emphasis added).

[26] *Letter to the Chairman of the Advisory Committee*, from the Assistant Superintendent of the Model School Division, November 5, 1964.

The fourth barrier, a lack of funds, also reflected the efforts of the school system to inhibit any outside involvement. The Committee's initial budget request was for less than $10,000. Yet, the Superintendent refused to submit a request for funds for it on the grounds that the Committee should be "independent" of the school system, free from any ties that might censor its opinion and advice.[27]

The local Community Action Agency, in the midst of trying to get its own review processes in operation, did not see the assurance of an independent Advisory Committee as its responsibility. Eventually, through the independent efforts of its members, the Committee received a seed grant of $2,000 from the Edgar H. Stern Family Fund and, six months later, the school system agreed to provide the salary for a staff member.

It is apparent therefore, that although the Advisory Committee was appointed, no effort was made to utilize it or any other group in the community for program planning. In fact, the Superintendent specifically recommended that the Committee concentrate on review of proposals submitted to it by the school administration subject to final determination by the Board of Education. He was quite explicit, stating that he did not construe the recommendation contained in his review of the draft report of the consultants, approved by the Board of Education, to require the school administrators in all instances to submit proposals to the Advisory Committee in advance of the Board of Education, or even necessarily to do so simultaneously.[28] The failure to ensure that the Committee, at a minimum, receive information and participate in the development of the Model School Division's initial projects and the refusal to help it secure funds reflect most accurately the attitudes of the school system toward the use of a citizens' advisory committee.

No one in the school system supported the use of an independent advisory committee to ensure that innovative programs would be implemented in the subsystem schools. Without support, the Committee was unable to act as an agent for change. If an advisory committee

. . . is to give meaningful advice, it has the right to demand infor-

[27]Notes of a meeting with the Chairman of the Advisory Committee and the Superintendent of the District of Columbia Public Schools, October 28, 1964.
[28]Minutes of the Advisory Committee of the Model School Division, November 24, 1964.

mation and a staff to obtain and assimilate it. It also has the right—because it is in effect *outside* the agency—to inform the public of its findings. Instead of being purely advisory, it now courts authority; it has captured an aspect of public opinion, making it a force in determining the shape of the program.[29]

It is true that since the Committee had been convened only a short time earlier, the pressure of time and the newness of the program would have limited the involvement of the Committee even if the local Community Action Agency and school officials had wanted its assistance.

The final barrier to citizen participation and change is the ability of the system to appeal to the numerous legitimate rules and regulations that govern its operations. Whereas some of the other barriers, even if generated by the demands of the system, might be minimized if specific individuals were replaced, a much larger number of restrictions have come to exist through the passage of time and are now removed from the purview of the people in power.

It must not be assumed that an administrator's reluctance to permit an autonomous unit to grow in his "territory" requires him to be active in preventing it. He need only be unimaginative about finding ways to create the structures for autonomy and citizen participation. For example, irrespective of the Superintendent's attitude towards the Advisory Committee and the concept of citizen participation, certain requirements such as submitting all supply orders to the public for bids, obtaining District Government approval of all new staff positions and restricting salaries to the amounts stipulated in the Teacher Salary Act could not be altered without an amendment of the laws of the District of Columbia; other regulations would require Board of Education approval. To achieve these changes would require such exceedingly inventive steps that it is difficult to blame the school officials for not thinking of them. It may be that citizen participation will be successful only if it confronts the system with specific steps for change that have been developed by outsiders.

The Superintendent, therefore, had a good case when he argued that:

we cannot, nor would I recommend it, and I hope that the Board would not approve it if I did, set up a division of the school system

[29] David S. Brown, "The Public Advisory Board as an Instrument of Government," *Public Administration Review*, Summer 1955, p. 201.

here which is not responsibe to the rules and regulations of this Board or to the legal requirements set forth by Congress on the operation of this school system.[30]

Similarly, when the school system submitted the Model School Division proposals for funding, the officials agreed that the Division must remain an integral part of the District Public Schools because

the Board of Education is charged by law with responsibility for the education of the approximately 17,000 young people served by the Model School Division as it is for all the children of the District of Columbia.[31]

Of course, although accurate, these arguments reflect the lack of commitment within the school system to create a sub-system. If the school officials had wanted to establish an independent administrative structure for the Model School Division, it could have hired a team of legal experts to ensure that the new structure conformed to the rules and regulations of the District of Columbia government and the Board of Education. The fact that the responsibility for the nineteen schools involved lay with the Board is unrelated to the various administration structures it is permitted to create. If anything, it could be argued that as long as the Board of Education was convinced that such steps would be of benefit to the 17,000 students, it would have been its responsibility to take them.

Thus, making the Division autonomous and, particularly, giving the Advisory Committee any authority would not have been inconsistent with the responsibilities of the Board of Education and the Superintendent. The Committee was advisory to the Board itself and could be dissolved by it, and the Assistant Superintendent of the Model School Division was accountable to the Superintendent. The acceptance by the Board of Education of the usefulness of a sub-system as a way of reaching the educationally disadvantaged cannot be reconciled with its failure to establish the ground rules to make it a reality.

In addition to the spurious legal argument, the school officials maintain that the Model School Division must be administratively bound to the rest of the system so that results of the successful experimental

[30]*Letter to the Chairman of the Advisory Committee*, from the Secretary of the Board of Education, October 25, 1965.

[31]*Projects for Funding*, Model School Division, submitted to the Office of Economic Opportunity, December 1965, p. 2.

efforts can "be adopted as rapidly as possible by the very large number of schools outside the Model School area."[32] But no evidence was offered to show that autonomy would preclude dissemination and one may question whether this argument did not also merely reflect the Administration's unwillingness to give the Division the autonomy needed to experiment freely.

On the other hand, the Advisory Committee seems to have erred in the direction that many citizens' groups err. Instead of pressing for changes in the system-based inhibitions to change, the Committee members viewed the opposition to change in terms of the individuals involved and objected to their lack of support for innovation. Instead, efforts should have been made to outline the areas in which existing laws would restrict the establishment of the sub-system proposed in the Superintendent's letter of June 11, 1964. Once these were determined, the Committee might have drafted legislation permitting a new organization, outside the school system to be created to handle the education component of the anti-poverty program. [33]

For example, a teacher's aide program included the innovative suggestion that the teachers be permitted to determine the salary increases of their own assistants. The idea was never discussed on its merits, but was rejected immediately by the school officials as impossible because it did not conform to the standard salary scales used to pay District of Government employees. Later investigation indicated that since the funds came from a special Federal grant, the rates controlling staff promotion did not have to follow that of the usual government scale and that a reasonable alternative could have been developed and submitted to the District Government for approval.

The second type of regulation or procedure, those which affected the internal management of the school system, required only the approval of the Board of Education. Yet, just as the responsibilities of the Advisory Committee were never defined, the relationship of the Model School Division to the regular system—its autonomy—was purposely ambiguous. As a result, all functions in support of any Model School Division project—hiring consultants, certifying teachers, ordering supplies, establishing payrolls—had to be processed by the regular school system. Although most officials were extremely helpful,

[32]*Ibid.*, p. 2.

[33]Office of Economic Opportunity funds were given subject to the rules and regulations of the locality. Efforts might nevertheless have been made to change laws which unreasonably interfered with the goals of a sound program.

the Model School Division programs were, understandably, viewed simply as imposing additional demands and, more often than not, demands of rather low priority. And, because the general workload of these officials was heavy, requests were rarely given immediate attention. A plan outlining in detail how these functions were to be performed in an independent sub-system was necessary if the Model School Division were ever to receive real autonomy. It is unlikely that the school officials opposing the idea would draw up such a proposal and there is no assurance that a plan developed by any outside group would be accepted. If, however, a group of citizens such as the Advisory Committee had such a document, they, no doubt, would be better able to force consideration of the needed change.

The Success of the Committee

On the whole the Advisory Committee never performed the role its most helpful members had anticipated it would play. It had some success, however, in one area—developing the teachers as a force for change. This suggests a possible strategy for other citizen's groups working to bring about change in a complete organization. The strategy is based on two principles:

1) Any outside group will be more effective if it seeks to build a constituency or other source of power within the institution it is trying to change.
2) Within any organization, there always exist some dissidents, sufficiently dissatisfied with the status quo or so situated as to serve to gain from any changes, who can be used as a part of the vanguard for change.

In the case of the Model School Division, the press, the concern of community organization workers, the Advisory Committee and others, by their very presence, put pressure on the District School System to try new ways of meeting the problem of educating the disadvantaged. All of these, however, were forces outside the school system. What was absent, however, were sources of pressure to change the status quo which arose from within the system itself and could join forces with the outside pressures.

On this point, studies of social change indicate that marginal members of any society or system, disenchanted with the status quo, are a potential force for change and can be a valuable source of innovation if their effective participation as a group can be elicited.[34] Teachers and principals, in this sense, are marginal to the administrators and boards of education. The following suggestions as to how existing school systems should be changed highlight the marginal role teachers occupy, despite their professional training, with regard to job-related decisions.

Teachers, administrators, and school boards have to operate not in a chain of command but in a bond of unity and common purpose. Responsibilities have to be divided not along the lines of hierarchy but according to what each group is best trained to handle. All teachers should have more of the responsibility for setting up the curriculum of the schools, for who knows better than a teacher the problems involved? Who can judge better what methods and materials should be used? A council of teachers in each school, with a head teacher elected by the others, could certainly handle the educational content of the schools as well as, if not better than, people who are no longer in the classroom. The idea that an administrator, by some magical power inherent in his position, knows more about educational content than all the teachers in a school creates a hardship on both sides. If administrators were relieved of this part of their role, they could then become what they are in fact most often today—business managers who keep the schools running smoothly.[35]

In order to try to create an internal mechanism for change, the Advisory Committee proposed the formation of a Teacher's Planning Committee, composed of two teachers from each of the nineteen Model School Division schools. Initially, the Teachers's Committee did little more than express the negative feelings the teachers in general felt about the Model School Division. Their remarks were summarized in a memorandum.

a) (The teachers) are somewhat skeptical about the likelihood promised innovations will be implemented since their *basic* teaching tools are inadequate. They point to outdated text

[34] Leonard Borman, *Institutions and the Institutionalized Patient*, University of Chicago School of Social Service Administration Club, January 26, 1963, pp. 5-6.

[35] Anne Mitchell, "The Crux of the Matter," *The Saturday Review*, January 15, 1966, p. 66.

books, old buildings, and most frequently, overcrowded conditions ...

b) The teachers doubt their suggestions will be welcomed and do not feel free to make them to administrative personnel ... The suggestions of various consultants seemed to be of more theoretical than practical interest to the teachers. They claimed that they would not be allowed to participate in such radical changes and that to continue the debate among themselves seemed pointless. Others claimed that they were so closely directed by visiting supervisors, they did not even have the freedom to arrange their rooms as they saw fit.[36]

The members of the Teacher's Committee, along with the Advisory Committee staff members and other Model School Division officials, did become involved in the planning and operation of a Summer Institute for 150 elementary teachers. The Institute, ostensibly an opportunity to learn about new curriculum techniques, was really viewed as a mechanism for creating a force for change within the school system. Only the most moderate success was attained the first year, although this included demanding and obtaining from the Superintendent the right to teach the new curriculum irrespective of school system regulations to the contrary. Yet, this was the first demand for autonomy that both was met and generated from within the system.

The true value of the use of change agents within the system can be seen in the fact that, although the Advisory Committee and original Teacher Planning Committee ceased to function the following year, the Summer Institutes have continued and their best graduates have been freed of all teaching duties to function as an "innovation team." The sole purpose of this team is to stimulate and support innovative ideas among all Model School Division teachers. The team received national recognition, for example, for their special curriculum on riots that it helped teachers develop after the violent response to Martin Luther King's death in April, 1968. Much of the credit for the continued battle to make the Model School Division a center of innovation is due to a single woman, who originally joined the experiment as a science consultant at the first Summer Institute. Like the Advisory Committee, it cannot be said she represents the community, but the impact of her determined efforts as an outsider to use

[36]Memorandum to the Advisory Committee, April 8, 1964.

individuals within the bureaucracy to bring about change suggests the usefulness of this technique for any citizen's group.

Conclusion

Citizen participation can be viewed as both an effort to implement the values inherent in classical democratic theory and a competitive organizational technique to help low-income groups obtain a voice in determining the allocation of resources. The concept of participation is, obviously, not a radical innovation in American political life; it is only its linkage with a federally funded national program that is new.

Daniel Moynihan argues that the conflict orientation inherent in the theory of the anti poverty programs has helped to undermine their impact.[37] To the extent that he is right, it is not, as he suggests, because there is no basis for conflict in social science research. The conflict orientation did not succeed because the existing power structures have had the advantages of inertia and resources in any confrontation with new groups attempting to alter the biases inherent in those structures.[38]

If, however, advocates of citizen participation understand the limitations and liabilities of their efforts, they can maximize the probability of success. The review of the Model School Division Advisory Committee's general ineffectiveness, although limited success in working with the teachers, suggests several considerations.

First, citizens' participation often assumes, erroneously, a commonality of attitudes where none exists. Other than sharing a common concern for "better education," the Advisory Committee members differed widely on the question of the kind of effort required to improve the school system. Perhaps it was fortunate that the school system confined the battle to the role of the Committee, thereby making this potential divisiveness irrelevant.

In the case of the poor, the problem is similar. Even if everyone in a well-defined geographical area, when such an area exists, suffers similar problems, it cannot be assumed that they will evolve an identical list of priorities regarding which problems are most critical

[37]Daniel Moynihan, *Maximum Feasible Misunderstanding*, MacMillan. The Free Press, New York, 1969.

[38]Adam Walinsky, review of Daniel Moynihan, *Maximum Feasible Misunderstanding*, New York *Times Book Review*, February 2, 1969, p. 1, presents a persuasive argument suggesting that the lack of adequate financial resources for the anti-poverty program was the real limit to its effectiveness.

247

or that they will agree on the methods to be used to solve them. More important, the objectives themselves are likely to conflict in ways that are difficult to resolve.

Second, although citizen participation among the lower class has special problems, most of the limitations lie in the difficulty of getting anyone to participate. Citizen participation, for example, usually requires an involvement on a volunteer basis for prolonged periods of time without tangible evidence of success. To generate continual interest among members, rich or poor, is a difficult task. It is necessary, therefore, to follow two strategies: initial projects should be limited to demands or confrontations that have a high probability of succeeding and citizen participation should focus on specific issues.

The Advisory Committee was ineffectual in confronting the school system in good part because it was not clear what it wanted the system to do. The successful suit initiated in the District of Columbia courts against the Superintendent and the Board of Education by Julius Hobson may have done more to force broad educational changes in the school system than both the Advisory Committee and the OEO-funded programs together, although its original purpose was simply to end tracking. Furthermore, by focusing on specific issues, citizen participation can co-opt other groups; the wider the scope of the conflict, the more the advantage accrues to the weaker group.[39]

The third consideration for citizen participation is to develop a strategy for dealing with the complex organization whose policies they hope to alter. The case study of the Advisory Committee and the Model School Division seemed to suggest the efficacy of obtaining support among some dissatisfied group within the bureaucracy and using them as a force for change.

This strategy assumes that in an industrial society it is inevitable that there be stratification and expertise; it is an efficient way of getting things done. The concept of citizen participation does not have to deny this and argue that the citizens must actually operate every organization serving them. Specialization is required to perfect any complex task. Different people have different talents. Instead, citizen participation can work to enhance the status and power of certain groups within the bureaucracy when that enhancement is likely to result in organizational policies that are more responsive to

[39]E. E. Schattschneider, *The Semi-Sovereign People: A Realist's View of Democracy in America*, New York, (Holt, Rinehart, and Winston), 1960.

248

the needs of the citizens.

The problem is not to oppose increased specialization and professionalization but to use the organization of the poor to end the biases inherent in current institutional decisions by changing the relative power of individuals in these institutions. The new hierarchy may, for example, be aware of the need to develop new techniques to teach ghetto children to read, just as the old hierarchy developed automated driver education courses when their clients, the middle class, wanted the school to perform this non-academic function.

At the same time, advocates of citizen participation should realize that many of the decisions in complex organizations are no longer in the hands of any one group. Superintendent contracts, teacher tenure, legal sanctions for union negotiations—all remove large numbers of decisions from everybody's review. To change these requires the substitution and acceptance of an alternative set of rules and regulations. These can be drafted and an organized group of citizens can, when desired, retain the staff to do so. The point is simply to recognize that, in many organizations, the issues of importance to the poor are no longer truly controlled by the bureaucrats either.

MANPOWER—T.W.O. AND THE BLACKSTONE RANGERS

by: Jerome Bernstein

Editor's Note:

The issue of where to place youth gangs, perhaps the most volatile of social groups in America, in the spectrum of citizen participation has long puzzled social analysts. Cloward and Ohlin's classic study, Delinquency and Opportunity, *showed the possibility of using the gang itself to build more socially acceptable behavioral norms.*

Experience with New York gangs and WYEAC in Wilmington, Delaware, among others, has shown that opportunity programs can work in the gang culture; but the obstacles are almost overwhelming. The most highly publicized and distorted gang story of the decade, however, concerns the Blackstone Rangers and East Side Disciples in Chicago and their adventures under an OEO grant.

Some questions:

1) Leaving aside the police and City Hall, what other examples are there of local agencies working to kill new participatory structures? How far outside America's broad middle-class "consensus" can innovative projects go? Relate Piven's and Fox's theses to the answers. How does the SWAFCA experience (see Zimmerman) compare?

2) Saul Alinsky worked in Woodlawn. What strategic prescription might he have offered the local leaders when OEO agreed to fund TWO and the gangs?

3) What peculiar obstacles are placed in the way of active citizen participation in the conduct of any manpower program?

Jerome Bernstein is now a senior consultant for Social Dynamics, Inc., Washington, D.C. His background, prior to the OEO service graphically detailed here, includes a number of significant positions in the field of manpower research. He was director of a vocational training center for the retarded in Washington and of a vocational rehabilitation research project funded by HEW.

Years of research and scores of demonstration programs concerned with alienated youth and youth gangs have provided abundant evidence that programs aimed at this population are destined to fail if they are not designed to deal with the values and cultural orientation of these youth in a manner which does not alienate them from the program. Techniques developed for use with individuals of different cultural orientation cannot be applied to the ghetto gang member. Such an approach would be tantamount to the State Department's sending a translator who is fluent in French to a conference where discussions are to be conducted in Russian.

Program approaches based on the assumption that alienated youth must adapt to the orientation of the professional workers in the program are doomed to failure. Programs which begin by assaulting the existing gang structure and demanding immediate change in that social organization will fail.

Social scientists have long theorized on the possibility of accepting the existing structure of youth gangs and producing changes in that structure by redirecting its focus and direction from within. The leadership within the gang structure will produce the desired results. This hypothesis provided the basis for the design of the youth manpower program discussed in this paper. The program illustrates citizen participation and indigenous leadership development in a youth gang

251

setting—one of the most critical forms to face American society.*

The TWO program was a radical departure from program designs which have been tried over the years. The experiment seemed more than warranted by the conditions that prevailed and the manifest failure of a more conventional endeavor. The OEO "highlight" memorandum summarized the principal reasons why TWO was prepared to try the untried:

> TWO's experience with alienated youth and the youth organizations in the Woodlawn community indicates that the principal reason alienated youth organize is to deal with the chaotic conditions with which they are confronted in the ghetto. These youth usually join such groups because they see the group structure as the only possible vehicle through which they can gain real power and socio-economic status to some degree. In essence, these youth organizations are illegitimate structures created to attain legitimate goals. There are few, if any, youth-serving programs which have been designed to come to grips with the problems of youth in the urban ghetto, and more particularly with the youth population of Woodlawn. The few programs which do exist tend to operate on a narrow recreational basis and are run through traditional youth-serving agencies. It is precisely because these agencies are bound by traditional rules and regulations that they do not adequately meet the needs of the alienated youth of the community. Inherent in the operation of traditional youth-serving agencies is the process of self-selection of clientele. The result of such a process is that only a minority of the alienated youth are served and those most in need of service are not recruited and remain both physically and psychologically alienated from the agency.

> A large proportion of the youth of Woodlawn belong to youth organizations in the area. The estimated membership of these groups in the Woodlawn area is 4,000 to 5,000 youths ranging from ages 13 to 25. Woodlawn Avenue is the basic dividing line between the "turf" of two of the area's largest youth organizations.

*As a staff member of the Community Action Program in the Office of Economic Opportunity (OEO), the author assisted The Woodlawn Organization (hereinafter TWO) in the development of an experimental program aimed at two youth gangs, the Blackstone Rangers and the East Side Disciples, in the Woodlawn area on the South Side of Chicago.

The police, schools, agencies, and churches have attempted to resolve the problems of these alienated youth and several "programs" have been instituted to discourage the destructive activities of these youths. However, over and over again, these programs have failed to attack the roots of the problem and have only pacified the symptoms.

The alienated youth looks upon the institutions of the community as being insincere and full of negative and meaningless social work cliches. To these youths, the police and schools represent very hostile authority figures and they act out their feelings in very hostile ways. They view the community of Woodlawn as they would a hostile Mother, with anger and disappointment, but with a dependency for nurture and security. The boundaries of their "turf" became their jail and their sanctuary. Seldom, if ever, will such a youth venture off his "turf"—even for employment or recreation.

The Woodlawn Organization feels that it is quite possible to redirect energies of the youth and the youth organizations to which they belong. It feels that youth can be involved in positive constructive programs that not only will be of direct and immediate benefit to them, but of benefit to the entire community.

At the present time, the youth of Woodlawn have no alternative to their traditional behaviors. Youth without a direction are youth headed for trouble. Every sign in Woodlawn at this time points to an eventful summer unless some type of intervention is provided to channel the activities of Woodlawn's youth into non-anti-social directions. CAP staff have met with the leadership of the youth organizations in Woodlawn and believe in the sincerity of their pleas for a manpower program to train and employ their membership. The proposed program is designed to eliminate the design errors of past programmatic attempts with this population. *For the first time, the youths themselves,* along with TWO and other professionals, *have participated in determining their own needs, planning solutions to their problems, and in designing a program to effectively deal with those problems.* Every responsible party in Chicago agrees that program intervention with this population in Woodlawn is badly needed. The proposed program is designed to meet that need now, before the pressures of a hot summer begin to agitate the youth of

253

Woodlawn, and on a long-range basis. It is uniquely designed to meet those needs. Past manpower efforts with similar populations have yielded disappointing results. Since the proposed program design has never before been tested, should it prove successful, it will offer a viable new programmatic approach in dealing with alienated youth and youth groups in a constructive way. We face the two alternatives of "giving up" and resigning ourselves to the social and personal disintegration of a segment of our youthful population, or trying again with more unique approaches in an effort to solve a problem which we must resolve.

The Demonstration Features of the Program

The program designed to cope with these conditions was structured to test certain fundamental hypotheses:

a) That the social structure of disadvantaged youth will provide a natural community-peer grouping that can play a strong positive role in self-help community unity and development.

b) That the natural structure of disadvantaged youth groups provides an excellent vehicle to develop skills and attitudes beneficial to the young adults of Woodlawn, the local community, and the larger community of Chicago.

c) That the natural structure of two street gang groups is a logical mechanism to shift attitudes of disaffiliation to productive adult concerns of employment, community development, and upward mobility.

d) That the primary peer group structure of the street gang provides a natural and logical mechanism to recruit and select subprofessional staff for a manpower program as well as a mechanism for the recruitment of client participants in a manpower program.

e) That a community-centered manpower program, planned with the cooperation of the leadership of youth organizations, is a natural and logical vehicle to reduce community tension and to bring about a cooperative and coordinated community concern by the youth, adults, and local institutions in Woodlawn and Chicago.

254

f) That the performance of youth participating in basic literacy training in this project will be consistent with the findings in the Greenleigh Literacy Study which found that the non- or sub-professional, using appropriate programmed educational materials, can, based on performance test measures, instruct undereducated "hard core" poor more effectively, efficiently, and less expensively than college graduates or certified teachers.

g) That the ability of sub-professionals in counseling roles to communicate, understand, and guide peer clients in a manpower program is more supportive and more acceptable to clients than the techniques used by professional counseling staff with alienated youth and young adults.

h) That part-time community developers, serving as intermediaries and interpreters in police-youth conflicts, can shift police-youth organization relationships and protect civil liberties.

i) That a community organization (TWO) can plan, develop, and run programs in cooperation with youth groups to the advantage of all members of the community.

j) That the involvement of alineated disadvantaged youth in the planning, developing, and staffing of a manpower program aimed at their peer group is central to the ultimate success of the program.

k) That the mutual planning and conducting of a special service component by university personnel and members of youth groups will provide more effective and prompt services than is generally the case in providing institutional services to the poor.

l) That a manpower program utilizing sub-professional peers in all direct service-training components is a more functional, successful, and less expensive method of conducting manpower programs for socially alienated young adults.

m) That the use of performance incentives for sub-professional personnel involved in a non-profit social service program is a functional, successful, and important ingredient in motivating staff to perform job functions with high effectiveness.

255

n) That a community-based and operated program will provide an effective mechanism for establishing functional communication (and ultimately programmatic coordination) with established agencies and programs regardless of the degree of alienation between the community and such established agencies.

Theory and practice went hand in hand, each modifying the other to produce a step-by-step plan of action.

Basic agreement between TWO and the gangs was necessary on a number of conditions if the experimental program was to be workable:

1. Gang leadership, as well as youth who are not members of a gang, will have a major role in the planning and design of the proposed programs.

2. The gang will effect a truce (effected April, 1967) *prior* to submission of a final proposal to the Office of Economic Opportunity. Such a truce would be viewed as tangible evidence of the sincerity of the gangs with respect to their desire to see the proposed program funded. It is further understood that this truce must remain in effect after the program is funded.

3. The proposed program will be funded to TWO, who will be the grantee, and no project funds will be made available to any gang at any time. No gang will receive a subcontract from TWO for any portion of the program.

4. Gang members, as well as other youth, may be employed in sub-professional positions on the staff of the proposed program. However, all job applicants must meet predetermined selection criteria. Final decisions for hiring (and firing) all project personnel shall rest with the Project Director and TWO. All project personnel will be subject to on-going evaluation and will be retained based on their ability to meet performance criteria for the job.

5. No prior commitment by the federal government nor any other funding source has been made to either TWO or the gangs with respect to funding the proposed program. No commitment will be made. The proposal will either be approved or rejected.

6. The purpose of the proposed program is to conduct a job training program for the unemployed youth of Woodlawn. To this extent, the program is aimed at a solution to specific problems of gangs as they relate to anti-social and destructive acts which may impair the success of the program. The gangs, therefore, have an obligation to insure, to the extent possible, that the support of their entire memberships is enlisted to assist the program in attaining its objectives. Should this

support be withdrawn or any of the above understandings violated, TWO will take appropriate action to resolve the problem, and if necessary, shut down the program.

7. TWO has requested the CAP Manpower Division, U.S. Office of Economic Opportunity, to provide for ongoing monitoring and evaluation of the project. This is to insure that the project is being operated consistent with the program design and in full compliance with all applicable government regulations; to further insure that there be no intrusion by gang organizations which would hamper TWO's ability to operate the program; and to further insure that the program is operated at an acceptable level of quality. (OEO contracted with the University of Chicago to evaluate the program. The evaluation report has been submitted but not yet released by OEO.)

8. TWO will establish a Program Policy Board which will be composed of adults, non-gang, and gang youth of the community. TWO reserves the right, to the extent necessary, to refuse to implement any recommendations of the proposed Program Policy Board.

9. TWO will be held accountable to the U.S. Office of Economic Opportunity for compliance with the terms and conditions of any grant which may ensue. Therefore, TWO shall be the final authority for any and all decisions made with respect to the personnel of the project and all aspects of project operation.

All of these "pre-condition" agreements were agreed to by TWO, the Blackstone Rangers and the East Side Disciples.

Once these fundamental ground rules were established, it became possible to put together the basic components of a workable manpower program for youth whom every prior effort had failed to reach. Thus the work program provided:

The target population for this manpower program will be 800 unemployed, poverty-level youth and young adults, approximately 700 of whom will receive training from the program.

The work program is structured into two tracks. Track #1 is designed primarily for those individuals who have had some work experience, whose literacy and math skills are at least eighth grade level, and who are motivated to work. Such individuals will receive quick brush-up instruction on their basic education skills and any vocational training as needed; and work orientation and counseling. Such individuals would be processed through Track #1 over a period of 1 to 10 weeks. When the staff of the program judge the individual to be ready for employment, the individual would be referred to a job.

Track #2 is specifically designed for the more severely disadvantaged individual who has little or no work experience, whose motivation may be low, and who needs extensive vocational training. Track #2 provides for extensive basic educational training, institutional vocational training prior to on-the-job training, and extensive work orientation and counseling. An individual may remain in Track #2 for a period of 10 to 50 weeks as required.

The Bureau of Apprenticeship and Training of the Department of Labor has committed a minimum of 300 and up to a maximum of 500 OJT (on-the-job training) slots to TWO to be used in conjunction with the proposed porgram. Thus, individuals completing training in both Tracks #1 and #2 may leave training and go directly into a job, or they may move from either track into an on-the-job training slot if it is deemed necessary to provide the individual with additional vocational training. The program is designed to provide follow-up services to individuals for a minimum period of 6 months after job placement.

The program is also designed to provide supportive health services and legal consultation. Funds will be provided to insure that each program participant receives a general physical examination and limited remedial health services if any serious health problems are diagnosed.

In many instances, TWO has found that individuals participating in its program have experienced problems which seriously affected their performance in the program and which could only be solved with the assistance of legal consultation. As has been indicated previously, the target population for the proposed manpower program will be 800 unemployed, poverty level young adults. Their legal problems run the gamut from housing, credit, personal injury, to domestic (marital, child support) and encounters with local police, etc. In most instances they will not be able to afford legal counsel and may have no notion as to their rights and the nature of the applicable laws with which they may be concerned. It is for this reason that the program proposes to make a limited amount of legal consultation available to sub-professional staff members and program participants. TWO has had several discussions with local police authorities in this regard and there is a working relationship between TWO and the police.

The program also provides for community workers who will be recruited from the University of Chicago. These individuals will work on a part-time basis in the evening and full-time on the weekend on the streets in the Woodlawn area. Their chief function will be to provide informal counseling to the youth of Woodlawn, particularly program participants, to "sell" the program at the community level, pick up information about community activities and problems which might have an impact on the success of the program operation or on the performance of individuals participating in the program.

Results Expected at the End of This Grant

This proposed program, if successful, will obtain gainful employment for a minimum of 800 youth and young adults in the Woodlawn area of Chicago. It will demonstrate, among other things (see item 3 above), that alienated youth can participate in a manpower program both as trainee participants and as sub-professional staff. The project should further show that there are alternatives for alienated youth other than anti-social behavior and that such anti-social behavior will have been markedly and demonstrably reduced as a result of the proposed program. The program should result in better overall relations between alienated youth and the organizations to which they belong and the police and gangs and the community of Woodlawn and the City of Chicago as a whole.

This is in essence the "model" which was funded. The "model" was never really tried. It was beset by obstacles, burdens, opposition and outright sabotage from the moment of conception to the date of execution, and beyond. That story is outlined below.*

Despite these handicaps, the program during its brief life did achieve certain tangible, demonstrable results which make it possible to justify the program on the basis of *performance* alone without resort to excuses drawn from the sordid tale of politics and sabotage set forth subsequently.

In terms of concrete achievements, it is possible to state unequivocally that the following concrete, documented results were produced by the expenditure of federal funds:

a. Cessation of gang warfare.

In June, 1966, violence between two black youth gangs—the East

*Other versions of the story have appeared in Chicago newspapers, *The Atlantic,* and the McClellan Senate Permanent Investigating Committee hearings.

Side Disciples and the Blackstone Rangers—was of such a magnitude that the adult community in Woodlawn, especially businessmen, was up in arms and demanding that TWO lobby for greater police coverage of the area, even though there was deep-rooted distrust of the police by the community. At that point in time these two youth gangs were engaged in constant warfare with each other, sometimes involving three or more "shoot-outs" in a given day. Yet condition #2, a truce and a total cessation of hostilities, (to demonstrate to the Government their good faith and the seriousness of their commitment to the objectives of the proposed program), was agreed to in writing. And from that date forward there was in fact a *total cessation of hostilities between the two gangs for approximately six months without a single violation of the truce.*

Certainly the extended absence of open hostility following the April, 1967, truce was a dramatic and historic event. It proved a major hypothesis of the program— namely, that alienated youth and gangs will radically alter their established patterns of behavior if they have a meaningful (to them) reason to do so and that such behavioral changes can be brought about without assaulting the gang structure.

This program afforded them the right to be participants in determining their own destiny, the right to have a say in the development and operation of a program which they perceived as a possible alternative to a way of life which they themselves admitted they wished to shed.

It should be noted that the police had obtained truce agreements with these youth gangs before. None of the agreements lasted for more than a week, if that long. From the point of view of the youth there was no reason for them to maintain such a truce, particularly when it had been their experience that the police themselves violated the terms of a previously agreed upon truce.

b. Riot prevention.

When riots tore apart over 80 cities during the summer of 1967, Chicago remained "cool". The TWO demonstration program and the two youth gangs were publicly credited by Commander Griffin of the Third District Police (Woodlawn); Chief Conlisk (Chief of Police for the City of Chicago) and the press with having prevented riots in Chicago during the summer of 1967. The youth gangs, of their own volition, went to Commander Griffin and offered their assistance in keeping the community quiet in the wake of Newark and Detroit. They worked actively with the police to keep the situation under control during one of the most tense periods in Chicago's history.

These two youth gangs were responsible for preventing a Black Panther meeting on August 1, 1967, which was to be held on the Westside of Chicago, allegedly to forge a coalition of youth gangs to "take on the City" during the summer of 1967. These two gangs proclaimed that there would be no riots and that there would be no Black Panther meeting.

There were no riots and there was no Black Panther meeting.

In July and August of 1967 the Chicago and national press publicly credited the activities of the gangs and the program in preventing violence and riots in the City. The Chicago *Sun Times* even ran an editorial acknowledging the signal contribution the gangs had made in averting civil disorder.

A year later, in April, 1968, the program and the two gangs again captured the press and television spotlight when holocaust ensued on the Westside of Chicago in the wake of the assassination of Martin Luther King. Woodlawn experienced only a few broken windows. Again, the program and the gangs were publicly credited with having kept things "cool" on the Southside. This time the press coverage was on a nationwide basis. The youths who were credited with having prevented riots and violence are sociologically identical to those on the Westside of Chicago and elsewhere in the country who were responsible for touching off and carrying out the disorders following the King assassination. In short, the TWO program was responsible for producing in an alienated population positive behavioral shifts.

c. Reduced crime rates.

According to police statistics there was a 44.4% *decrease* in serious assaults in the Third Police District (which is mainly comprised of the Woodlawn area) of Chicago during the summer of 1967 over the summer of 1966, the only decrease of any magnitude in any major city in the country.

The University of Chicago evaluators stated:
The evidence is clear and unequivocal that crime in Police District 3 was either absolutely reduced over the previous year or relatively lowered compared to other similar districts of the City as a whole. The only major exception was the increase in the occurrence of murder and non-negligent manslaughter. There was, however, a

consistent and general increase of crime in the City of Chicago as a whole.

There are other details which are also relevant. The evaluation of the TWO program by the University of Chicago found that there were significant reductions in the arrest and police pick-up rates for youth participating in the program, that the incidence of youths carrying weapons decreased significantly; that, in the judgement of storekeepers in Woodlawn, these two youth gangs were major factors in keeping the area quiet before and after the riots which took place on the *Westside* of Chicago in the Spring of 1968; and that at the same time the storekeepers perceived the activities of *other* gangs as having become more violent.

d. Improved police-community relations.

Shortly after the truce was signed relations between the two youth gangs and the police in the Woodlawn District, Commander Griffin's District (separate and apart from the Gang Intelligence Unit), shifted from a totally negative to a positive relationship. Commander Griffin was a man whom the youth gangs had once threatened to shoot on sight. He was now willing to give written as well as verbal support to the program.

In August, 1967, Griffin wrote the Reverend Brazier, President of TWO, praising the program and the activities of the two gangs in preventing violence and riots in Woodlawn. Subsequently, Commander Griffin informally deputized members of the East Side Disciples as "assistants" to his Department at a time of extreme racial tension in Woodlawn. Commander Griffin even went so far as to complain of the provocation and harassing activities of Lt. Buckney and the Gang Intelligence Unit (GIU). He asked the Chief of Police to keep Buckney out of his District in Woodlawn because Buckney was aggravating the already tense situation in Woodlawn. Griffin's support for a special out-of-town outing on Bud Billikin Day (a notorious and often boisterously destructive local holiday) for the two gangs figured prominently in OEO's decision to permit TWO to use project funds for the outing. Griffin stated publicly at the monitoring meetings that he thought that the program had brought about a marked reduction in gang violence and reiterated his support for the program.

e. Job placement.

The project placed over 100 trainees in gainful employment. The University of Chicago estimated that:

... the success ratio of job placement was 1 in 9 or 1 in 7 or even better, depending on which base figure is used. Other manpower projects experience an average ratio of job placement of 1 in 9. The TWO program did as well, if not better, than most programs.

SUMMARY

The program produced certain results which no other program can point to. In the narrow realm of manpower training and job placement, its performance record was adequate. Yet the program was killed.

What really happened—
a successful project deliberately aborted?

In analyzing the historical development of the project, the University of Chicago evaluation observed that:

The Youth Project was under attack from the beginning of its program operation, and indeed even before it was funded. The Project was opposed by the Mayor's office, Chicago Committee on Urban Opportunity (CCUO), the Chicago Commission on Youth Welfare, powerful voluntary social agencies, including the YMCA, as well as the Chicago Police Department. There was little organized support for the program, except within the Woodlawn Community, individuals at the University of Chicago, and the Chicago Urban League.

Cirticism against the program developed at a very early point and was evidenced by two major investigations, one by the Government Accounting Office (GAO) and the other by the Midwest Regional Unit of the Office of Economic Opportunity, early and in the middle of the program year. A third major investigation was initiated in the Spring of 1968 by Senator McClellan's Permanent Subcommittee on Investigations of the Committee on Government Operations. The newspapers, particularly the Chicago *Tribune*, also engaged in investigation and attack on the program.

263

Pressures opposing the project were enormous. The staff and program participants were in a continuing state of tension and anxiety about the status of the program. The barrage of inquiry and hostility was overwhelming. The staff and trainees reacted not only defensively in order to protect themselves, their personal, professional and organizational reputations but after a while probably became "punch drunk" and even somewhat disoriented. Each day of the program was in essence another day of crisis and cataclysm. Project operations were immobilized repeatedly, if not continually, by waves of increasing hostility and fury.

The organization which led the attack in the winter of 1967 was the Chicago Police Department, particularly its Gang Intelligence Unit. The community force probably more responsible than any other for directly hindering and destroying the project was the Chicago Police Department. Its lack of commitment to the objectives of the program, its gross failure to understand the complexity of the problem of gang delinquency in the Black ghetto, its reluctance to cooperate with The Woodlawn Organization in the implementation of the program, and its punitive law enforcement attitudes and activities were elements in the systematic attack.

This summary makes clear that the destruction of the project was achieved by the cooperation of a number of forces. Opposed to the project were John Root, Executive Director of the Chicago YMCA; Deton J. Brooks, the Executive Director of the Chicago Committee on Urban Opportunity (CCUO), Chicago's antipoverty agency; Mayor Richard Daley, who reluctantly officially supported the funding of the program even though he gave the green light to Brooks to try to prevent its existence; Lieutenant Edward Buckney (recently promoted to Captain as a result of his performance on the TWO program and before the McClellan Committee), the first (and only) director of the Gang Intelligence Unit of the Chicago Police; Congressmen Pucinski and Rostenkowski of Illinois, who are said to have put considerable pressure on OEO to have the program cancelled; and R. Sargent Shriver, formerly Director of the Office of Economic Opportunity.

Mayor Daley had shown his clout at the highest level of government when the President himself disavowed his own Commissioner of Education, Francis Keppel, and sided with the Mayor on the Chicago school desegregation issue. OEO Director Shriver was vulnerable in another

at the project was a failure. These issues, we
...tially political and inter-organizational. It is clear
...ul groups and organizations acted in such a way as
...ure of the project. The fact that the program had
...remarkable in view of the opposition.

...at a pioneering approach to youth manpower devel-
...e ghetto has been offered. The need is to test the
...a far wider scale in Chicago and other urban centers
...he country. Program design and administrative and
...ons have been learned. . .

...ct it seems clear that the Gang Intelligence Unit of the
...ioning as direct agents of Mayor Daley and his poverty
...ctor played the most visible and central role in destroying
...n, provoking the gangs to violence and disrupting the
...s, but fragile, relationship of mutual confidence and coopera-
...volved between the gangs and Police Commander Griffin who
...arge of the Precinct in which Woodlawn is located. As the
...y of Chicago evaluators concluded:

...underlying rationale of the Manpower Project was repugnant to
...Police Department and went counter to its own basic mission,
...ticularly as this mission was viewed by the Gang Intelligence
...it. The purpose of the GIU, a new unit or task force in the Police
...epàrtment organized in the Spring of 1967, was to break up gangs,
...ainly through surveillance, control, and harassment of its leader-
...hip.

By definition, the purposes of the Police Department, especially the
GIU, was directly contrary to those of the Youth Manpower Project.
One organization sought to utilize the gang structure, particularly its
leadership, to redirect the energies of the gang and its members
towards more productive pursuits, mainly basic education, training
and job placement. The other organization sought, with single
minded purpose, to destroy the gang structure. The assumption of
the GIU was that the gangs were negative and evil forces; they could
not and should not be dealt with, except in relations to their swift
destruction.

way, since he was known to be interested in the Democratic nomination for Governor of Illinois and the Mayor was the most powerful
Democrat in the state.

The McClellan Committee started out its investigation with a set of
conclusions and created "facts" to support its conclusions. The record
of his committee's investigation of the project is also clear, both in
terms of who was called before the committee and who was not. The
committee's two star witnesses, Watusi Rose and Annabelle Martin
were, at the least, of questionable credibility. Rose had previously been
convicted of two felonies in the State of Illinois. Shortly before his
appearance before the committee, TWO officials aver, he was charged
with another felony. In Illinois conviction for three felonies usually
means a life sentence. It is reported that the charge pending against him
was dropped prior to the committee's opening of its public hearings
into the TWO program.

Mrs. Martin's situation was quite similar. Two of her sons had been
charged by the police with murder. Shortly before hearings began, it is
reported these charges against her sons were dropped by the police
(although a leader of the Rangers had been convicted of bribing her two
sons to commit murder and is now in prison for this conviction).

From Birth to Death—Some Narrative Highlights

On June 2, 1967, the project was funded to the Woodlawn Organization by OEO in the amount of $927,341. It took one year to obtain
funding for the program. The difficulties of negotiating a program
concept with TWO and particularly the Blackstone Rangers and the
East Side Disciples, developing a highly innovative program design,
bringing about communication between the two gangs, getting them to
cease acts of violence towards each other, obtaining support from
various organizations and programs both in the federal government and
in Chicago, negotiating an on-the-job training contract, and completing
all of the paperwork involved was an overwhelming and nearly
impossible job under the best of circumstances. (TWO, for example,
was required to submit many pounds of paper in support of the project
application although it was understaffed and had no additional
resources, personnel or dollar, to meet the demands made upon it.) To
add to this burden, the program concept met immediate opposition by
the forces described above.

The evaluation report of the University of Chicago made the following observation:

The acting director of the project reported that trainees and particularly subprofessionals, who were a target for GIU attention, were very frequently arrested on the charge of disorderly conduct outside the centers. For some of the youth, such arrests were reported as occurring almost daily. Each time a boy was arrested he had to find bail money, and the cost of staying on the street was becoming prohibitive. The charge was also made that the GIU was picking up Ranger or Disciple leadership and "dumping them" in each other's territory. This kind of action could easily heighten tension between gangs and precipitate additional group conflict. The head of the GIU admitted that this had occurred once or twice.

The report further stated:

In all likelihood, members both of the uniformed and non-uniformed force, *i.e.*, regular police officers of the Third Police District and the Gang Intelligence Unit were responsible for these punitive actions. While both the Commander of the Third Police District and the head of the Gang Intelligence Unit denied that their men engaged in brutal activities, they did admit that such activities were committed by policemen in the Woodlawn Area, generally by men not in their units. They insisted these occurrences were of an isolated nature.

Over time, the harassment took its toll—and a threatened breach of the all-important truce appeared imminent. In the face of a likely resumption of gang warfare that would destroy the entire program, OEO officials took action to avert disaster—action which was successful, but which led to new attacks on the program and ultimately to its demise.

In late July, 1967, it was feared at OEO that violence between the two gangs was likely to touch off wide-spread riots in Chicago on the scale of Newark and Detroit. After exhortation from OEO superiors (particularly Donald Hess, director of program planning for CAP) to do something to prevent violence, the author suggested that OEO bring to Chicago some black militants, so-called "black power" types with police records, from Watts to intervene with the leadership of the Blackstone Rangers.

On July 25 a meeting was held in Chicago involving black power advocates from Watts, the leadership of one of the two gangs, two staff members of TWO, and the author. This meeting resulted in an im-

266

mediate "cooling off"
in concert to pre
Immediately
services to
preventing ri

Another by-
1967 was the a
individuals from
Gang Intelligence
pistols in the room o
TWO officials had wr
their fears that the
premises of the project o
of project staff and/or oth
to create the kind of incid
funding of the program.*

The rest of the story can
along as best it could—without
Brooks' opposition to the candid
broke the always precarious truce
between the gangs resumed in the
refunding was turned down and the p

The University of Chicago evaluation

On the basis of available evidence, there
reason for terminating or failing to ex
Modification of design elements, especia
entirely feasible and already planned. 1
effective demonstration were at hand and n
better organization, and a more sophisticated

The inescapable conclusion was that there wer
those of program effectiveness, which must have

policy decision th
believe, were esse
that many power
to encourage fai
positive results is

We conclude th
opment in th
approach on
throughout
technical less

In retrospe
police, funct
program dire
the progra
harmoniou
tion that e
was in ch
Universit

The
the
par
Ur
D

* The author was fired by OEO shortly thereafter. Shriver denie
was being subjected to pressure from Daley and the police. Pr
the author had received an offer of a good job elsewhere in
peaceful resignation. He was then reassigned to a regional office a
in November, the reason given being his refusal to accept the reas
an appeal before the Civil Service Commission, the author's right to
upheld. OEO has appealed the decision in his favor and the case
pending in July, 1969.

267

Yet it is equally clear that the Gang Intelligence Unit was only an instrument of the Mayor and that the program could probably have sustained and survived the ferocity of those continuous attacks had not the so-called forces of good succumbed to self-interest and/or expediency.

On the local scene, the program was deserted and covertly opposed. At the national level, the program's official protectors similarly deserted the program. Bertrand Harding, the Deputy Director and subsequently the Director who turned down the proposal for refunding, played an active role in removing all sources of support for the program within the Office of Economic Opportunity. Lower echelon officials in OEO with two or three notable exceptions did not fight back—and those who did defend the program found themselves shut off from access to information and removed from any significant role in the decision making processes of the agency.

The significance of this case history lies not in terms of the destruction of the project itself, but rather in the reasons why it was destroyed and who destroyed it. The forces which successfully opposed the TWO youth demonstration program are the very forces which, on a national level, play a major causal role in the racial polarization of the country, the programmed destruction of an effective antipoverty program, the increasing disruption of our social institutions, the increasing violent clashes between "the establishment" and various segments (middle class as well as lower class) in our society, and the increasing "confidence gap" between government and the citizenry. The story is also revealing in terms of how the federal government moves toward dangerous self-insulation by way of eliminating personnel within it who propose policy and program alternatives and recruits career bureaucratic and professional "yes-men". Finally the story sheds revealing light on why many segments of society see no alternative to increasingly violent assaults on the existing social order.

The TWO project sought to utilize the participation of indigenous organizations as a means of reaching the alienated and creating new avenues to economic opportunity where all previous approaches had failed.

The lawlessness of the police—and the sanctioning of this lawlessness by public officials on the local and national level—does more than pose an academic question, how far government will go within the framework of the law to enfranchise the disenfranchised and to remove the barriers to opportunity which the powerful have placed in the path of the powerless.*

The issue takes on symbolic dimensions here—because the police possess a monopoly on the lawful use of deadly force. The TWO story becomes one of confrontation between the police, exercising their power lawlessly, and the poor, seeking to create something important for themselves within the confines of the law. Ultimately, however, citizen participation—in this context—becomes more than a phrase. For the viability of the concept, its ability to survive despite continuous setbacks such as the death of the TWO program may ultimately determine the viability of democracy itself. None are free when some are suppressed. And in Chicago, we have had all too recent a demonstration of the meaning of the TWO controversy writ large.

*See *Rights in Conflict* ("The Walker Report") for further views on the Chicago police and this issue.

MODEL CITIES–DAYTON PLAYS THE GAME

by: Ginger Rosenberg

Editor's Note:

The Federal Model Cities program, with its focus on local planning, provides an excellent gauge of the success and failure of citizen participation. Ginger Rosenberg offers a case study of how the groundwork for Model Cities was built in one city, Dayton, Ohio. By most standards, the efforts there by residents to gain a real say in transforming their neighborhood constitutes a rousing success story. And yet, finally it must be judged as the most disheartening kind of success —— the sort so familiar in surgery, where the operation is a success but the patient dies.

Mrs. Rosenberg first relates the saga of how citizens, making effective use of the existing antipoverty structure, defeated step-by-step attempts by the city to dominate the planning process. Then, in an epilogue that is really an autopsy, she divulges the patient's fatal illness —— if not death —— and details some of the causes: internecine knifing among the citizen allies who had won the victory, strangulation by governmental paperwork, inertia and audit.

In the 1950's, Mrs. Rosenberg was executive director for the Citizens Housing Association. She formally edited an East Detroit community newspaper and served as public relations director for the Social Welfare Planning Council in New Orleans. She is now Associate Director, Development Department, at Antioch College.

1) How does the Dayton story relate to the Fox monograph on Federal regulations?

2) Was the Dayton experience, in effect, a form of "participation as ritual" —— the type described in the Piven monograph?

271

3) What are the implications of what Mrs. Rosenberg calls the "new kind of means test" for the poor?

It has been observed, perhaps uncharitably, that the War on Poverty could most accurately be characterized as an adult civics course, complete with role playing with a friendly bureaucracy, lessons in grantsmanship and negotiation, exercises in management, internal intrigue and confrontation. To the extent that this characterization is accurate, then the value of the War on Poverty as a form of adult education in citizenship will depend upon the extent to which the poor succeed in applying the lessons they learn to the larger realm of politics and to the vast array of programs administered by other federal departments and agencies with no *a priori* commitment to be responsive to the poor.

Recent history has shown that alert mayors and governors have learned the lesson well —— if indeed they ever needed it. Change the name of the game from Public Housing to Urban Renewal, to War on Poverty, to Elementary and Secondary Education Act to Food Stamps to Model Cities —— and they were ready, application in hand, rules and regulations mastered, rhetoric and jargon up-dated, budget request expanded and impregnable.

The establishment passes the test with flying colors. "Citizen participation" was a form of compulsory remedial education law for the poor. But the first test for the poor of their ability to shift when the rules of the game changed came with the enactment of the Model Cities Program. The returns are not yet in on whether the poor have mastered those lessons sufficiently to apply them effectively to the general business of society. However, one city, Dayton, Ohio, provides significant indication that the poverty program disseminated sufficient knowledge, generated new groups and leaders, raised expectations sufficiently and provided an adequate base of resources and skills to enable the poor and minority groups to wrest control of the

273

Model Cities program in a way the would have been unthinkable five years ago.

The Dayton Model Cities story began in the usual way. By the time the Model Cities program had been enacted, the powers that be had already done their homework, and put together an application.

The modus operandi was typical. A private organization, SCOUR (Special Committee on Urban Renewal), was established and raised ten thousand dollars to pay a private university constultant to draw up the initial Model Cities plan. In October, 1966, the president of SCOUR headed a Dayton delegation to Washington, and reported that federal officials were "overwhelmed at the large size of the Dayton delegation and the amount of preliminary planning that has already been done." As could have been predicted, that plan proposed a structure which relegated the poor to a token advisory role while perpetuating the ruling oligarchy of municipal agencies and private social-welfare agencies.

The plan took no account even of the existence of the local poverty agency, Supporting Council on Preventive Effort (SCOPE).

Once the Model Cities program became law, the city moved swiftly to convert this plan into Dayton's official application for planning funds. At that point, a new city manager, Graham Watt, took office. In preparing the application, he relied on the plan he inherited despite incipient rumblings from the black community and explicit admonitions from SCOPE that the earlier proposal was unsatisfactory — so unsatisfactory that SCOPE had refused to concur in it as required by HUD's coordinating "check point" procedures. City Manager Watt presented the proposal, declaring that "the key innovation concept is to assure participation of the residents of the target area through establishment of a Model Cities Planning Council."

But local residents in the target area, assisted by technicians at SCOPE, had learned to read the small print. They fully comprehended the implications of City Manager Watt's statement that their power would consist only of "authority to review and comment on all staff ideas and proposals before they are transmitted to the Policy Committee for final review and approval."

The poor understood that they would have no real say; actual power would be vested in the Policy Committee where three representatives from the model neighborhood area, West Dayton, would be out-manned, out-voted and out-gunned by representatives from the city government, the county government, the Board of Education, the Housing Authority, the Health and Welfare Planning Council, the Chamber of Commerce and other groups. In addition, they saw themselves flanked by still another box on the organization chart, the Technical Advisory Committee, which would be staffed entirely by representatives of the old-line city agencies; in theory the members would be technical advisors, but in fact they would use that committee as the point of leverage to assure dominance of the Model Cities Program by the existing agencies within the Dayton municipal government. That was where things stood in the spring of 1967.

By 1969, however, an entirely different structure had been created completely superseding the earlier one and reversing the role to which the residents of the model neighborhood had been consigned.

The new structure has the following key features:

1. The key planning and policy-making function is vested in a council drawn entirely from the target area and elected by residents of the target area. It is called the Model Cities Planning Council. This Council is not a public governmental body; it is a private, nonprofit corporation with staff of its own, resources to hire technicians and consultants to assist in the design of various program elements, and legal authority to enter into agreements with private agencies and city agencies, such as the Board of Education, to design and implement specific programs in specific areas. Though legal responsibility ultimately rests with the municipal government, this delegation of planning authority goes as far as the Model Cities Act permits in providing for resident control of the planning and administration of the Model Cities program. In terms of power realities, representatives of the residents are at the hub of the process.

2. Technical assistance and consultants are to be provided to this Council by city agencies and by private groups. But the Council retains the right (and is to be provided with funds) to select its own consultants and staff and is under no compulsion to accept those offered by the city or by private groups.

3. Priority program areas have been selected -- employment, education, health, housing, crime and delinquency, etc. -- and subcommittees of the Planning Council are charged with responsibility for drawing up the program components. The basic principle for each component will be community control, using the community corporation as the chief organizational vehicle for insuring control by the residents of the target area.

275

The Planning Council's plan became the City of Dayton's official application. In effect, the citizens recaptured the Model Cities Program.

The steps by which this was done are at least as important as the organizational structure that emerged.

1. The nucleus of resistance to "business as usual" already existed in the West Dayton target area. An Alinsky-oriented, social protest group had operated there for several years, with some notable successes but with substantial internal organization problems. It had been funded, in part, by the poverty agency SCOPE and had been assisted by professors and students from nearby Antioch College. That group was defunct by the time the Model Cities issue came to the surface. But the Model Cities Program served as a catalyst; a citizens group, calling itself a Steering Committee for the Model Cities program, emerged spontaneously under the leadership of Floyd Johnson, a teacher, to resist the token participation of residents provided for under the proposed Model Cities plan.

2. The resident Steering Committee contacted SCOPE to seek assistance in formulating demands and strategies and to inquire into the possibility of funding for a resident group whose sole function would be to insure real resident participation in the Model Cities Program. SCOPE agreed to fund the group as a delegate agency for this purpose -- but not until the group had a recognized status, both within the West Dayton Area and vis-a-vis the City Demonstration Agency (CDA), the municipal agency established to administer Model Cities.

SCOPE proceeded to give technical and other assistance to help the group broaden its base of community support and win full recognition from the city.

3. At this point, the City of Dayton received a planning grant from HUD to plan Model Cities. It engaged a white director despite considerable local protest that the director should have been black.

4. The new director turned to the Steering Committee to work out a suitable method of providing for representation of the residents of the model neighborhood. At that point the Steering Committee became the Ad Hoc Committee with quasi-official status. Its limited mandate was to devise a method for selecting the membership of the official resident-participation group to insure that it would be representative of the target area. The question of the power that group would exercise was left open by design. Differences were papered

276

over by rhetoric.

5. A method was carefully thrashed out which provided for election of the membership of the Model Cities Planning Council from the 27 geographic units into which the target area was divided. This involved a community battle with private agencies which had established "block clubs" to engage in clean-up and neighborhood improvement projects. These agencies wished to control the program and fought to have their block clubs given the power to chose the members of the Planning Council, and even to give representation to block clubs *outside* the target area. The attempt at a takeover through the block clubs was repulsed. Exchanges such as the following are illustrative:

"We're tired of you people outside our area telling us what we need," said Mrs. King Heard, a resident of inner West Dayton. "We know what we need."

Another resident, Mrs. Delores Winslow, remarked that "people in the area just don't trust government programs" and "nothing will be accomplished unless people in the area are all assured they have the controlling vote." She also pointed out that the "little men don't come to such meetings, it's the organized, meeting-happy people who turn out with the voting power."

Melvin Jackson of the West Dayton Self-Help Center cautioned: "Let's not get into a family fight. . . let's not become so fearful we can't trust each other." But Mrs. Wisnlow countered that the poor Negro distrusts other Negroes and "the Negro will do the same thing to you a white man will."

6. Once the method of election was agreed upon and incorporated into the plan, the critical issue of the power of the group called the Model Cities Planning Council emerged.

The confrontation on the power of the planning council required a great deal of homework. First, the basic plan had to be worked out -- and this was done by SCOPE working in conjunction with the Ad Hoc Committee. Then the timing for presentation of the demand had to be worked out and the Ad Hoc Committee had to be sure that the community would back its demands. The organizational effort tactically focused on the selection process for members of the Planning Council. Discussion of this issue in public meetings helped to unify the community behind the Ad Hoc Committee.

The Ad Hoc Committee then walked in with considerable bargaining power: it had a unified community behind it; it had a carefully

277

designed plan worked out; and it had firm assurances that SCOPE would fund the Planning Council as a delegate agency to insure that the resident participation element of Model Cities was effectively implemented.

The City Manager advanced a series of technical and legal objections as to whether delegation to the Council constituted an improper delegation of governmental power to a private, non-profit corporation.

The most decisive answer was the threat that, if the City did not enter into the "partnership agreement" on the terms proposed by the Ad Hoc Committee, there would be no election, no resident participation and no Model Cities program. While the City Manager remained cautiously neutral, the Commission voted to enter into the "partnership agreement" on the terms demanded. This was the pivotal document giving legal status to the resident-elected Model Cities Planning Council.

That agreement stated:

WHEREAS, While it must be understood that the Commission carries the ultimate responsibility for final decisions in this and all other neighborhoods, it is imperative that the City Commission and the administration of The City of Dayton recognize the elected representatives of the target area residents, the Planning Council; now, therefore,

BE IT RESOLVED BY THE COMMISSION
OF THE CITY OF DAYTON:

That the Commission of the City of Dayton, Ohio, declares that the Planning Council shall be a full partner in all programs, decisions and planning related to the target area and the decisions of the Planning Council shall at all times be given full consideration in all decisions made by the Commission affecting the welfare of the target area residents.

Be It Further Resolved, that all proposals from either the City Commission or the Planning Council affecting the Welfare of the target area residents shall be set forth in written memoranda and transmitted to the City Commission, the Planning Council and the City Manager.

7. Once the agreement was final, SCOPE proceeded to enter into a contract with the Planning Council making it a delegate agency.

The work plan stated that the Model Cities Planning Council as a delegate agency of SCOPE would:

278

review all Model Cities (M.C.) programs submitted by any agency in the community. . .

. . . have the authority to also approve said programs before submission to any Federal funding source, *e.g.*, H.U.D., Labor Department, etc. . . .

. . . have the prerogative to initiate its own action programming and submit for funding as part of the 5-year M.C. Master Plan.

. . . be the "Advocate" of the target area residents; it will be the "connector," the "linkage," the "agent," . . . between the consumer of the M.C. Programs, and the "Establishment."

The Planning Council in its role of representing the target area residents, will be concerned about knowledgable matters, and involved in all M.C. programming. Among its areas of concern and involvement will be:

—Physical Improvements
—Housing Choice and Supply
—Public Facilities
—Employment Opportunities
—Health Services
—Education Services

. . . In order for the P.C. to effectively discharge its responsibilities to the target area it represents, and to the total M.C. effort, it must have a staff. . . .

. . . Their major function will be to provide a variety of staff services for the P.C. and to act as continuous linkage between the target area neighborhoods and the P.C. Such functions do not include the delivery of direct services. . . nor organizing them around social issues; in this vital respect, they will not be duplicating what the aides of other programs are now doing. . . .

8. The master agreement had been hammered out, the Model Cities Planning Council given both status and funding (from three sources: the city, HUD and OEO). The next step was to hammer out similar partnership agreements regarding each component of the planning process. Controversy erupted most dramatically over the control of the education component of the Model Cities program. The Planning Council sought to enter into a partnership agreement with the Board of Education which had named Arthur Thomas, a militant black educator, as the coordinator of the Model Cities education program. Just as the terms of that agreement were being worked out

279

in final form, the Board of Education removed Thomas from that position in what was seen as an attempt to sabotage the efforts to create a community-controlled school system as part of Model Cities. Community protest, demonstrations, and newspaper editorials forced the Board of Education to retreat and reinstate Thomas. He then proceeded to develop with the community a detailed plan for educational innovation.

The role of SCOPE was critically important:

It refused to endorse the original program.

It provided technical assistance to the embryonic Steering Committee.

It helped work out the basic organization plan and partnership agreement.

It secured staff and personnel to stimulate community discussion and participation of the election proposal.

It backed the Ad Hoc Committee in its demands for a central role for the Model Cities Planning Council.

It funded the Model Cities Planning Council to implement the resident participation requirements of the Model Cities Act.

It continues to play an important role—as technician and public advocate, pointing up the threats to citizen participation, which are masked in seemingly attractive proposals, and backing the Model Cities Planning Council resisting such maneuvers. The following excerpt from a letter by the Director of SCOPE to Floyd B. Johnson, the Director of the Planning Council is illustrative of both the guidance, the style and the role which the anti-poverty program has played in its continuing consultative capacity:

The Schmidt plan calls for employment and supervision of technical specialists by City of Dayton Model Cities Administrative Office .... assigned to work with Model Cities Planning Council subcommittees. ... This is a denial of the Model Cities Planning Council's agreed-upon role in the program planning. For the Model Cities Planning Council to continue an effective planning role, it must be able to have available to its committees technicians acceptable to the citizen group. Rather than specialists employed and supervised by the CDA, as Mr. Schmidt proposes, the Model Cities Planning Council should have a budget adequate to employ the necessary technicians who have, in addition to the technical competence, proven ability to work effectively with the community representatives.

280

The concept of advocacy planning, now established in many communities which respect and take seriously the citizen contribution, is left out in Mr. Schmidt's statement. Implementation of the above phase of the CDA plan will scuttle meaningful citizen participation, as has been proven time and again in the dismal failure of programs all over the country.

We take issue with the proposition that the City Demonstration Agency will retain responsibility for all Model Cities activity "including the Satellite Corporations established to carry out certain action programs." The Satellite Corporations to be controlled by the City are the community schools proposed in the educational component, the multi-service center, . . . the multi-service health care center . . . . the not-for-profit housing corporation, the one stop manpower development center . . . . It is proposed that the direction of these organizations be similar to that of the already existing CEP . . . . " Prior to the release of this document citizens of the target area had every reason to believe that public officials entrusted with administration of the Model Cities Program acknowledged the concept of community corporations as a major part of the development of new services. The suggestion that the pattern of CEP be followed is, to put it mildly, unfortunate. Because of certain statutory requirements, CEP is at this time operated by two co-sponsors -- the City of Dayton and by frustration and vaguely defined responsibility. The proposed new corporations, responsible for operation of activities to serve the residents of the West Dayton area, should be directed by boards composed of West Dayton citizens.

The Dayton experience is a model of how the anti-poverty program can be used as a technical assistance base from which the poor and minority group residents can move to exact accountability from other programs. Such programs always help them but in fact often are designed and structured in such a way as to be unresponsive to their needs. A newspaper story reported:

The local program has attracted the participation of Negroes "whose anger and frustration had provided the basis for the disorders in 1966 and 1967," said the firm of Marshall, Kaplan, Gans, and Kahn, an evaluating consultant hired by the U.S. Department of Housing and Urban Development (HUD).

"Significantly, Dayton enjoyed relative surface calm during the 1968 planning year," the report said adding:

"While tensions still exist, it may be possible that the Dayton Model Cities program purchased the necessary time to cool tempers and establish a successful mechanism for continuing community dialogue."

The report covers the planning phase of Model Cities, which ended when the program was submitted to HUD in February. The consultant studied Dayton, Seattle and Atlanta, three cities generally cited by HUD officials as among the most advanced in the nation.

"The creation of a meaningful coalition between (target area) residents and city hall, able to survive tensions of the ghetto, must be rated an innovation," the consultants added.

However, the report noted this coalition did not come about easily.

"Contention" between city officials and the Model Neighborhood was more "abrasive" in Dayton than in Seattle or Atlanta. This led to a larger role for Model Neighborhood residents in the planning process and an equal partnership with city hall.

The initial distrust of target residents and the later friction with city hall were not "all confrontation and petty politics," the report said.

". . . a dialogue; moreover, it established a process. Viewed in these terms alone, Dayton's Model Cities program could be seen as a pronounced success," it said.

Only in Dayton was the citizen-arm group, the Model Cities Planning Council, elected by target area residents. Also, Dayton was the only one of the three cities in which the planning council hired its own technical staff.

EPILOGUE

Subsequent events are worth summarizing, both to update the story and to make clear the dangers and problems which any such effort appears almost certain to encounter.

First, and perhaps most critical, Model Cities encountered extensive delay in funding; so the package that was sent remained in limbo -- and with it, the initiative and leadership of the Planning Council.

Second, the Model Cities Planning Council was never adequately funded to engage in the kind of organizing effort and staffing necessary to insure full resident participation, either in the elections that ensued or other efforts to involve citizens more broadly in the design of specific program components. Organization and involvement take staff, time and money to hire technicians, organizers, etc. Thus, its success in designing specific program components has been largely a matter of luck. Contracts to provide technical assistance were entered into by the city as a form of patronage and paying off debts to local agencies and private groups. The Model Cities Administrator moved to control the technicians and thus, in effect, to control the actual program design.

In the education area, where the School Board had appointed a creative, militant and capable person as coordinator for the education component of Model Cities, an extraordinarily innovative program emerged as one newspaper reported:

> The evaluation of past performance repeatedly praised the education component of Dayton's plan and those who prepared it, including Arthur Thomas, Model Cities education co-ordinator because:

> > Thomas 'stumped the neighborhood, gathered petitions, wrote articles, gave speeches downtown, yelled when it appeared politic ...' to inform the West Dayton residents of the program and involve many of them in its planning.

283

The housing component is cited as the other extreme. The reports says it 'developed little consultation with residents of the area.'

In other areas technicians were assigned to citizen panels and were thrust on the Planning Council by Schmidt. The technicians were drawn from old-line city agencies and from old-line private social welfare organizations whose agenda was control and perpetuation of their own role.

Third, the Model Cities Planning Council was subjected to a series of audits and the auditors decided that seven thousand dollars had been spent improperly in connection with a regional meeting of citizens' groups involved in Model Cities. As a result, all funds to the Model Cities Planning Council dried up immediately. The City, HUD, and OEO found they could not legally continue to fund the Planning Council; it has been kept alive only becuase SCOPE hired for its staff three of the top staff of the Planning Council then assigned them to continue work on Model Cities. But an impasse has been reached because of the funds alleged to have been improperly spent. Until that decision is contested and reversed, or the Council reorganized by bankruptcy or other proceedings that make it eligible for funding, it may be barred from access to vitally important resources.

Fourth, with everything in limbo, the Model Cities Planning Council found itself doing what resident groups throughout the country have done when they needed an issue: they have attacked the structure and operations of SCOPE -- and called for its dismantling. The response of the Director of SCOPE was rather startling. He conceded the validity of most of the criticism about his own organization's unwieldy structure and inadequate performance and concurred heartily in the request for a restructuring of the poverty program in Dayton.

Such internecine warfare, which so often characterizes citizen participation can either revitalize the poverty program or destroy it as a power base from which the poor can effectively secure accountability from other agencies and organizations.

Fifth and finally, it must be observed that much of the leadership that emerged in the battle for resident control was middle class. To be sure, many of those elected to the Planning Council were poor. But many were black and middle class. Some saw Model Cities as an opportunity to create a black patronage system -- using their position, like the ward heeler of old, to dispense services to friends, procure jobs, secure preferred treatment, run interference for the favored few. Yet, their actions do not appear likely to generate the kind of political

284

power base that would give the black residents of Dayton any genuine increase in traditional political power. The elected council began to lose its standing because it did not work to maintain its power base in the community -- in part through lack of funding, staff and experience, and in particular because of the autocratic style of the chairman. One newspaper account reports:

The muscle of the council increased the day it was officially born -- when an unexpected 23 percent of eligible voters turned out to elect the council's 27 members.

The members, in turn, have used this turnout during the last year to argue that because they were chosen by the people, not by someone "downtown," they were the only legitimate spokesmen for Inner West Dayton.

But the demise of the council's power also began that day because of the council's apparent willingness to leave its constituents right there -- at the polls.

Council critics say, and some of its members admit, that to build a real solid power base the council should have pulled its voter constituents along, maintaining frequent contact with them so they would be ready to support the council visibly in its dealing with "the establishment."

Council member James Payne confirms that "if citizens had been informed, they would have been in a better position to have supported us."

Complaints of lack of council communication with constituents were sounded hardly a month after the council's first meeting and they grew louder and more frequent.

And this alleged communication gap not only left the council without a constituent-supplied power base but made it vulnerable to these attacks from its own community that further impaired its credibility and weakened its muscle.

Council chairman Roger Prear said recently: "One of the things we have recognized is an inability to communicate to the broad spectrum of the community."

Other council members say they had little previous experience in community planning and had so much to learn they couldn't spend large amounts of time getting the message to the community.

Development of broadly based power was not even encouraged inside the council. Chairman Prear has dominated meetings, leaving little time for other members to speak or develop their own images.

Prear is verbose and articulate and has never followed normal parliamentary procedure of stepping down from the chair when taking a position on an issue.

Supported by West Dayton council critics, some council members admitted last February that they had wanted to speak up earlier but had felt inadequate in the face of the poise and apparent knowledgeability of council leadership.

Prear defends his domination of meetings, saying "You must have a strong personality to hold a group together until they (members) feel knowledgeable and secure enough to participate in free debate."

Perhaps one of the major unsolved problems of citizen participation is what to do after a victory. Before the shift takes place from organization and confrontation to program management, there is always a waiting period, and during that time, unity is likely to dissipate. The leadership turns on the coalition of friends, allies, well wishers and responsive organizations that proved indispensable to past victories. All the internecine, separatist, factional impulses previously subordinated to a united drive for common causes rise to the surface.

These predictable periods of limbo, of waiting, of transition, are part of the pattern by which government damps down the rate of social change, frustrates expectations, generates cynicism, and turns constructive impulses to destructive ones.

Primary blame must be assigned to the federal government, to local officials and to private social welfare groups who use delay to break the momentum of a movement, to perpetuate themselves and to insure that those with resources and staying power ultimately prevail. The paperwork delay and vastly expanded application requirements that cause delay, rewrites, review, reevaluation are consciously and unconsciously used as a form of rationing limited funds -- a new kind of means test which doles out limited dollars only to the "worthy and deserving" poor. Then the search for "qualified" cities echoes the old slogan "we can't find any qualified Negroes." The fault lies only secondarily with those who respond out of bitterness, frustration, disappointment and who, to buy time and maintain their credibility, are left with little choice as to their mode of response.

RESIDENT PARTICIPATION IN THE MASS MEDIA

by: Patricia A. Wood

Editor's Note:

The mass media in America are businesses. No citizen involvement is appreciated, except in buying the products that keep the airwaves filled and the newspapers thick.

Successes of public or educational television have usually been limited to small or specialized audiences. There have been sporadic recent attempts to involve specific parts of the media in the problems of the nation and vice versa. These include radio talk shows and opening of newspaper society pages to blacks (who now are described as being born, married and buried as well as arrested). Network television shows integrated commercials.

Patricia Wood, a research assistant and writer at the New Jersey Community Action Training Institute, in Trenton, describes a new venture: involvement of a large, ethnic-based "TV market" in a leadership development training series.

Some questions:

1) *Is the "Ya Es Tiempo" model workable in the general English-speaking TV market? Or can it only be successful with a "captive" ethnic audience?*
2) *Granted that TV has great audience attraction powers and training potential, can community development be "sold" like soap and viable organizations be built through soap operas?*
3) *Can other media be used to further similar goals? What programs might be devised for citizen participation in radio? newspapers? magazines?*

"Ya Es Tiempo – It's About Time"

While the "Ya Es Tiempo" television series received national attention as a pioneer in the field of community television and a first in community action training through the mass media, resident participation played a major role in the development and execution of the project. The major share of the credit belongs to the Puerto Rican and other Spanish-speaking residents of the New York/New Jersey metropolitan area.

Early attempts at participant recruitment were directed toward the established Puerto Rican leadership in the Spanish *barrios* of New York City and northern New Jersey. When that attempt met with little effective interest, the main thrust of the project's recruitment campaign was redirected toward the grass-roots population of those same Spanish-speaking communities. News of the project and its need for local participants was spread via church and social action club meetings, local CAP delegate agencies, neighborhood workers and the intra-ghetto communications system known as the "grapevine." Throughout the project, it was the block resident rather than the community leader who was responsible for the success of "Ya Es Tiempo."

The five half-hour television show series was financed by the U.S. Office of Economic Opportunity under a $100,000 grant and coordinated by the New Jersey Community Action Training Institute. The programs were telecast in prime week-night time over UHF Channel 47 to an audience of more than 250,000 adults in the New York City metropolitan area. The project was planned and coordinated by David W. Parker of the CATI staff. Professional television technicians from Channel 47 aided in the actual studio work, and the station donated the time.

At the beginning of the project, the basic training and community development goals governing the OEO grant were to explore the feasibility of effective community action training through the television media and to produce a series of five half-hour television programs to fulfill that aim.

Supplementing those agreed-upon objectives, the Training Institute set eight additional goals. Of the eight, six are directly related to resident participation.

. . . All the actors in the television programs are to be local Spanish residents from the disadvantaged *barrios* of the New York/New Jersey metropolitan area.

288

... Neighborhood people are to decide on the topics of the shows and help in the development of the program (scripts).

... Community residents are to assist in the production of the television programs.

... Three hundred (300) neighborhood Spanish-speaking residents are to be recruited and trained to serve as local group leaders. Their task is to gather ten neighbors in each home on the evenings the programs are televised, and to conduct a training session with the group after the programs are viewed.
... The trainers necessary to prepare the group leaders are to be recruited from the local Spanish neighborhoods.
... The project is to be done completely in Spanish. Three thousand (3,000) neighborhood residents are to be involved in the project by participating in the groups set up by the trained group leaders.

A Look at the Process Time Table

One of the most common complaints lodged against the use of resident participation is that it takes time. The consensus seems to be that resident participation slows the process and complicates the completion of even simple tasks, particularly when the nature of the project, its content and method of completion are foreign to the community residents.

Certainly the development and production of television programs were largely foreign to the residents of the Puerto Rican *barrios*, but a look at the project's timetable from beginning to end demonstrates something other than a slowing up of the process by the participants.

The project proposal was submitted to OEO in April, 1967. It was approved in July for funding from November 1, 1967, to October 31, 1968.

After much planning and consultation with television and community leaders, and a false start, the Institute began implementation of the action phase on May 1, 1968.

The group leaders were recruited and had completed their training by August 22, 1968. The shows were aired on five consecutive Tuesday evenings, starting August 27 and ending September 24, 1968.

The Office of Economic Opportunity consumed a total of four

months in approving the proposal. Once it was approved, the Institute took a total of nine months to begin action implementation of the project. After the recruitment of actors and group leaders was started, the entire development and production of the shows took only five months. It took the local participants only one month longer to complete the entire project than it took OEO to approve the proposal.

The Action Implementation Phase

During the planning stage of Ya Es Tiempo, the actual production of the shows and all steps leading to the project's completion were divided into four major tasks.

Task Number One

The first of these tasks was the development of the shows. From the very beginning, target area residents played a principal role. The name of the project and the titles of the shows were chosen by the neighborhood participants. The content of the programs was also the result of the combined efforts of members of the Spanish community. The Institute staff had prepared and presented a list of suggestions, but the five program-content areas finally used were decided by the local citizens.

Each of the four neighborhoods whose residents showed the greatest initial interest in the project was chosen to be in charge of a single program. Residents from the Williamsburg, Brooklyn, area worked out the consumer education program; East Harlem participants developed the segment on housing problems; Newark, employment problems; and Brownsville, Brooklyn, took charge of the education problems program. The fifth show, on leadership formation, was developed by residents from many different neighborhoods and there were typically no more than two community people from any one neighborhood working on that program.

The shows were done in a dramatic "soap opera" type of format. The story line was an important factor in the presentation of the shows, as illustrated by the segment on housing problems: at the opening of the show, a party is in progress. During the course of the evening, a rat gets into the home where the party is being held and bites a baby sleeping in its crib. This incident begins to mobilize, first, the people present at the party and later, as more people are brought in on the meetings, other residents of the community. Block leaders develop. They contact a local neighborhood worker to get help in organizing around the issue of the poor housing conditions.

In this way, situation drama and true-to-life issues helped the viewing audience identify with the problems being portrayed and apply their learnings to their own situations.

Task Number Two

Group leaders had to be recruited and trained. A total of 340 group leaders, ranging in age from 17 to 65, were recruited from 23 neighborhoods. The only requirements were that a candidate be both a neighborhood resident and have the ability to speak Spanish. Of those recruited, 287 completed the four evenings of training delivered by Institute trainers, Spanish-speaking consultants and a number of neighborhood residents. The neighborhood residents recruited as trainers were given a crash train-the-trainers program by the Institute.

The areas of skills development emphasized during the training were:
a) the purpose and method of the Y.E.T. training project
b) how to organize a group of 10 to 15 neighbors for a home viewer training group
c) principles of group leadership
d) pulling group learnings from the training programs
e) training content of each of the five shows
f) evaluation of their work as group leaders and of their group's work

One of those trained as a group leader was Mrs. Marcelina Diaz, a resident of Brownsville and mother of five. Mrs. Diaz had never before been actively involved in any kind of community action or organization. She had attended a few meetings of a Brownsville Tenants Council but had given up on the idea. After having played an extremely active role in the Ya Es Tiempo project as group leader and helping in other phases of the project, she has since formed two Tenant Action clubs of about 10 to 12 members each, and has also started a Tenants Association of between 50 and 60 members in the new low-income housing project where she lives.

Of the 287 group leaders who finished the training, 240 served as group leaders for all five programs and helped in the evaluation process by evaluating their own training performance, their group's participation and interest, and the programs themselves.

Task Number Three

Training materials, booklets for group leaders' use, had to be developed, printed and distributed. At the completion of the taping for each show, Institute staff developed a brief outline encompassing what had taken place during that program. Those outlines provided the first section of each of the five corresponding booklets written to supplement the series. The rest of each booklet was developed around the subject matter of the show.

Institute staff developed rough drafts of all five booklets which were then distributed to local residents who gave feedback and suggestions. The booklets were then redrafted and printed.

The booklets were used during the project, being distributed at the completion of each show. They were also sent to anyone who wrote to Channel 47 requesting copies.

Task Number Four

The programs had to be publicized and promoted.

Group leaders, actors, CAP agency workers, churches and local organizations in New York City and northern New Jersey -- some 400 people from 25 neighborhoods -- aided in the promotional campaign. That combined effort was responsible for the distribution of more than 3,000 posters and 50,000 throw away announcements reaching 36 Spanish *barrios* in the metropolitan target area. Channel 47 donated free air time for short promotional spot announcements. Some of the actors went on live televison to promote the series.

Evaluating the "Ya Es Tiempo" Program

Eighteen months after its inception, the last program in the series of five was aired. But the process was far from complete. The evaluation of the program would play an extremely important part in determining what future efforts would be made in the area of resident participation in the mass media.

The evaluation process was thorough. The resulting myriad of statistics can be summarized in three major categories: the general television audience, television professionals and participants.

Of the general audience reporting through random telephone interviews, personal interviews and letters received by the television station, approximately 5 per cent felt that the use of non-professional actors was damaging to the program. Approximately 95 per cent expressed approval of the shows and a desire to see more similar programs and to become involved in any future project of this nature.

The project coordinator talked with more than 15 television professionals. Although skeptical at the outset of the project, they responded favorably to the programs and thought the video part was live and well-placed, except for a few scenes. They mentioned two problem areas in particular. One was an audio problem caused when two or three actors spoke at once. The other: they thought some of the sets could have been more realistic. They commented very little on the content and were amazed to learn that none of the actors were professionals.

The majority of the third reporting group, consisting of the actors, group leaders and home viewing groups, were in almost unanimous agreement on all aspects of the project. They thought that the use of non-professional actors and group leaders was greatly beneficial to the project as a whole. Many expressed the desire to become involved in further projects of this kind. The major complaint was that there was not enough -- not enough shows, not enough time, the shows were too short, there should have been ten evenings of training instead of four for the preparation of group leaders, etc.

Effects of the Project

"Ya Es Tiempo" was designed as a community action project. Therefore, the most meaningful measure of its success is calculated by the amount of actual community action and organization it spurred. As a result of the project, over 50 group leaders have initiated buyer's clubs, block clubs or other action type clubs. Forty of the group leaders in Union City, Hoboken, West New York, and North Bergen (all New Jersey) have formed themselves into a "federation" for community action and development. They meet together monthly and requested further training. Many group leaders have reported that for the first time they are now involved in community action work in their neighborhoods.

It is impossible, as the length of time from the completion of the project increases, to keep an accurate account of how many action groups and clubs have formed as a result of the project; but the numbers available have been encouraging.

A national conference of Spanish-speaking community leaders was held in October, 1968, to view the "Ya Es Tiempo" films. The group critiqued the product, which was then made available for national distribution -- with the strong admonition that each locality should develop its own community-based approach to the mass media.

The most unexpected measure of the success of the project came in the form of a nomination as one of the ten finalists in the 1969 Emmy Award Contest of the National Academy of Television Arts and Sciences, in the category of Public Service for Station Citation Award.

ABOUT THE EDITORS

EDGAR S. CAHN is Director of the Citizens Advocate Center, Washington, D.C. He served as special assistant to R. Sargent Shriver, the Director of the Office of Economic Opportunity, and has a doctorate in law from Yale University.

BARRY A. PASSETT is President of Systems for Change, Inc., Trenton, N.J., and was formally Director of the New Jersey Community Action Training Institute. Mr. Passett has served in the Alliance for Progress and the OEO. He holds an M.P.A. from the Woodrow Wilson School of Public and International Affairs, Princeton University.